The COMPLETE HOUSE AND GROUNDS

The COMPLETE HOUSE AND GROUNDS

Learning from Andrew Jackson Downing's Domestic Architecture

Caren Yglesias, AIA

CENTER FOR AMERICAN PLACES AT COLUMBIA COLLEGE CHICAGO

Published in 2011. First Edition.
Published in the United States on acid-free paper.

The Center for American Places
at Columbia College Chicago
600 South Michigan Avenue
Chicago, Illinois 60605-1996, U.S.A.
www.colum.edu/centerbooks

Distributed by the University of Chicago Press
www.press.chicago.edu

20 19 18 17 16 15 14 13 12   1 2 3 4 5

Library of Congress Cataloging-in-Publication Data

Yglesias, Caren.
The complete house and grounds : learning from Andrew Jackson Downing's domestic architecture / Caren Yglesias. — 1st ed.
p. cm.
ISBN 978-1-935195-24-5 (alk. paper)
1. Downing, A. J. (Andrew Jackson), 1815–1852—Criticism and interpretation. 2. Architecture, Domestic—United States—History—19th century. 3. Country homes—Landscape architecture—United States—History—19th century. 4. Architects—United States—Biography. I. Downing, A. J. (Andrew Jackson), 1815–1852. II. Title. III. Title: Learning from Andrew Jackson Downing's domestic architecture.

NA737.D675Y39 2011
728.092—dc23

2011039470

For my wonderful husband, John.

CONTENTS

ILLUSTRATIONS

Downing's books are indicated by the following abbreviations:

ACH, figure numbers from the 1968 reprint of *The Architecture of Country Houses* (1850).

CR, figure numbers from the 1981 reprint of the 4th edition of 1852 of *Cottage Residences* (1842).

TPLG, figure numbers from the 1991 reprint of the 4th edition of 1849 of *A Treatise on the Theory and Practice of Landscape Gardening* (1841).

Other sources are abbreviated as:

MMA for The Metropolitan Museum of Art, Harris Brisbane Dick Fund, 1924, A. J. Davis Documents.

BIOGRAPHICAL IMAGES

ACKNOWLEDGMENTS

MY GRATITUDE extends to David Leatherbarrow, Joseph Rykwert, and William Braham for their guidance during the first steps of this project. I am indebted to the work of Downing scholars including Arthur C. Downs, Jr., Francis R. Kowsky, Judith K. Major, Daniel D. Reiff, David Schuyler, Adam W. Sweeting, and George R. Tatum. Richard Jenrette generously granted permission to use rare Downing-to-Robert Donaldson letters in this work. Thank you, Cathy Ensor, for listening. Colette Silver read the entire manuscript with care, patience, and kindness; thank you for its many improvements and your encouragement. This project has been supported by a 2010 David R. Coffin Publication Grant awarded by the Foundation for Landscape Studies in partial support of image publication. My appreciation extends to George F. Thompson, Brandy Savarese, and Anne Sanow for bringing the manuscript forward to publication with skill. Finally, I thank my father, Jose J. Yglesias, for all his support and interest in this effort throughout the years—it mattered; and I remember my mother, Magenta C. Yglesias, who died before I was finished—I know you would have thrown a little party.

The COMPLETE HOUSE AND GROUNDS

INTRODUCTION

> We will not do more at present than throw out these suggestions, in the hope that those about to build in the country will reflect that an entirely satisfactory house is one in which there are not only pretty forms and details, but one which has some *meaning* in its beauty, considered in relation to their own position, character, and daily lives.
>
> —Downing, "A Few Words on Rural Architecture" [1]

THE SMITHSONIAN Institution in Washington, D.C., the large museum complex lining the Mall between the Capitol and the Washington Monument, is often referred to as America's front yard. These grounds are the site of significant historic events, and the museums are the repository of America's finest cultural and scientific achievements. Next to the Smithsonian Castle, a monumental urn stands in a small garden (Fig. I.1). It honors the work of one man, Andrew Jackson Downing, an early nineteenth-century American once considered the foremost authority on horticulture, garden design, rural architecture, and the emerging interest in public landscapes.

Downing (1815–1852) lived during times Russell Lynes calls "the age of public taste." Regarding Downing's influence, Lynes observes that "there is scarcely a monument left, scarcely a garden or a house or a terraced hillside, to which we can now point and say Downing did that. But there is scarcely a building still standing from the 1840s and 50s or a city park in which Downing's ideas, sometimes distorted almost beyond recognition, cannot be detected."[2] This circumstance sums up Downing's legacy to American design. Although his early death, the Civil War, and superseding directions in architecture diminished his influence, Downing's work still provides lessons for

Fig. I.1. Downing Urn, Smithsonian Institution Grounds, Washington, D. C.

dwelling with grace and satisfaction. If Downing's mission was to promote cultivation, his ability to write clearly and with sentiment delivered his message. His obituary notes that "we are compelled to admire the symmetry of his character, the vigor of his mind, the versatility of his talents, and that healthful flow of enthusiastic feeling which marks his writings."[3]

Andrew Jackson Downing's *Cottage Residences* is a slim book—pleasant to read—that has held my attention for many years (Fig. I.2). In my own career as an architect, I have observed that people often choose their houses based on location and size, but then long for some degree of charm in its appearance, and struggle with rooms that do not take advantage of natural daylight and lack views to the garden. I look at Downing's designs and think about

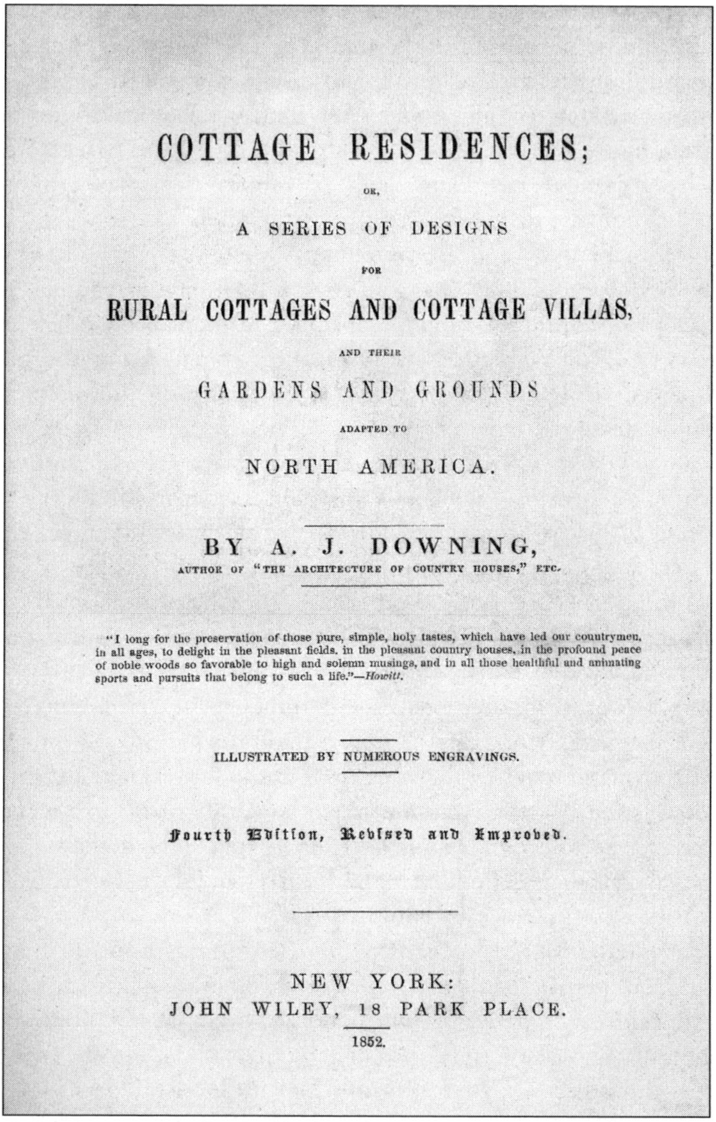

COTTAGE RESIDENCES;

OR,

A SERIES OF DESIGNS

FOR

RURAL COTTAGES AND COTTAGE VILLAS,

AND THEIR

GARDENS AND GROUNDS

ADAPTED TO

NORTH AMERICA.

BY A. J. DOWNING,

AUTHOR OF "THE ARCHITECTURE OF COUNTRY HOUSES," ETC.

"I long for the preservation of those pure, simple, holy tastes, which have led our countrymen, in all ages, to delight in the pleasant fields, in the pleasant country houses, in the profound peace of noble woods so favorable to high and solemn musings, and in all those healthful and animating sports and pursuits that belong to such a life."—*Howitt.*

ILLUSTRATED BY NUMEROUS ENGRAVINGS.

Fourth Edition, Revised and Improved.

NEW YORK:
JOHN WILEY, 18 PARK PLACE.

1852.

Fig. I.2. Title page, *Cottage Residences.*

what better houses they are for what people desire in a home. Published in 1842, the book presents architectural principles for house and garden design, and Downing's influence is evident still today in our communities. Understanding Downing's work reminds us of what we once considered necessary and desirable for satisfactory dwelling, and leads us to reconsider what kind of domestic design supports living in a positive and uplifting manner.

Cottage Residences is the first American treatise on architecture and landscape architecture. In contrast to the comprehensive treatment of civic, commercial, and domestic architecture theorized by Roman architect Vitruvius and Renaissance architect and writer Leon Battista Alberti, Downing's book features ten house designs set within cultivated landscapes. There are floor plans for rural cottages, farmhouses, and villas shown in pleasure grounds and gardens, and animated by people engaged in leisurely activities. The houses range in size and style, and are suitable to different regions of the country with varying geographic characteristics and climatic situations. Unlike the encyclopedic efforts of contemporaneous European authors such as J. C. Loudon and Eugène Viollet-le-Duc, or the diagrammatic American builder's guides and pattern books that served as the typical source for architectural construction detailing, Downing's book clarifies design principles. Satisfactory dwelling, he felt, was the confluence of many factors but depended most on matching the person to the land and its improvement. His motive was to educate and to inspire people with diverse backgrounds intent on creating new lives by defining new social structures and cultural institutions.

In Victorian-era America, Downing's work resonated for several reasons. His writing is elegant and direct, with an appealing tone. And it was well timed. Taking advantage of recent technical developments in printing and publishing, Downing inserted images within the text at a far lower cost than the metal plate engravings that had been traditionally inserted on separate pages with tissue overlays so that readers could follow examples easily. Economic production made his well-illustrated books affordable to a wide audience. The images satisfied his audience's visual appetite and allowed readers to imagine their own tasteful homes and gardens, and the accompanying text described the ways in which to achieve this.

As an internationally recognized horticultural authority, Downing expanded his expertise to what he called "rural improvements." In the mid-nineteenth century, 80 percent of all Americans lived in rural locations. People sought advice on how to lay out new homesteads, and to improve their properties and villages. Often locations had no local builders, only journeymen carpenters and craftsmen. Access to an architect or architectural authority in the form of a pattern book allowed the homebuilder to have information on the vocabulary of a particular architectural style's composition as well as the latest technological innovations, including dumbwaiters, indoor plumbing, and central heating.

Having been brought up in his family's nursery business in Newburgh, New York, fifty miles north of New York City on the Hudson River, Downing saw immigrants and homesteaders crossing the river at Newburgh to make their way west. Newburgh was also a convenient stop for steamships heading from New York City to Albany and the Erie Canal. Many were en route to the developing territories of the Ohio River Valley, or beyond. Downing's Botanic Garden and Nurseries supplied seed for vegetable and flower gardens, and cuttings for orchards and vineyards. The young man's horticultural experience allowed him to offer landscape design services; this experience, in turn, led to his writing on the subject. Downing believed that with his instruction, a settler's desire for a new life would become a desire to settle the land and thus improve the culture and character of the proprietor as well as that of the land and of the country.

Even before he weighed in with architectural plans, Downing had established his authority on the subject of rural improvements with his first book, *A Treatise on the Theory and Practice of Landscape Gardening* (1841). Primarily focused on horticulture and plant cultivation, the final sections were devoted to landscape or rural architecture, and architectural, rustic, and floral embellishments. This was Downing's first attempt at outlining architectural principles, distinguishing styles, and illustrating how well-executed houses and gardens might reflect a proprietor's character. Thinking about homeowners as proprietors, as Downing did, demonstrates that he wanted to encourage a sense of engagement with the landscape that would likely lead to greater commitment to sound improvements. Homeowners evidently embraced this point of view; the book became a favorite wedding gift of the time.[4]

After *A Treatise on the Theory and Practice of Landscape Gardening* and then *Cottage Residences*, Downing went on to write *The Fruits and Fruit-Trees of America* (1845), which systematically categorized fruit trees and illustrated the fruit's characteristic appearance. In 1850 he published *The Architecture of Country Houses*, depicting thirty-two architectural designs (without ground plans) in the format of *Cottage Residences*. By this time Downing was a Victorian celebrity; novelist Catharine Sedgwick noted that "nobody, whether he be rich or poor, builds a house or lays out a garden without consulting Downing's works; every young couple who sets up housekeeping buys them."[5] An expanded fourth edition of *Cottage Residences* was published in 1852, including five new designs.

As the founding editor of *The Horticulturist and Journal of Rural Art and Rural Taste,* a monthly periodical first published in July 1846 (Fig. I.3), Downing furthered his exposure to the American audience. According to publisher Luther Tucker, at the time of Downing's death six years later it was the most widely read publication in America after the Bible. Tucker thanked subscribers for their patronage and noted that the enthusiasm with which they had received *The Horticulturist* in its first three years resulted in a circu-

Fig. I.3. Cover, *Horticulturist* 1, August, 1846.

lation “equal to that of any similar magazine in Europe and far beyond any of its class hitherto attempted in America.”[6] The year after Downing’s death in 1852, many of his editorial essays were compiled and published in a book called *Rural Essays*.

THE MID-NINETEENTH century was a time of rapid change for Americans, with controversial issues of the safety and health of city life, territorial expansion, and good taste hotly debated among landowners, politicians, and artists. No longer a brand-new nation, the country was forging its identity. The Greek Revival style—popularized in part by Thomas Jefferson, and employed to grand effect by Benjamin Latrobe in many public buildings—was, in Downing’s opinion, ill-suited to domestic architecture. While architectural references to the temples of democracy were well-suited to civic pursuits in the new republic, a shed with a portico and columns was inappropriate to the varied national landscape and its settlement by people of varied backgrounds. Downing was determined to provide alternatives, and the reasoning behind them.

In adapting European ideas for the American middle class, Downing was influenced by the work of Scottish botanist John Claudius Loudon, and English art critic and social thinker John Ruskin. Borrowing from Loudon's landscape and design theories, Downing's adaptations required changes in materials—avoiding thatched roofs for instance—and adjustments to roof shape, chimney location, and porches in response to drier and sunnier climates typical of much of America. Ruskin's elegant writing helped Downing articulate the need for clarity and directness in the expression of purpose. Displaying certain physical elements, such as chimney tops and deep roof overhangs, indicated that a building was a house and not a barn or shop. Other writers thought that expression of purpose and style were important too, but Downing's position was unique in his belief that improvements should be made to both the land's physical character and to those who settled it.

Downing's chief complaint against "temple" houses of the Greek Revival style was their inability to accommodate multiple facets of habitation. The alternatives he offered engaged architectural thinking beyond style selection alone to the consideration of how a house's design relates to site and to the proprietor's character. In order to do this, Downing designed two kinds of floor plans. Floor plans either had a regular shape subdivided into rooms or an irregular shape with rooms assembled into an irregular plan composition. The subdivided floor plans were intended to appeal to the proprietor who valued common sense above all else and who wanted architecture with symmetry and unity tempered by economic and efficient considerations. Assembled floor plans were meant to appeal more to people with a bold imagination, who desired their land and architecture to have variety in the topography, buildings, and view. In either case, Downing's intent was for design to have meaning beyond utilitarian purpose:

Benjamin Henry Boneval Latrobe (1764–1820)

English architect and engineer, Latrobe immigrated to America in 1796 where his prominent work included the Bank of Pennsylvania in Philadelphia (1798), the first institutional building designed in the Greek Revival style, and Sedgeley (1799), outside Philadelphia, the first house designed in the Gothic Revival style. As the Surveyor of Public Buildings, he was involved in the construction (and reconstruction after it burned in the War of 1812) of the U.S. Capitol in Washington where he designed outstanding Neoclassical interiors in the invented American Order of columns with corn-cob and tobacco inspired capitals.

John Claudius Loudon (1783–1843)

Scottish botanist, landscape designer, inventor, prominent and prolific writer on horticulture and landscape design. Born in 1783 in a village southwest of Edinburgh and educated at Edinburgh, Loudon lived in London from 1803 to 1816 at which time he moved to Bayswater, a country house with large garden he called the Hermitage. In 1816 Loudon invented and patented a wrought-iron sash bar for curved greenhouse glass construction. Among numerous publications, his best-known were the Encyclopaedia of Cottage, Farm, and Villa Architecture and Furniture *(1832–1833), the* Architectural Magazine *(1834–1839), the* Suburban Gardener *(1839), and the* Arboretum et Fruiticetum Britannicum *(1838). Loudon died in 1843, deeply in debt due to his publishing activities.*

a person's civic responsibility extended the cultivated landscape beyond their property to the community in the form of improved villages, which led to publicly supported education and cultural institutions (Fig. I.4).

What Downing instinctively understood—and what he aimed to impart to all Americans—was the idea that when one designs or builds a house, or even thinks about a house as a home, satisfaction comes not just from accommodating fundamental needs, but by inspiring desires. A house is more than a number of rooms with assigned functions gathered under a roof; humans seek a place to *dwell.* How this is achieved has been a subject of continual interest to designers and a thriving industry today: publications such as *Better Homes and Gardens*, *Architectural Digest*, and the appropriately named *Dwell* instruct us not just on how to build, but how to live in what we build.

Recognizing dwelling type origins reinforces our appreciation for the reason *why* we feel the way we do in certain places. At this Downing excelled. Following the architectural principles of the early nineteenth-century French architect and writer Antoine

Fig. I.4. Study for a Rural Church by Richard Upjohn.

Chrysostôme Quatremère de Quincy, who identified the three original dwelling types of cave, tent, and hut, Downing incorporated in architectural form all three into the houses he designed. Original dwelling types in expressive architectural elements are critical to any home because they address the fundamental human need to hunt, wander, and cultivate.

The cave type, for instance, fulfills the desire for smaller, secure, and intimate zones within a larger space. These are places of rest and retreat. The tent type usually appears in Downing's designs as a porch or veranda occupying a position between house and grounds; it is a place for contemplation, a transition from outdoors to inside where one is protected from the elements while remaining close to nature. The hut type is the constructed shelter keeping handy equipment that supports comfortable and convenient operations. These include technological innovations newly available as manufactured products as well as nonmechanical objects such as window hoods. The recurrence of these original dwelling types in Downing's work accounts for the appeal of Downing's domestic designs, and their enduring relevance.

Downing identifies architectural details as a vocabulary for dwelling, but how are these physical elements capable of *expressing* certain human sensibilities? If elements are affirmed with techniques of animation, the accoutrements of dwelling and what they do become a grammar allowing design principles to be transcribed into a full architectural language. When architecture grows through addition, regenerates through repetitious and patterned space, and stimulates movement, it supports dwelling in a more comprehensive way by personifying life's fundamental definition.

While Downing did not write about architectural theory in terms familiar to today's designers and readers, his ideas about the expression of the real meaning of architecture—truth, propriety, senti-

John Ruskin
(1819–1900)

London writer, artist, and moralist of the Victorian era, Ruskin's work commented on aesthetic, social, and environmental issues. Champion of J.M.W. Turner's modern art and its depiction of nature's wonder and terror, Ruskin also wrote and illustrated two important treatises, The Seven Lamps of Architecture *(1849), and* The Stones of Venice *(1851-53). Loudon published Ruskin's first work on vernacular architecture,* The Poetry of Architecture, *in monthly chapters in his* Architectural Magazine *(1837–1838), and noted that these essays were for the young and unprejudiced artist looking to improve the art of design and taste.*

Antoine Chrysostôme Quatremère de Quincy (1755–1849)

French writer on architectural and aesthetic theory, architect, and Secrétaire Perpétual of l'Académie des Beaux-Arts from 1816 to 1839. Quatremère de Quincy's Essay on the Nature, the End, and the Means of Imitation in the Fine Arts *(1823) was published in Loudon's* Architectural Magazine *(1837). Loudon states the translation into English was made at his request and credits it for his thinking about aesthetic issues. Loudon recommended it to "every thinking man of taste." Quatremère's seminal work was* Le Dictionnaire Historique d' Architecture *(1832), which discussed history, nature, and the role of imitation and invention in design.*

ment, and beauty—nevertheless resonate. The terms may have changed, but what people need for satisfactory and comfortable dwelling remains the same. What may be taken from Downing's work and applied now are his strategies. The complete house and grounds infers the harmony he thought attainable through thoughtful design. His designs are not model houses, and they do not promote the illusions of unobtainable domestic perfection; Downing simply saw Americans as individuals needing instruction in the concepts of settlement and cultivation, in order to create a full life.

Imagine young nineteenth-century couples pouring over Downing's designs, debating their different advantages, and being intuitively attracted to one design in ways difficult to articulate. They respond to visual representations of their own sense of dwelling and lifestyle—their sense of who they want to be. The idea of dwelling has not changed—if anything, it has become more necessary and yet more challenging to achieve as more time is spent in, and commuting between, machine-dominated worlds. In cities and suburbs, Americans live in apartments, rowhouses, duplexes, and single-family houses. There is no reason that every scale of housing cannot accommodate human dwelling needs as laid out in Downing's vision. And yet most residences fail to meet these needs in a profound way.

In the chapters that follow, I provide an account of Downing's life, his influences and training, and his stellar (if all-too-brief) professional career. Chapter 2 examines his development of design principles and the ways in which they were adapted—and made new—for the mid-nineteenth century American middle class. Descriptions and plans for house and grounds design are presented in chapter 3, and chapter 4 describes how Downing so successfully incorporated the original dwelling types of cave, hut, and tent into these designs. In chapter 5, I focus on

Downing's contribution to the language of architectural expression. Finally, I conclude with some thoughts on Downing's considerable legacy. I hope this book makes apparent that the design principles that satisfied nineteenth-century ideas for domestic architecture may guide decisions about domestic design in the twenty-first century as well.

I

A. J. DOWNING

A Life

> I am employing my 8 or 10 weeks of winter's leisure in preparing a thin 8vo on "Cottage Residences." I undertake this partly *con amore,* and partly at the solicitation of a great many persons who want *plans* having some degree of adaptation to our country; & which also come within the means of the middle classes.
>
> —Downing to Robert Donaldson, January 21, 1842[1]

FROM GARDENER to horticulturalist, and from self-taught architect to the leading theorist of his day, A. J. Downing's lasting contribution to the field came from the clear understanding and convincing publication of design principles. Yet little in Downing's background could have predicted his accomplishments. The following account of his life and activities are worth examining as they serve as the foundation for understanding his ideas.

His father Samuel Downing (1761–1822) married Susanna Brown Bridge, and they lived in Lexington, Massachusetts. Around 1800, Samuel left his wife and children and moved to Newburgh, New York with Susanna's younger sister Eunice Bridge (1773–1838). The Bridge sisters were daughters of Eunice Brown and John Bridge, early Puritan settlers in Cambridge, Massachusetts. On five acres of land just north of Newburgh, Samuel worked as a wheelwright and nurseryman, and invested in local real estate.[2] Samuel and Eunice had five children: Emily (1801–1864), Charles (1802–1885), George Washington (1804–1846), Fanny (1808), and Andrew Jackson, born on October 31, 1815. Downing was seven when his father died; his mother lived until 1838, the year he married.

Downing's formal education at the Montgomery Academy in Orange County ended when he was sixteen years old. Although his mother wanted him to clerk for a local dry goods retailer, he preferred to work in the family's nursery business. In 1834, at the age of nineteen, he joined his brother Charles, his senior by fourteen years, in producing saplings, cuttings, and seeds.[3] This practical horticultural training supplemented time Downing spent with several well-educated and refined people who advanced his thinking. His acquaintance with Baron Alois Freiherr von Lederer, the Austrian Consul General and an amateur naturalist with a summer place in Newburgh, extended Downing's education over long walks when they discussed botany and mineralogy. The Baron invited Downing to a dance where he met his future wife, Caroline, and he introduced Downing to aristocratic circles including his neighbor Edward Armstrong, a cultured country gentleman and connoisseur of leisurely pursuits. Frequent visitors to the Armstrong estate included Raphael Hoyle, son of English immigrants living in Newburgh, a landscape painter familiar with theories of landscape gardening as pictorial design. Before the invention of photography, artists such as Hoyle were included on expeditions to record the landscape through drawings and paintings. (Hoyle was to be one of three artists on the Wilkes Exploring Expedition to the Pacific Northwest, but he died before its departure in 1838.) Downing also met Charles Augustus Murray, English gentleman and travel writer.[4] These friendships developed Downing's definition of a gentleman as one who appreciated nature, pursued scientific reasoning in his work, and displayed refined habits in society.

A catalogue for C. & A. J. Downing's Botanic Gardens and Nurseries dated 1838 gives a sense of their business production, advertising 112 varieties of apple tree saplings selling for $.20 each and 106 varieties of pears for $.37½, in addition to peaches, plums, cherries, apricots, and nectarines. Currants, raspberries, grapes, and strawberry cuttings and nine species of roses sorted by color were also available. The town of Newburgh was well situated for good business, on the Hudson River's west side about fifty miles north of New York City and seventy miles south of Albany. Settlers from Boston crossed the Hudson on ferries and passed through the Highlands at Newburgh.[5] Brick manufacturing was the chief industry, along with a large iron foundry and brewery. Once the Erie Canal opened in 1825, more reliable and less weather-dependent steamboats replaced sailing sloops, and railroads offered an alternative to poorly built roads, wealthy New Yorkers wanted country estates. These estates took advantage of the healthy conditions and scenic vistas of rural life while allowing businessmen to remain in contact with their urban enterprises.

One record from Washington Irving gives an account illustrating the effect of these changes. In a letter from 1802, Irving recounts a journey from New York City to Albany as taking ten days by sailing sloop. In 1835, the same trip was possible by steamboat in twenty-four to thirty hours for $7 round-trip—about twice the monthly salary of Irving's Irish servant girl. In 1848, three years after Irving finished building his home in Tarrytown, the Hudson River Railroad turned the New York to Albany trip into a six-hour commute.[6]

As the nursery business grew, Downing began to provide landscape design services for owners of estates along the Hudson River. Historians have concluded Downing was not a particularly profitable businessman and facing financial difficulties, Downing sold his interest in the family nursery and two-thirds of his inherited property to the supervisor Andrew Saul in 1847. This allowed Downing to devote more time to literary pursuits, activities he thought more likely to be successful vehicles of influence, and to work on commissions throughout the country.

Downing's friends from estates in Newburgh and beyond joined him in forming the Horticultural Society of the Valley of the Hudson in May of 1838. In June of that same year, he married Caroline Elizabeth DeWint (1815–1905), the oldest of eleven children.[7] Although there are no surviving images of Caroline, the Swedish author, correspondent, and family friend Frederika Bremer described her as "a delicate, pretty little woman; of a bird-like nature; charming, merry, and amiable little creature, of a highly cultivated mind, and equal to her husband."[8] Andrew and Caroline Downing had no children.

Caroline's background was wealthier and more established than Downing's. Her father was John Peter DeWint, Esq. (1786/87–1870), a wealthy businessman and amateur horticulturist.[9] DeWint was from a Dutch family who made their fortune in the West Indies sugar trade and settled in New York in 1784. DeWint's local business interests included owning the Wiltse river ferry, the Long Dock for his freight activities, a sloop named *Caroline*, and a saloon. He served as director of the Unitarian Church, of a local newspaper, and at the First National Bank of Fishkill Landing. As a philanthropist, DeWint gave land for a village graveyard. The DeWint home, Locust Grove, was a two-thousand-acre estate in Fishkill Landing (now Beacon), on the east side of the Hudson opposite Newburgh.

Caroline's mother, Caroline Amelia Smith (1795–1852), was the granddaughter of John Adams, second president of the United States, and the niece of John Quincy Adams, the sixth president. Downing dedicated his first book to John Quincy Adams, identifying him as, "the lover of rural pursuits, as well as the distinguished patriot, statesman, and sage, this volume, by permission, is respectfully and affectionately dedicated, by his friend, the author."

The young couple lived with Caroline's family after they were married, while Downing designed and built a new house on the nursery property (Figs. 1.1, 1.2, and 1.3).[10] The design reflected the influence of an Elizabethan villa published in English architect Francis Goodwin's portfolio, *Rural Architecture* (Fig. 1.4). Downing's version added a veranda on either side of the entry hall providing a place for leisurely contemplation of river views. Sometimes called Highland Garden, it was Downing's first attempt to put into practice principles of design where a house and grounds fit together. Downing's house reinforced his rejection of the Greek Revival style for a more progressive way of building, while demonstrating that tasteful architecture was possible on a smaller, more affordable scale. The grounds contained plants and architectural elements in compositions of interest to amateur gentleman gardeners and lovers of nature.

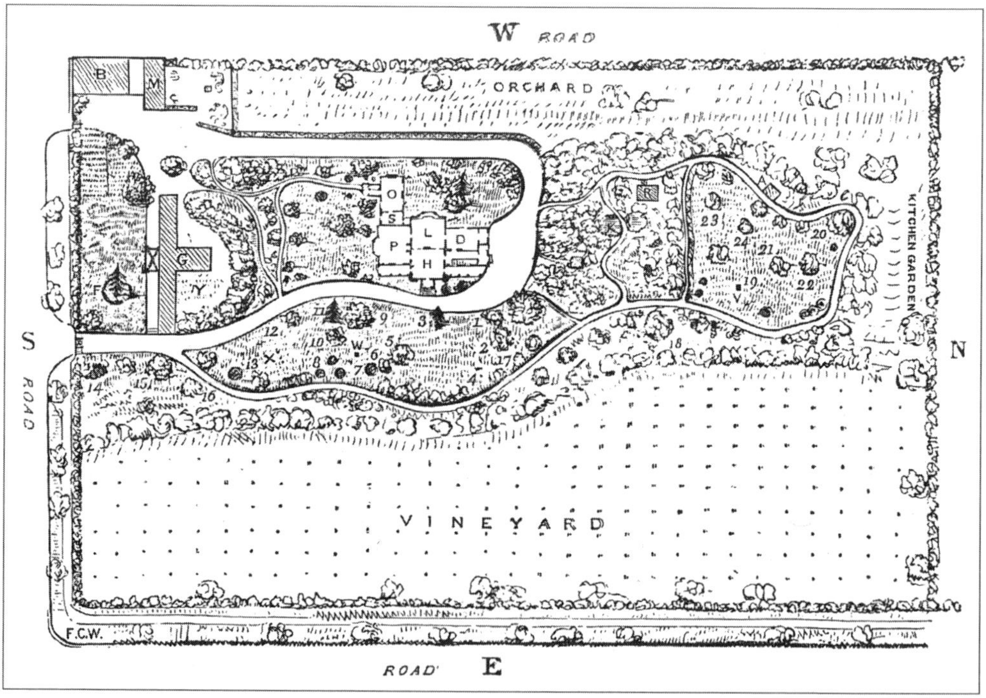

Fig. 1.1. Residence of the late A. J. Downing, Newburgh, on the Hudson, Frederick Clarke Withers drawing of Downing's house, 1852.

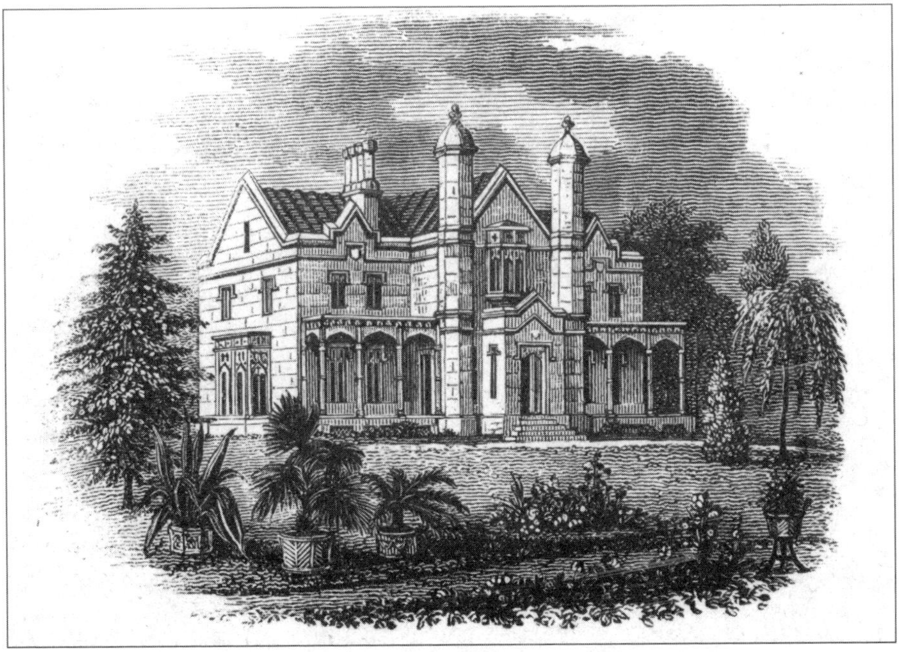

Fig. 1.2. Alexander Jackson Davis drawing of Downing's Highland Garden, Perspective View.

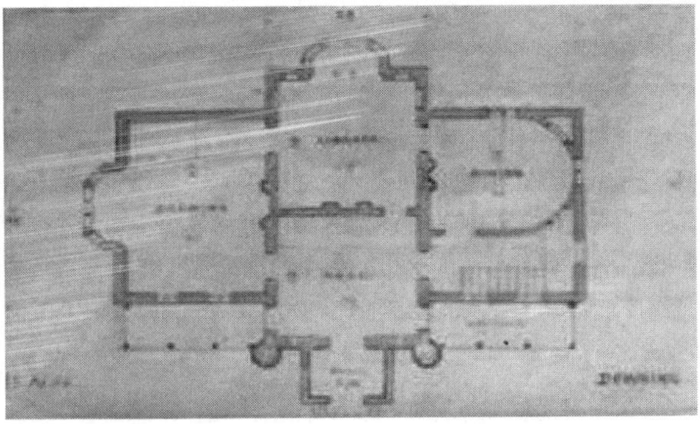

Fig. 1.3. Alexander Jackson Davis drawing of Downing's Highland Garden, Principal Floor Plan.

Fig. 1.4. A Villa in the Elizabethan Style, Design 10.

Two of Caroline's younger sisters married men who worked for Downing. Clarence Chatham Cook (1828–1900), a Harvard graduate with little architectural experience at the beginning of his career, married Caroline's sister Louisa in 1852. Cook later wrote articles for *Scribner's Monthly*, some of which were later collected in his popular book *The House Beautiful* (1877). Cook was also an inspiring poet and interested in art criticism. In 1869, Cook wrote *A Description of the New York Central Park* to attract support for the various phases of development. The book included engaging vignettes showing people enjoying leisurely activities. Francis Kowsky claims, "More than anyone in the latter part of the century, Cook was the spokesman for the spirit of Downing's teachings."[11]

Frederick Clarke Withers was a London architect. Responding to a newspaper advertisement, Withers joined the practice only six months before Downing's death. He continued working with Downing's partner Calvert Vaux until 1856, the year after he married Caroline's sister Emily Augusta. Withers had "a distinguished career as a Gothic Revival church architect."[12]

More personal observations about Downing are provided in a "Memoir" and "Letter to His Friends," published with his collected essays after his death. George William Curtis, a friend with a shared interest in Transcendentalism and a leader of public opinion on political and social reform, described

Fig. 1.5. Daguerreotype of Andrew Jackson Downing, c. 1851.

Downing as tall and slight with thick black hair worn long, large dark brown eyes, and a quiet, thoughtful, reserved nature coupled with great scientific intelligence (Fig. 1.5). Bremer described his character as noble, intelligent, and refined, recalling his search for perfection in rural beauty and in its improvements. She observed that Downing conducted his business deal-

Frederick Clarke Withers (1828–1901)

An English architect who immigrated to America in 1852, where he became Downing's second office employee. After Downing's death he partnered with Vaux, designing thirteen houses credited as by Vaux & Withers in Vaux's book Villas and Cottages *(1857 and 1864). Withers established his practice remaining in Newburg through the Civil War. After 1864, Withers moved his family and practice to New York City, where his work was important to the High Victorian Gothic style movement. His significant projects includes the Jefferson Market Courthouse in New York and Gallaudet College in Washington, D.C. Withers wrote* Church Architecture *(1873), documenting the history and his chief contributions to ecclesiastic architecture.*

ings with an apparent careless ease and presented an appearance of leisure and grace. Bremer noted that his chief intent was to instruct others about the country's future by advocating public parks and gardens, public libraries, schools and universities, and art galleries—the civic institutions needed to elevate middle-class taste and cultivation in a republican social order.

BORN WITH intelligence, curiosity and talent, enriched with field observation, fortuitous acquaintances and reading, and experienced in horticultural endeavors, Downing was prepared for his work. Formal training as we know it was difficult because there were no architecture or horticulture schools in America. A sort of trade school for architects and builders, The Carpenters' Company of Philadelphia, operated from 1833 to 1842.[13] In any case, Downing's family was not financially able to send him to Europe for further study. As scanty as Downing's architectural training seems, it was not unusual or unreasonable for the times. The 1850 census lists 591 architects in the entire country, the majority of them foreign-born and educated.[14] English architect Benjamin Latrobe is a typical example. Richard Morris Hunt was the first American to receive a formal architectural education studying at the École des Beaux-Arts in Paris from 1846 and returning in 1855. Five years later, the second American, Henry Hobson Richardson began his studies at the same institution.[15]

Downing's architectural training advanced through an unusual apprenticeship. In late 1838 or early 1839, a client and friend, Robert Donaldson, Esq., introduced Downing to Alexander Jackson Davis, a New York City architect.[16] Their twelve-year collaboration was a reciprocal arrangement where Downing referred potential clients for house designs to Davis, and Davis prepared architectural drawings from Downing's sketches for engraving. Downing valued Davis's skill in representing his design intent and there are surviving Downing letters requesting Davis to use his architectural experience to adjust the design for errors as needed. Clearly Downing admired Davis, noting that "for invention, and scientific knowledge of his art, we do not know his superior in this country."[17] Davis later used Downing's popularity to advance his own career. Evidence of this is found in Davis's stated list of qualifications in his portfolio book of designs, where he called himself an "illustrator of old New York (fine drawings of significant buildings much like tourist postcards), New York Mirror, Valentine's Manuel, Hoilon's History, and Downing's Publications."[18]

To enhance his knowledge, Downing read American authors including Ralph Waldo Emerson, the poetry of William Cullen Bryant and James Russell Lowell, and English authors on landscape design theory.[19] Downing thought that the most important theoretical work was Sir Uvedale Price's *An Essay on the Picturesque* (1794)—"with which I am thoroughly familiar"—where the picturesque category is added to the sublime and the beautiful.[20] His favorite romantic writings were Sir Walter Scott's Waverley novels and poems. In his work, Downing frequently quotes English writers on theory and aesthetics, including Sir Archibald Alison and Victor Cousins on taste, Edmund Burke on romanticism, Sir William Chambers on architecture, Reverend William Gilpin on tourism and "sight seeing," the painter William Hogarth on beauty, Richard Payne Knight on the picturesque, poet William Mason on the English garden, Humphry Repton and Thomas Whately on landscape gardening theory, and John Ruskin. French authors included René Girardin's essay on landscape composition and Quatremère de Quincy on the history of fine arts. Also referenced in Downing's writings are American authorities on farming

Alexander J. Davis (1803–1892)

Born in New York City in 1803, Davis first trained as a printer and lithographer, and in 1825 was a founding member of the National Academy of Design. In 1829 he joined the prominent Greek Revival architect Ithiel Town, who had the most extensive architectural library in the country. This partnership lasted until 1835 although they worked together again from 1842 until Town's death in 1844. Their projects included houses—some in the new Italianate style—and many state capitols and university building designed in the Collegiate Gothic style. Davis met Robert Donaldson while working at the University of North Carolina at Chapel Hill. Davis and Downing both worked on improvements to Donaldson's estate Blithewood in Barrytown, New York from 1841. In 1853, entrepreneur Llewellyn S. Haskell, a former client of Downing, commissioned Davis to design the first residential community in the United States, called Llewellyn Park, in West Orange, New Jersey. Davis was invited to join the newly formed American Institute of Architects in 1857. Davis died in 1892 with his last project a redesign of his summer lodge in West Orange, New Jersey.

Calvert Bowyer Vaux (1824–1895)

London architect who apprenticed under Lewis Nockalls Cottingham, a Gothic Revival architect. Returning to Newburgh with Downing in September, 1850, much of their production over the next two years was published in Vaux's Villas and Cottages: A Series of Designs Prepared for Execution in the United States *(1857). In 1854, Vaux married Mary Swan McEntee of Kingston, New York, who was the sister of landscape painter Jervis McEntee, a Hudson River School painter. They had four children, naming their second son Downing. After a partnership with Withers from 1853 to 1856 (and periodically throughout the 1860s and 70s) Vaux moved to New York City and joined the National Academy of Design. Vaux and Olmsted worked on Central Park from 1858, and again in different capacities during its uneven development at various points from 1866 to1895 where Vaux designed numerous bridges and park structures. Their formal partnership—Olmsted, Vaux and Company—operated from 1865 to 1872. In 1874, Vaux formed an architectural partnership with George Kent Ratford to work on the Metropolitan Museum of Art. Olmsted and Vaux worked together for the last time in 1889 on Newburgh's Downing Park (see Fig. C.3).*

such as Richard Lamb Allen and David Low. Downing's library had busts of Scott, Linnaeus, Franklin, Milton, Dante, and Petrarch mounted above the bookshelves.[21] Downing read William Hazlitt, considered one of the masters of the English essay, to develop writing proficiency.[22]

Downing often professed his greatest debt to his self-appointed mentor, John Claudius Loudon, a man he never met. Loudon is the father of English landscape architecture; a claim based more on his vast literary achievement than his built work.[23] Considered the most prominent and prolific writer on horticulture and landscape design during the first half of the nineteenth century, Loudon's work allowed "the art of garden design with all its new modes and styles [to be] codified and broadcast through printed texts and journals."[24] This followed the work of professional landscape designer Lancelot "Capability" Brown (1716–1783), designer of pastoral landscapes with gently undulating topography, water bodies with indistinct edges, and belts of trees to conceal or reveal distant prospects. This constructed landscape is now considered quintessentially English. Humphry Repton (English, 1751–1818), who sought to be Brown's successor, was a skillful artist and writer, unlike Brown who left no written accounts of his ideas.[25] Repton's work included hundreds of projects and numerous historical, practical and theoretical books that advanced the landscape design profession. He demonstrated proposals to clients with "before and after" rendered views of composed landscapes. Loudon was at first critical of this approach, but then published a collection of Repton's writings in 1840. Downing used Repton and Loudon to understand English landscape theory and the visual relationship between architecture and landscape, as well as the emerging profession of landscape design. After Loudon died, Downing edited an American edition of his wife Jane Loudon's *Gardening for Ladies*.

Fig. 1.6. *Pastoral Landscape,* Claude Lorraine, 1638.

One significant difference between Loudon and Downing was how they saw social classes. Unlike England with its Enclosure Laws, new industries, and a slowly emerging middle class, Downing observed unique opportunities for all Americans. As historian Dell Upton notes, "While Loudon bitterly attacked the ruling class, Downing, who did not admit that there was such a thing in America, cultivated it."[26] Downing's audience was decidedly middle-class—that is, the first generation with sufficient means to buy and cultivate land, and to build a home.

Seeing important landscape painters was part of the European Grand Tour experience, and these paintings influenced nineteenth-century authors and landscape designers in thinking of landscape design as composing a scene. The French artist Claude Gellée from Lorrain, known as Claude Lorrain (c. 1600–1682), painted what came to be considered "the Beautiful" in landscape theory (Fig. 1.6).[27] Scenes of calm repose presented worlds of harmony and unity between the simple, flowing forms of nature and of the man-made. Another seventeenth-century landscape painting master, Salvator Rosa (1615–1673), illustrated the contrasting "Sublime" with haunting, wild views of gloomy yet spirited irregularity in an intriguing world of great variety (Fig. 1.7). In America, Niagara Falls, the Natural Bridge of Virginia, and Yosemite Valley were considered to be examples of the sublime found in

Fig. 1.7. *Bandits on a Rocky Coast,* Salvator Rosa, c. 1656.

nature. Given that such landscapes cannot be created, the Sublime as it could be made became the "Picturesque," which was considered the contrasting style to the Beautiful. The idea of the guiding hand of taste as art embellishng nature became an inherent premise in Downing's work.

DOWNING BEGAN his literary career in 1835 by contributing an essay to the *New York Mirror*, three articles to *The Horticultural Register and Gardener's Magazine*, and five articles to Hovey's *Magazine of Horticulture*, with eighteen more in 1836.[28] In 1841, Downing wrote a preface and added notes along with Asa Gray, Harvard Professor of Natural History, in the American edition of John Lindley's *Theory of Horticulture*, in which he notes it is "free from superfluous technicalities, and at the same time truly scientific." These efforts prepared Downing for his first book, *A Treatise on the Theory and Practice of Landscape Gardening*, published in New York and London in 1841. In technical terms, John Crowley has concluded that the book "was the first American architectural publication issued in machine-sewn cloth bindings, and the first with extensive use of wood engravings."[29] Downing published an enlarged and revised edition with additional illustrations in 1844 and with a new preface in 1849. There were reissues in New York and London in 1850 and 1852. After Downing's death, a fifth edition was published in 1853, with reissues in 1854, 1855, 1856 and 1857, and a sixth edition with a supplement by his friend, horticulturist Henry Winthrop Sargent, was published in 1859.

The first edition contained only a few examples of homes with landscapes Downing thought worthy of publication. The expanded 1849 edition contained more. Notable estates include Robert Donaldson's Blithewood, Mrs. Edward Livingston's Montgomery Place, Henry Winthrop Sargent's Wodenethe, W. Langdon's Hyde Park with grounds designed by André Parmentier, and William P. van Rensselaer's Beaverwyck near Albany.[30] The residence of George Sheaff, Esq. was included because Downing considered it a model farm. Other houses offered examples of specific styles or modes of building, such as Samuel Lyon's Cottage for the Tudor style, the Ludlow Cottage for the Rural Gothic style, and John Notman's 1838 design for Bishop Doane's Riverside Villa in Burlington, New Jersey, "the first Italianate house to be erected in the United States."[31]

In addition to providing critical horticultural information, it included a chapter called "Landscape or Rural Architecture." Here Downing discussed principles of fitness, expression of purpose, and the art of taste. New constructions were to attempt a harmonious union between buildings and setting where the concepts of the Beautiful or Classical, and the Picturesque or Romantic, were presented as two distinct approaches. This book set expectations for suburban development with idealized images of individual houses in pastoral settings on winding streets following undulating topography.

Given the middle-class audience he attempted to reach and the message of taste he conveyed, Downing employed the most advanced bookmaking techniques for affordable publications. This book's popularity is partly due to economic reasons, but also because of the comprehensive content and clear writing. Downing saw that his audience was looking for applicable principles about domestic architecture, and he expanded his horticultural experience to address a broad range of improvements to rural properties, eventually describing himself as a "rural architect."[32]

Downing's second book on rural architecture, *Cottage Residences*, had ten designs in six styles, each with an arrangement of the grounds. The book included a single hand-painted, water-colored page of six exterior color choices with light grey tones meant for shady situations, and drab or fawn tones for sunny situations. Each design chapter ended with plant lists for

Fig. 1.8. View in the Grounds at Blithewood, Dutchess Co., NY, The Residence of Robert Donaldson, Esq., Frontispiece, *TPLG,* Alexander Jackson Davis.

kitchen gardens, perennial border flowers (classified by flowering peak over six months and by height), deciduous and evergreen trees and shrubs, grape vines, and fruit trees, including over fifty varieties of pears alone. It is dedicated to Donaldson, *Arbiter Elegantiarum,* who paid for a steel engraving of Davis's addition to Blithewood that Downing used for his first book's frontispiece (Fig. 1.8). *Cottage Residences* was reissued in 1844 and 1847, and expanded in the fourth edition of 1852 by adding five designs, although without landscape plans.[33]

New printing technologies allowed Downing to insert detailed, white-line wood engravings directly into the text, and he did so generously. The typical procedure for illustrating his books was for Downing to design and sketch the house with views of the appropriate landscape on a single piece of paper, usually about 7 x 10 inches (Fig. 1.9). Davis prepared drawings from the sketches for engraving by the notable book illustrator Dr. Alexander Anderson (Fig. 1.10).[34] This relief process achieved a greater delicacy of line and tone than woodcuts, and the image could be inserted and printed simultaneously with the text.[35] George Tatum notes that Davis's highly regarded drawing skill was a key factor in Downing's literary popularity, where "the most successful architectural design was apt to be considered the one that appeared to greatest advantage in a wood engraving."[36] Because

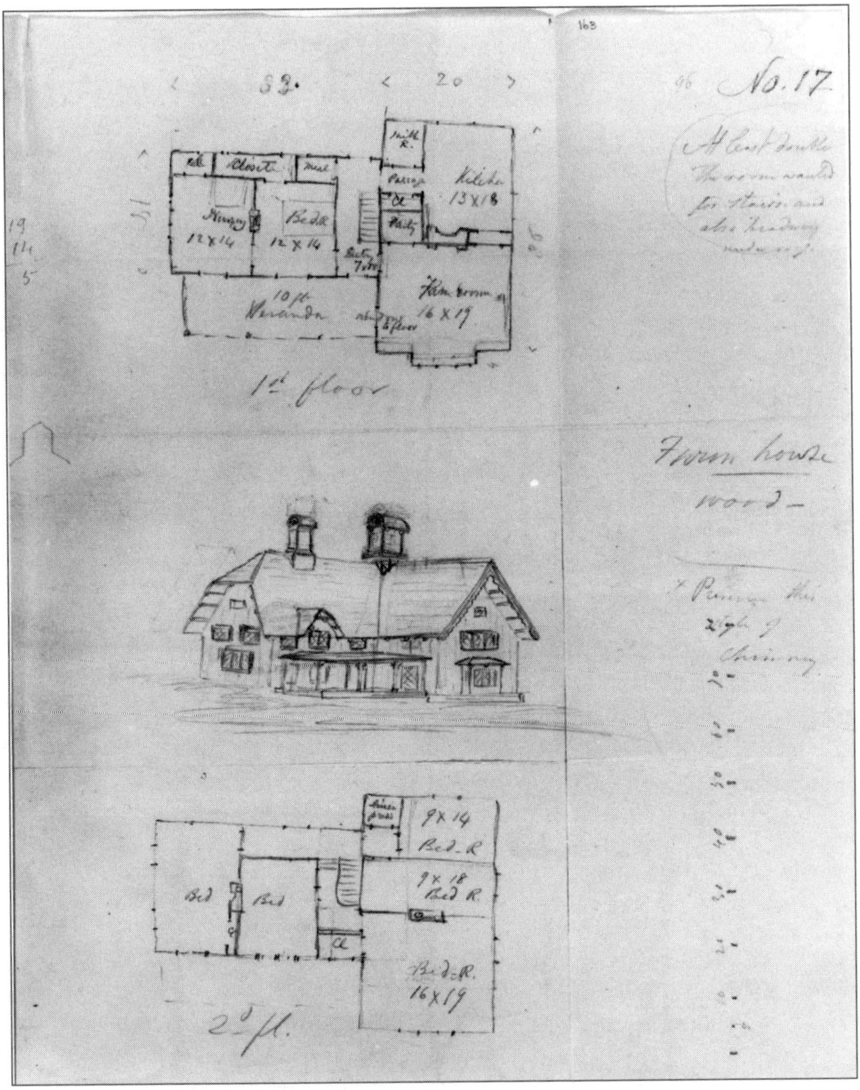

Fig. 1.9. Downing sketch of Design XVII, *ACH*.

some Downing sketches survive, it is certain that Downing designed and sketched, Davis drew, and Anderson engraved six designs in Downing's first book on architecture, and fourteen in his second. There is no evidence to dispute that they could have executed five more designs in the first book and ten more in the second. In all, this exceptional team made the illustrations for between twenty and thirty-five of the thirty-nine published house designs.

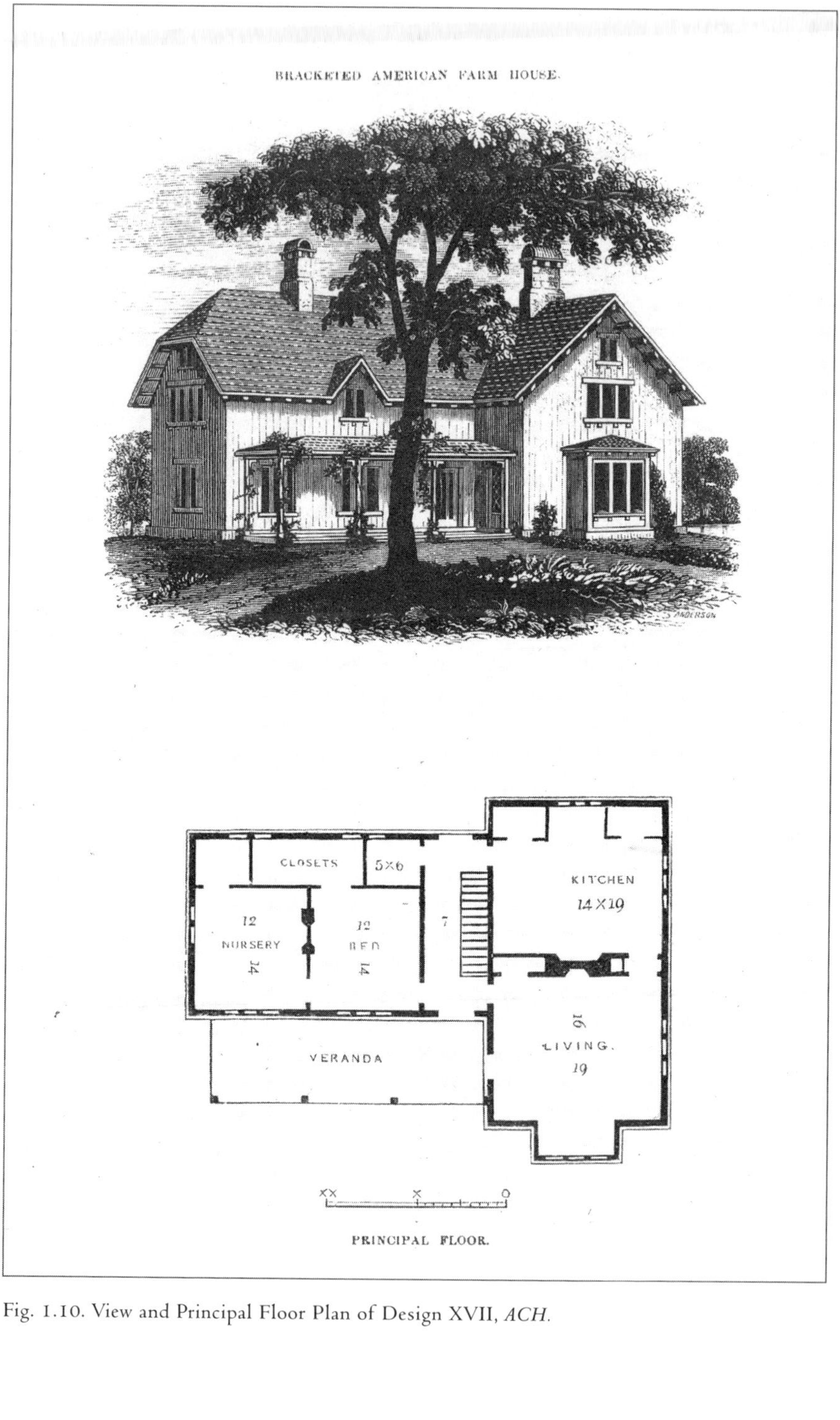

Fig. 1.10. View and Principal Floor Plan of Design XVII, *ACH*.

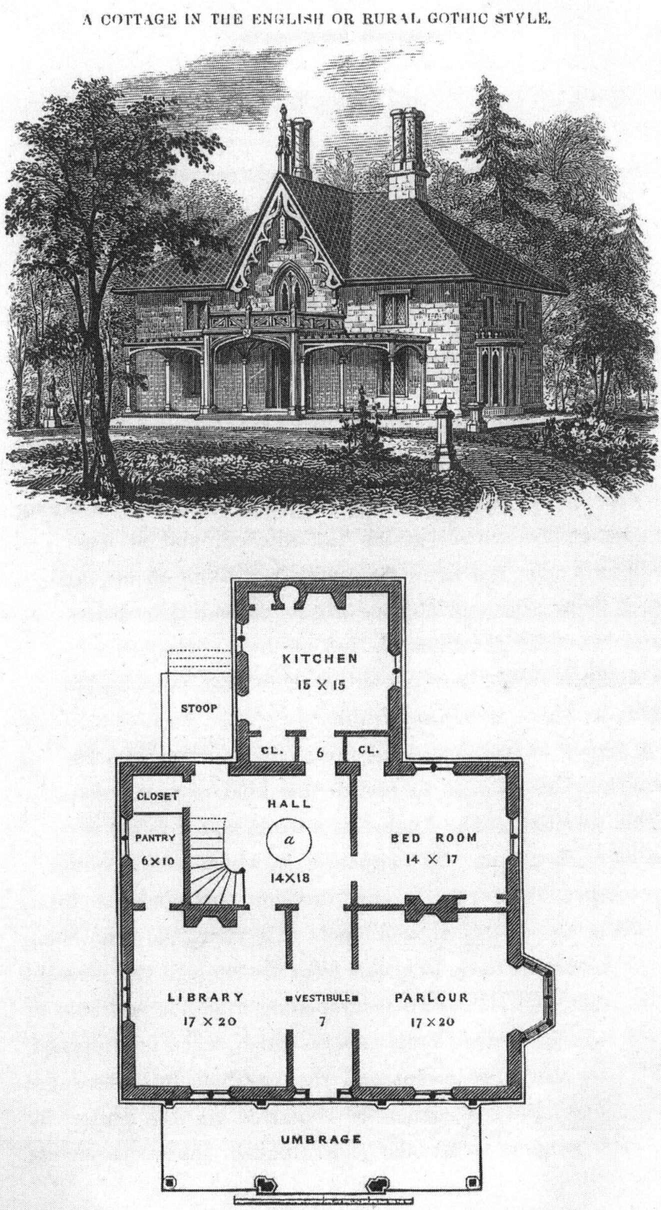

Fig. 1.11. View and Principal Floor Plan of Design II, *CR*.

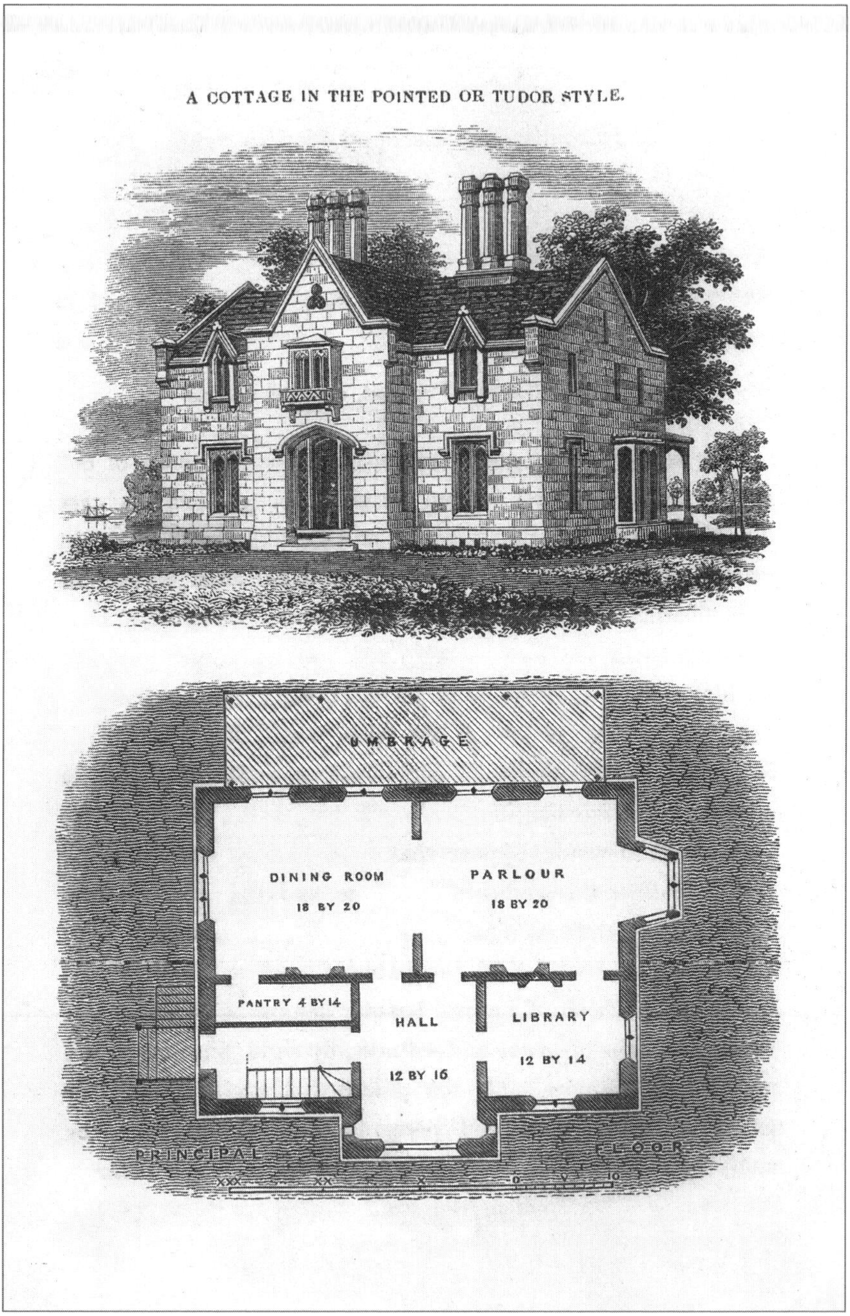

Fig. 1.12. View and Principal Floor Plan of Design III, *CR*.

Fig. 1.13. George Washington Downing House with front addition, different roof configuration and porch. 87 Broad Street, Newburgh, New York.

Downing designed eight houses in the first edition of *Cottage Residences*, with Davis and another English architect practicing in America, John Notman, providing one design each. Of Downing's designs, only two were built projects. Construction costs were estimated to range from $830 or about $.41 per square foot for Design VII, a two-story wood cottage or gate lodge, to between $12,000 to $15,000 depending on the finishes, or between $1.67 to $2.08 per square foot, for Design X, the three-story stone villa Davis designed for Joel Rathbone, Esq. in Albany. Downing's expertise with construction methods and costs came from designing and building at least three houses of similar size. Besides his own house, Downing's most reliable and timely information was from Design II, which was built for his wife's relative, John B. Angier in Medford, Massachusetts in 1842 (Fig. 1.11), and Design III, built for his brother George on property across from the nursery in 1841–1842 (Figs. 1.12 and 1.13).[37]

Downing's designs included two or three floor plan drawings, some details, and an elevation perspective view. This kind of drawing helped the design enter the imagination more readily than straight-on elevation drawings because the context was shown as a complete scene with plants, distant views, and people. The reader could longingly imagine his home in such a setting and the tranquil life it projected. No evidence of toil or farm chores was indicated, for this world was for gentlemen and ladies above the survival level. The depicted way of life was not intended to be unobtainable, but as Downing thought possible to achieve.

This book was unlike other books on architecture, many of which were project portfolios. Builder's guides included construction details. Asher Benjamin and Minard Lafever supplied pattern books for carpenters. For theory, history of art books sometimes had dedicated sections on architecture. Louisa Tuthill's *History of Architecture*, published in Philadelphia in 1848, is such an example.[38] A rare surviving Downing letter outlines how his intent with his book differed from standard practice at the time: "This little work will contain elevations, plans & some essential details of the buildings—and plans of grounds, lists of fruit & ornamental trees, etc. Mr. Notman, the ablest architect in Phila(delphia), has volunteered two plans—Mr. Davis one—and I have prepared six which before engraving are corrected as to the accuracy of details ect. by Mr. D(avis) & I trust the work without being one of much pretension will, in the absence of any thing American of the kind, be found of some use in directing the public taste."[39]

Downing's third book, *The Fruits and Fruit Trees of America*, was so popular that it was reissued annually for seven years from its first edition in 1845 until 1852, with a color plate edition in 1847, and sold 15,000 copies before 1853. Drawings of fruit showed distinguishing characteristics and the size a common home orchard was likely to produce. This systematic catalogue of fruit and fruit trees had great impact on the country's agricultural development.[40] The economic value of consistent names and commonly accepted attributes of each fruit species cannot be overstated. As with any developing economy, surpluses supply markets and promote trade—so long as the commodity is reliably identified and defined. European horticultural societies recognized Downing's contribution and his international reputation continued to grow. The book title identified Downing as a "corresponding member of the Royal Botanic Society of London; and of the Horticultural Societies of Berlin; the Low Countries" and numerous American societies. Frederick William IV of Prussia awarded Downing his country's Gold Medal of Science, and Anna Pavlova Romanova, Queen of Holland, sent him a carbuncle and diamond ring.[41]

The success of these books and their national and international recognition established Downing as an important figure for his scientific contribution and as an arbiter of good taste. Perhaps this accomplishment, along with the desire to elevate his professional status, gave him the confidence to write Donaldson suggesting that they form "a kind of country club . . . composed of gentlemen interested in agriculture and gardening. . . . our number should be limited, say to 10. I already know several who are inclined to join but it is better that little should be said about it until a plan is decided upon. Pray tell me what you think of this little matter—and if you think favourably of it, propose some names of the most desirable persons between Hudson and Hyde Park. If it could be nicely constructed & managed would it not render our noble river residences more agreeable still?"[42]

Calling it their "rural club," there is no evidence this society of gentlemen formed, and it is questionable whether Downing would have been considered on equal social status with the others he proposed as members. While his interests in rural pursuits coincided with theirs, Downing was in business; he may have been a friend and frequent guest at the Donaldson estate, but he did charge a fee for his services. Even though Downing believed that "every laborer is a possible gentleman, not by the possession of money or fine clothes—but through the refining influence of intellectual and moral culture," this does not mean that the wealthy agreed.[43]

Downing's early effort to establish himself as a gentleman *and* a professional reflected other newly emerging domestic design businesses, where architects and landscape architects courted clients who sought their expertise and appreciated their cultivated taste. In 1842, Downing advertised his services as flat fees for landscape design of various sizes and $15 per day plus traveling expenses for sketches of any ornamental garden building of rustic work, a gate lodge, gardener's house, or greenhouse.[44] Downing noted five per cent of the construction cost as the usual fee for complete services in the 1852 edition of *Cottage Residences*—half of what he predicted an owner would pay to remedy problems if he acted as his own architect.

Following the successful reception of these three books, Downing became the first editor of Luther Tucker's new journal, *The Horticulturist and Journal of Rural Art and Rural Taste*, simultaneously published in Albany, Boston, New York and Philadelphia.[45] Downing edited 74 monthly issues from July of 1846 until his death in 1852. This journal of approximately fifty pages per issue covered house and garden design, as well as commentary promoting public parks, rural cemeteries, schoolhouses, agricultural colleges, and country churches. Subscriptions cost $3.00 per year, and advertisements were sold at $5.00 per page. Within the first year, *The Horticulturalist* had subscribers in twenty-nine states and British provinces in Canada—a testimony to Downing's widespread influence.

Each issue had an engraved frontispiece, sometimes already published in one of Downing's books, as well as more illustrations inserted into the text. In addition to writing editorials and editing numerous reviews, foreign and domestic notices, letters, and reports from state horticultural societies,

Downing contributed monthly essays and articles sometimes under the appellation "an old digger." After Downing's death, sixty-six essays, eight letters, and a few images were published as *Rural Essays*.

In 1847, Downing wrote a thirty-three-page supplement for the American edition of George Wightwick's *Hints to Young Architects.*[46] Downing's review in *The Horticulturist* declared that the supplement added advice on siting buildings, principles of fitness and propriety, style and material choice, and finally on the advantages of proper planning to Wightwick's practical details and specifications.[47] Capitalizing on Downing's popularity, the 1859 edition of *Hints* reversed the book title, giving Downing's contribution more prominence. One reason for Downing's interest was Wightwick's earlier book *The Palace of Architecture*, published in 1840. Downing claimed to be an "associationist," who was defined in this book as one who believed that expressive artistic production prompted elevated human response.[48]

Downing's fourth book, *The Architecture of Country Houses*, was dedicated to his friend Henry Winthrop Sargent and was published in 1850, with nine reissues to 1866 and nineteen printings by 1886.[49] The book contained Downing designs for twelve cottages, seven farmhouses, and seven villas, with three other architects contributing eight designs. Downing defined cottages as houses for families who had some domestic assistance but without need for additional accommodations, while villas were designed for families with three or more live-in servants. Farmhouses needed large attics to accommodate seasonal workers. The design descriptions do not include site plans, although exterior views continue to show composed settings appropriate to each particular style. Wood cottages average $.45 per square foot, farmhouses built with fieldstone average $.80 per square foot, and villas average $1.07 for wood, $1.27 for stone, and $1.56 per square foot for brick with stucco-finish construction. Responding to criticism about an insufficient number of low-cost designs in *Cottage Residences*—and therefore not being the true republican he claimed to be—Downing showed more wood exteriors and included a greater range of styles for small cottages. Other improvements included chapters on interior finishing, manufactured furniture, and mechanical heating and ventilating equipment along with their suppliers.

Critical comments about Downing's illusion of practicality were well founded. In *Cottage Residences*, the Ornamental Farm House, for instance, was for the "intelligent" farmer who wanted some architectural beauty in a fieldstone house, making a *ferme ornée* (Fig. 1.14). The site plan designated as the "ornamental portion of the farm" showed a front lawn (shown as *a*) with a curved road (*b*), an orchard (*c*), a parterre-like kitchen garden (*d*),

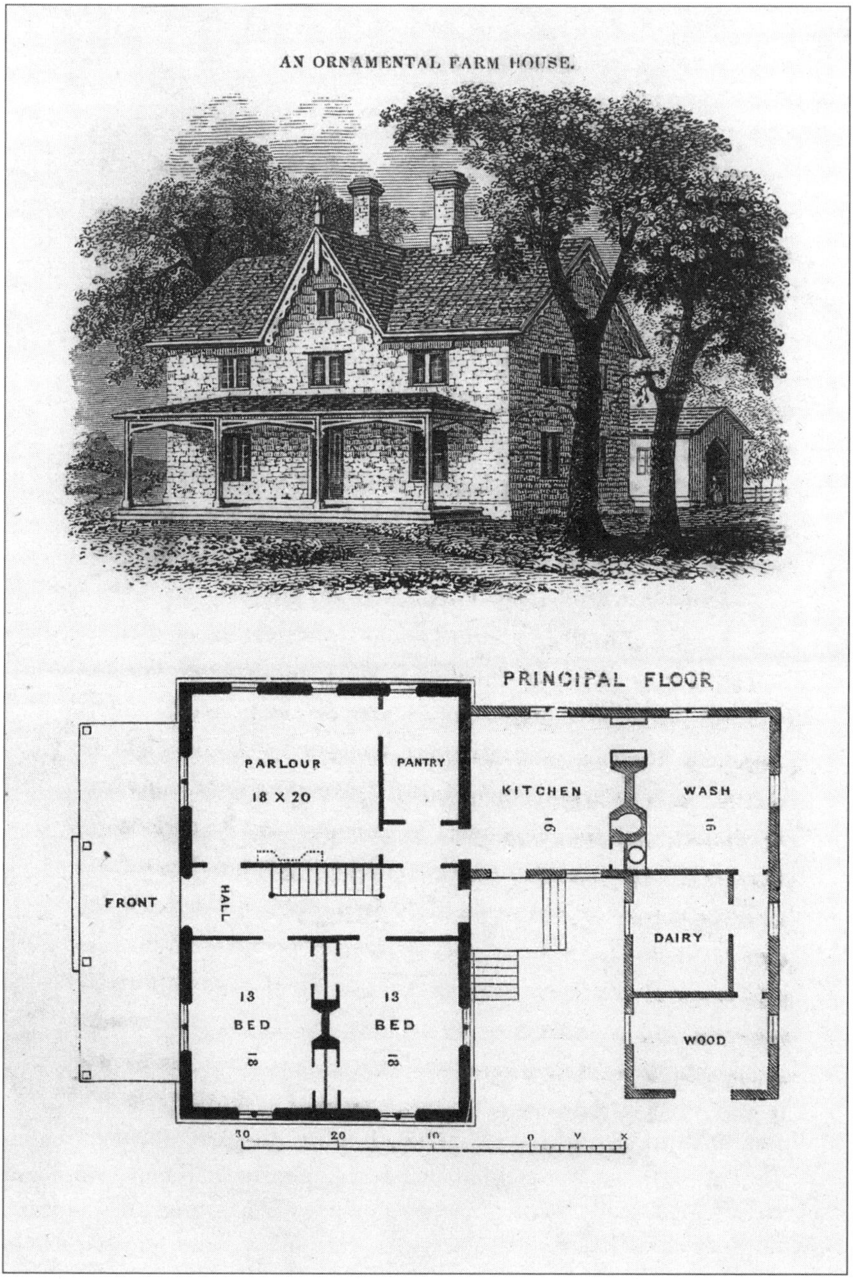

Fig. 1.14. View and Principal Floor Plan of Design IV, *CR*.

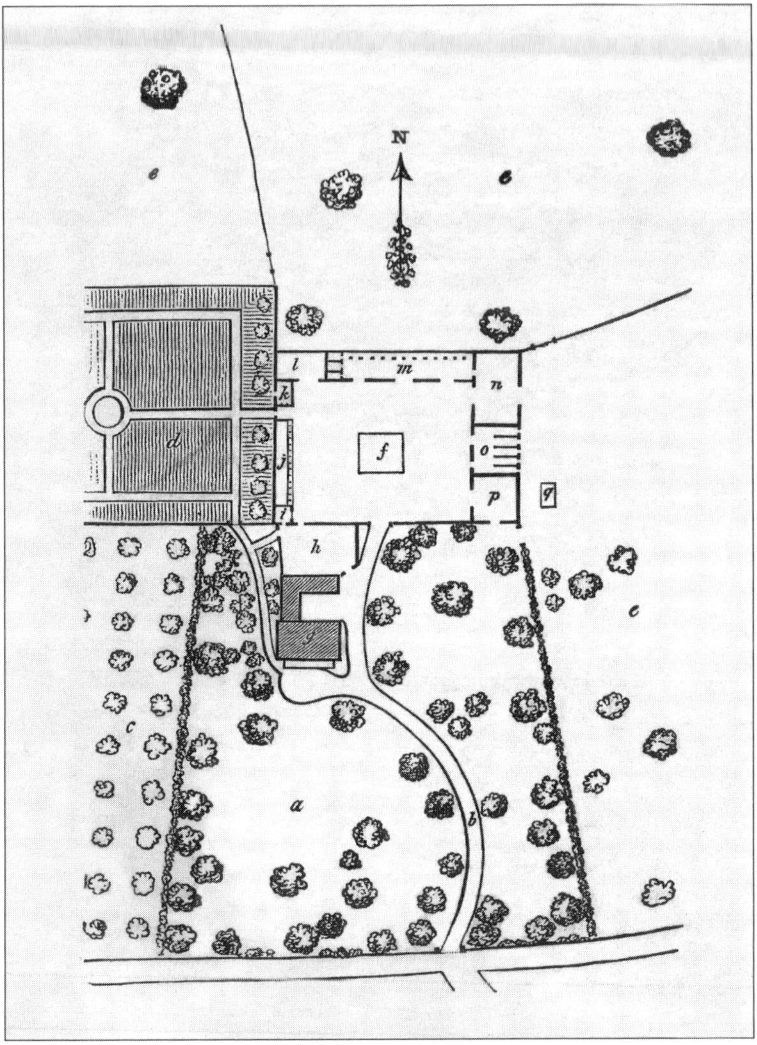

Fig. 1.15. Plan of the Grounds of Design IV, *CR*.

adjoining fields in turf or under the plough (*e*), and a yard for the outbuildings (*f*) (Fig. 1.15). Such a gentleman farmer appears well above mundane concerns of subsistence. While he may not possess paintings or sculpture, Downing declared that the presence of nature offered the finer view.[50] In other words, the farmer had time to consider his land a landscape, in accordance with Downing's directive to unite purpose and beauty.

IN ADDITION to his literary pursuits, Downing wanted to build projects. In late 1849 and early 1850, Downing and Davis worked together on an agricultural college design with Davis as architect and Downing laying out the grounds. Downing's letters reveal a somewhat uneven partnership; at one point, he directed Davis to change his work on behalf of the client commissioners.[51] Perhaps Davis grew tired of this, because when Downing proposed a closer business alliance, he declined. As a result, Downing no longer referred potential clients to Davis or published comments recommending him, and Davis added landscape gardening to his list of potential professional services.[52] Now they competed for the same clients, often people such as Donaldson. Previously, Davis had designed Blithewood additions including covered verandas and a gatehouse, published in his 1838 book as an example of the rustic cottage style. Downing had provided plants and landscape designs, and now published an octagon springhouse design, calling it the New Gate Lodge in the 1849 reissue of his *Treatise on the Theory and Practice of Landscape Gardening* (Fig. 1.16).[53]

Because of their close collaboration, some historians attribute Downing's designs to Davis. Although Davis was an accomplished illustrator and a Greek Revival and Gothic-style architect with commissions for collegiate and ecclesiastical buildings, state capitols, court houses, and a classically styled Smithsonian Institution competition entry, he lacked the ability to reach a popular audience. In 1838, Davis published his portfolio as *Rural Residences.* It was poorly received, primarily because it was very expensive and unluckily coincided with a financial panic and subsequent depression.[54] Offering little text explaining the designs, it also failed because the houses were impractical for farmers and unappealing to people looking for charming cottages, of which Davis included one in the oriental style and two with tree-trunk columns. His most elaborate villa was a stone villa in the English collegiate style with a fifty-foot-tall octagon tower, turrets, and battlement detailing, intended to inspire Donaldson to build at an estimated cost of $12,000. The remaining books of a projected six-part series were not published.

The question of artistic authorship is settled by a comparison of Downing's sketches to Davis's published drawings. Davis had fourteen Downing sketches bound in his copy of *The Architecture of Country Houses,* which is preserved with other Davis documents at the Metropolitan Museum of Art in New York. It is apparent that Davis sometimes made some minor changes such as room names or sizes, and some chimney, stair, and adjoining closet locations, but it is also clear that Downing designed the building. More significant Davis changes to some exteriors include additional or

Fig. 1.16. The New Gate Lodge at Blithewood.

altered windows and gables, and veranda post locations. Nevertheless, Davis did not have a free hand. Downing asked him to re-draw Design V at larger scale, for example, because it did "not convey my idea well."[55] Downing consistently attributed the work of Davis and other architects in his books and included six Davis houses in his *Treatise on the Theory and Practice of Landscape Gardening*, one in *Cottage Residences*, and three in *The Architecture of Country Houses*.

After 1850, without Davis to call upon and intent on expanding his architectural practice, Downing went to England in July. Downing saw the architect Calvert Vaux's landscape watercolors of his tour to the continent at an Architectural Association Exhibition. He persuaded Vaux to return with him in September. While touring England, Downing saw London's great parks—perhaps influencing his thinking about public parks later incorporated in the Washington Mall design. Downing wrote letters in *The Horticulturist* about Kew Gardens and the Botanic Garden in Regent's Park, as well as the great country estates of Chatsworth, Warwick Castle, and Woburn Abbey. His description of Warwick Castle reveals his appreciation: "Whoever designed this front, made up as it is of lofty towers and irregular wall, must have been a poet as well as architect, for its composition and details struck me as having the proportions and congruity of a fine scene in nature, which we feel is not to be measured and defined by the ordinary rules of art."[56] In other letters from the trip Downing noted the impressive size of London parks in general, their beautiful plantings, and accessibility to the public. Downing also saw Loudon's Derby Arboretum, the first park in England designed to be public, whose particular elements included dense border vegetation, serpentine perimeter paths, and lodges with toilets and facilities for purchasing hot water for tea. (He also made a brief visit to Paris, but did not send letters about his experience there.)

Within the first year of working with Downing, Vaux rose from draftsman to partner. One early project was to build a one-story office addition to Downing's house, connected through a bookcase door off the library. Other employees soon joined the practice, including future brothers-in-law Cook and Withers, and landscape garden designer Frank Jessup Scott.[57] Proud of his growing business, Downing wrote to his friend John Jay Smith, "I wish I could show you my 'Bureau of Architecture,' in my new wing of my residence—full of commissions, and young architects, and planning for all parts of the country."[58]

By all accounts, Downing's practice was successful. In 1851, Downing wrote Smith, "I am deeply immersed in practical works—architectural and rural—turning my theories into practice all over the country."[59] These building commissions included a house for Joel T. Headley, Esq. called Hudson Highlands in New Windsor, New York, just south of Newburgh, built in 1852 and published as Design XIV, "A Cottage in the Rhine Style," in the expanded edition of *Cottage Residences* (Figs. 1.17 and 1.18).[60] Matthew Vassar, Esq. hired Downing to design his estate called Springside in Poughkeepsie, New York. Besides seventeen gardens in the forty-four-acre landscape, Downing designed numerous buildings including a gardener's cottage completed in 1850 and published as Design III, "A Symmetrical Bracketed Cottage," in *The Architecture of Country Houses* (Figs. 1.19 and 1.20) and a carriage house and stable published in *The Horticulturist* in February, 1851 and *Cottage Residences* as Design XV (Fig. 1.21).[61]

Downing's oeuvre must also recognize some contribution to the six constructed commissions Vaux published in 1857, as designed by "D. & V." The historian Francis Kowsky argues that they display a sophistication reflecting Vaux's more experienced hand than the "genial influence" of Downing.[62] These included the following (house numbers are from the expanded second edition of 1864):

DESIGN NO. 14, "A Symmetrical Country House and Design for a Coach-house and Stable," for William L. Findlay of Balmville, New York, built 1852 (Fig. 1.22). The house was demolished in the mid-1900s.

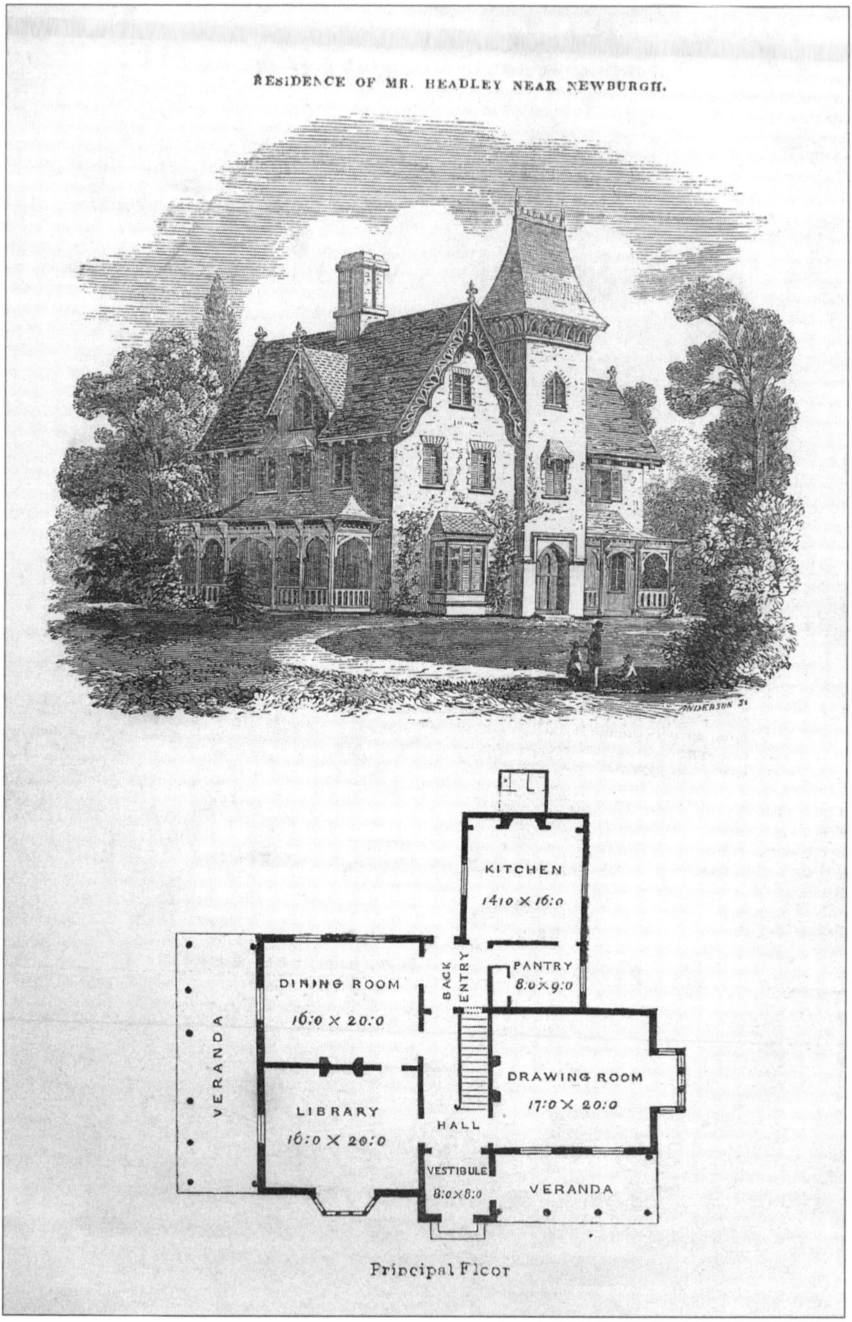

Fig. 1.17. View and Principal Floor Plan of Design XIV, *CR*.

Fig. 1.18. Former Headley House, New Windsor, New York.

DESIGN NO. 18, "A Picturesque Square House," for David Moore of Newburgh, New York, built 1852; additions in 1871 (Fig. 1.23); extant (Fig. 1.24).

DESIGN NO. 19, "A Suburban Villa," built 1850–1853 (Fig. 1.25), for Robert Perley Dodge and Francis Dodge of Georgetown, Washington, DC. The designs have similar floor plans and different exterior elevations. R. Dodge's house (28th and Q streets) had a side addition in 1930 and the interior was remodeled c. 1936 (Fig. 1.26), and F. Dodge's house (30th and Q streets) was renovated for condominiums (Fig. 1.27).[63]

DESIGN NO. 22, "A Suburban House with Curved Roof and Design for a Dormer-window," for Dr. William A. M. Culbert of Newburgh, New York, built 1850–1852 (Fig. 1.28). After a fire in 1981, only the brick shell remains (Fig. 1.29).[64]

DESIGN NO. 35, "A Marine Villa and Design for a Coach-house and Stable," for Daniel Parish of Newport, Rhode Island, built 1852 (Fig. 1.30). The house burned in 1855 and was rebuilt by Vaux in 1857 closer to the ocean; in 1889 the Astor family remodeled the house and named it Beechwood.[65]

Fig. 1.19. View and Principal Floor Plan of Design III, *ACH*.

Fig. 1.20. Springside Cottage, Poughkeepsie, New York.

Fig. 1.21. View of Design XV, *CR*.

Fig. 1.22. View and Plans of Principal and Chamber Floors of Design No. 14.

DESIGN No. 18.—(D. & V.)

PERSPECTIVE VIEW.

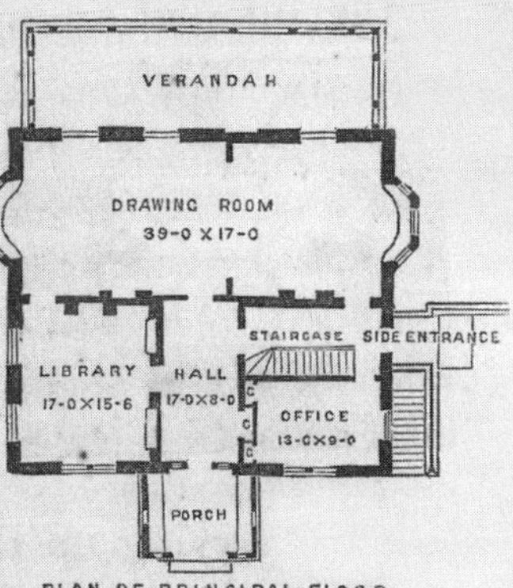

PLAN OF PRINCIPAL FLOOR

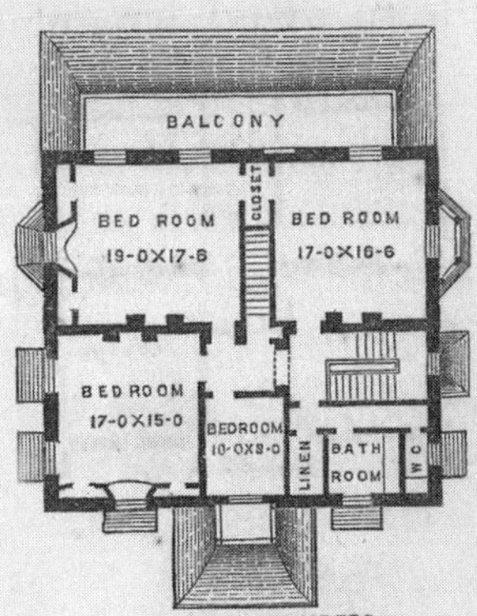

PLAN OF CHAMBERS

Fig. 1.23. View and Plans of Principal and Chamber Floors of Design No. 18.

Fig. 1.24. Moore House, 55 Broad Street, Newburg, New York.

Fig. 1.25. Views and Plans of Principal Floors of Design No. 19.

Fig. 1.26. Robert Perley Dodge House, 28th and Q streets, NW, Washington, D. C.

Fig. 1.27. Francis Dodge House, 30th and Q streets, NW, Washington, D. C.

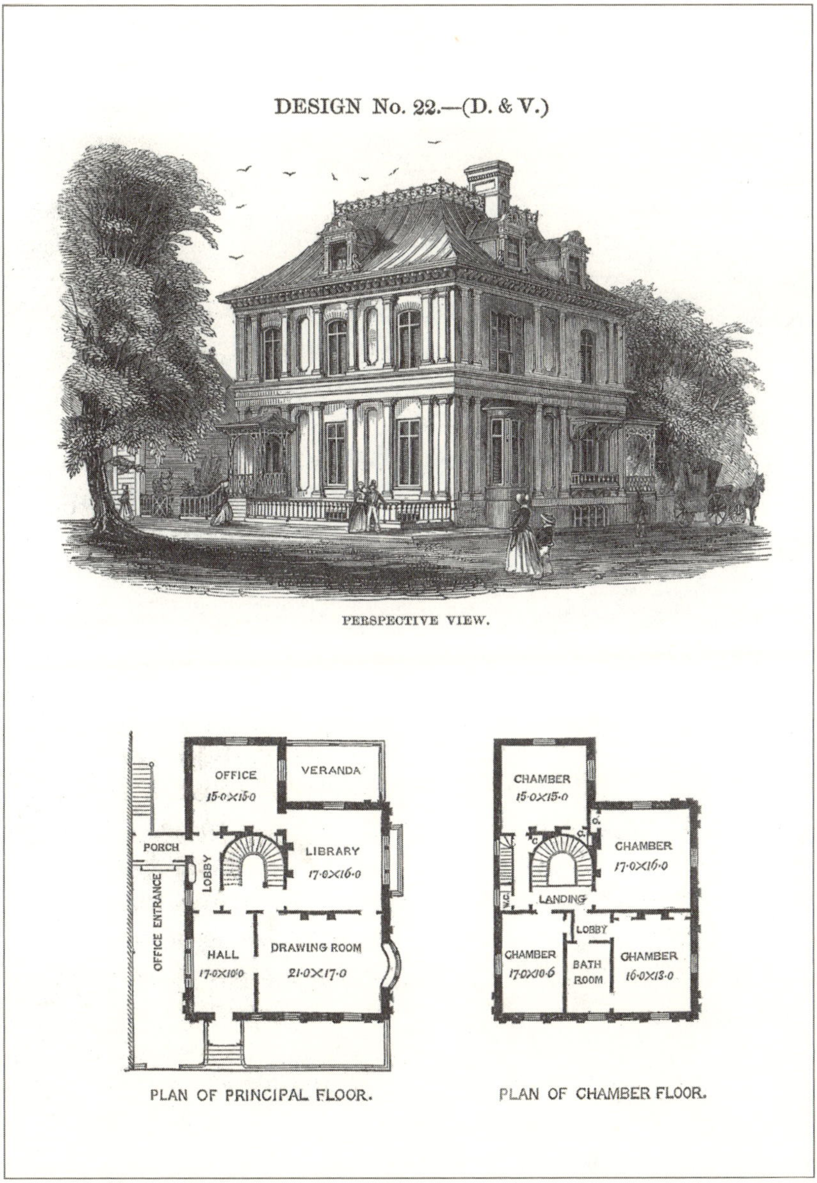

Fig. 1.28. View and Plans of Principal and Chamber Floors of Design No. 22.

Fig. 1.29. Culbert House, 120 Grand Street, Newburgh, New York.

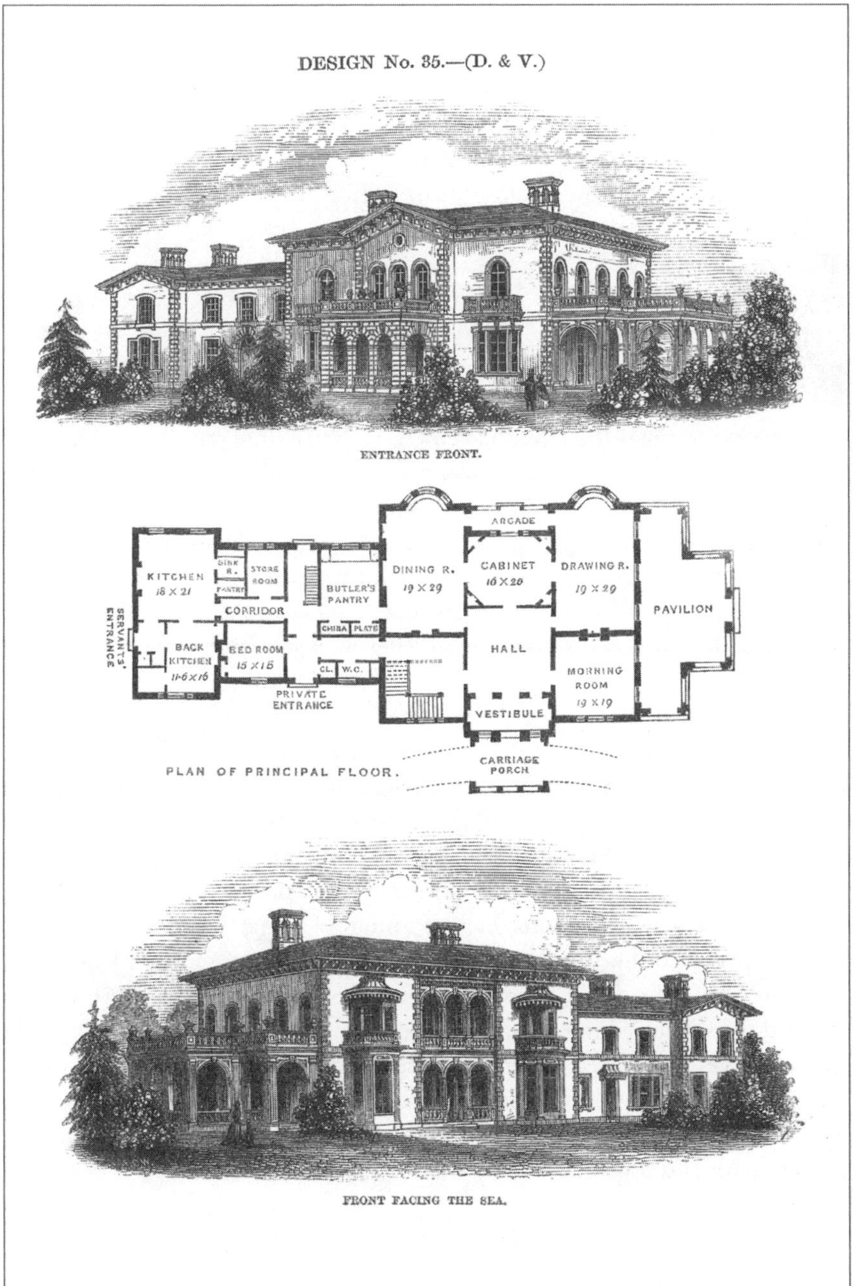

DESIGN No. 35.—(D. & V.)

ENTRANCE FRONT.

FRONT FACING THE SEA.

Fig. 1.30. Entrance Front, Plan of Principal Floor and Front Facing the Sea of Design No. 35.

Not all built projects were published. Houses executed with Davis include the Rankin House remodeling in Fishkill, New York (1844), the B. Phelps villa in Springfield, Massachusetts (1847), and James Chambers's Highland Villa near West Point, New York (1850).[66] Unpublished built projects executed with Vaux include Warren Delano's Algonac in Newburgh (1851) and the Cornelius Barber villa, Observatory Hill, in Washington, D.C. (1851–1852, demolished c. 1891).[67]

Little remains of the landscapes and gardens Downing designed for his Hudson River estate clients. His work for Matthew Vassar turned out to be his most enduring landscape. Vassar's wealth came from a successful ale brewery business in Poughkeepsie, New York. As part of his philanthropic work, Vassar founded Vassar College for Women and purchased forty-four acres on the edge of town for a public cemetery. When another site was used for the cemetery instead, the land became Vassar's country estate, called Springside (Fig. 1.31).[68] Vassar and his wife occupied the original gardener's cottage (shown as *11*) and (see Figs. 1.19 and 1.20). Childless, they saw no need for a large villa, (proposed site is shown as *16*), for which Downing's firm prepared a complete set of inked construction drawings, signed A. J. D. 1850.[69] Vaux published the proposed design as a "Villa of Brick and Stone" (Fig. 1.32). In his descriptive narrative of the Vassar grounds, nineteenth-century historian Benson Lossing describes other estate construction including a gatehouse completed in the autumn of 1852 and the only surviving structure, (*1*) (Figs. 1.33 and 1.34); a coach house (*10*); a "summerhouse" structure on a hill with a view to the Hudson and Catskills beyond (*12*); grapery and a greenhouse (*22*); a gardener's cottage (*23*); pagoda (*24*); stables and office (*26*); an aviary (*27*); the apiary or bee house (*30*); and ice house, dairy cottage, and granary (*36*).[70] The grounds had more than two miles of gravel paths unfolding presentations of park-like leveled meadows with fountains and ponds, in what Downing considered the Beautiful style. The Picturesque style is found in wooded dells, planted mounds, and rocky outcroppings (Fig. 1.35).[71] Together the sequence of enclosed and revealed scenes was Downing's most complete landscape design, combining "function and form, utility and art, unity, variety and harmony. It united the grounds in a manageable balance between garden, park and forest appropriate to a large American estate."[72]

DOWNING'S MOST significant pubic commission was for The Public Grounds at Washington, known today as the National Mall and Memorial Parks, or

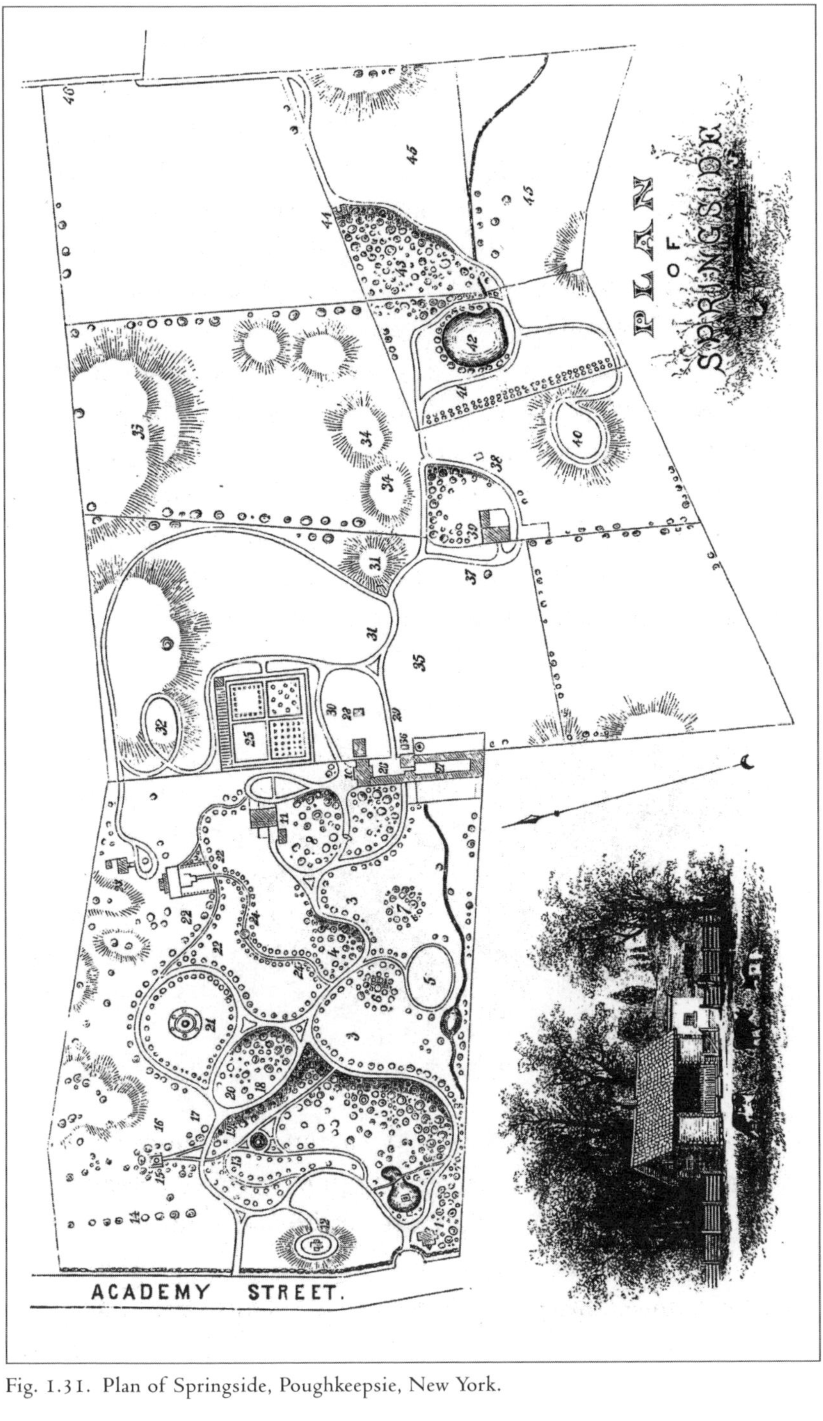

Fig. 1.31. Plan of Springside, Poughkeepsie, New York.

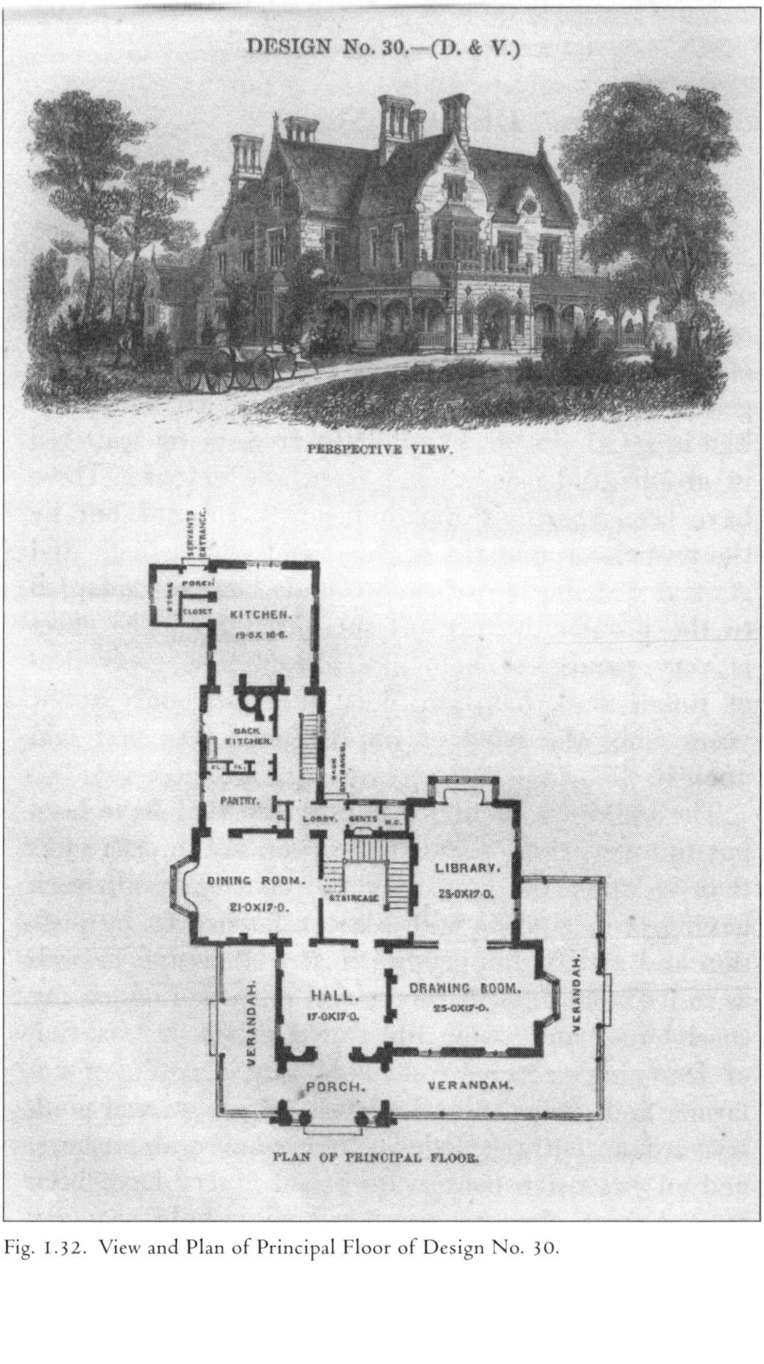

Fig. 1.32. View and Plan of Principal Floor of Design No. 30.

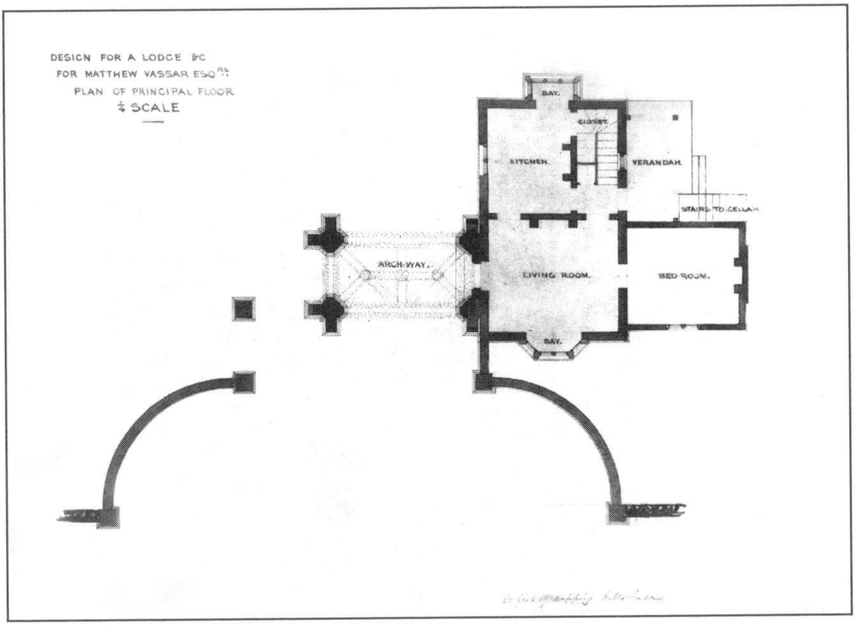

Fig. 1.33. Downing drawing of the Gate Lodge Plan of the Principal Floor, Springside.

Fig. 1.34. Springside Gatehouse, Poughkeepsie, New York.

Fig. 1.35. Entrance to Springside.

more simply the Mall (Fig. 1.36). Joseph Henry, first secretary of the Smithsonian Institution, encouraged Downing to visit Washington and meet President Millard Fillmore in November of 1850, and to look at the Mall's poor condition. The previous president, Zachary Taylor, had died just sixteen months into his presidency after attending a blistering hot Fourth of July celebration on the swampy grounds. The French-born American architect and engineer Pierre L'Enfant had situated the President's House (now the White House) on a rise with a southern prospect above the Tiber Creek, which emptied into the Potomac River. The creek was channelized into the Washington Canal in 1815 to provide a transportation route between the Eastern Branch (now the Anacostia River) and the Potomac. In reality, the wooden canal was an open sewer that attracted mosquitoes and was a serious health threat. The new president agreed with Henry that something had to be done.

Sixty years after L'Enfant's 1791 city plan for Washington was designed, many significant elements remained unexecuted (Fig. 1.37). The original intention for the Mall included the four-hundred-foot-wide Grand Avenue (shown as *H*), extending straight west from the Congress House or Capitol, as Thomas Jefferson renamed it (*L*), bordered with gardens sloping up to buildings for embassies and refined public places of resort, such as theaters, assembly rooms, and academies.[73] L'Enfant's plan located high points for squares or circles connected with diagonal avenues named for the states. These intersections, called reserves, were public places that visually united the different areas of the city. Lots around the squares and circles were for sale to each designated state for development or places of worship. This was L'Enfant's idea for settling the new city: use public avenues to link representative neighborhoods. Downing's Mall design followed this brilliant urban plan as originally envisioned with public footpaths, carriageways, and a relocated canal uniting a large park with six different and distinct gardens.

When Downing inspected the site, he saw various completed federal buildings and some under construction. These included the neoclassical President's House (officially the White House after 1901); the Capitol, located on Jenkins Hill with westerly views; and the partially completed Washington Monument, designed by Robert Mills and begun in 1848, which substituted for the equestrian monument the Continental Congress had approved in 1783.[74] Near the Capitol grounds were Botanic Garden greenhouses used for expedition plant collections, and close to the Mall's center was the Norman-style Smithsonian Institution designed by James Renwick, Jr., begun in 1847.[75] Downing found the Washington Canal to be a "pestiferous ditch," useful for transport and drainage, yet far from an intended public amenity it had to potential to be.[76]

Downing submitted a design for 150 acres between the President's House, the Capitol, and the Washington Monument. Smithsonian regents reviewed the design in February, and the president approved it on April 12, 1851. The design included almost five miles of carriage drives and many pedestrian walks through the landscape. The canal's eastern end was made large enough for pleasure boating activities. The portion west of Seventh Street was

Pierre Charles L'Enfant (1754–1825)

French artist, engineer, architect, and city planner, L'Enfant was the son of a painter for the court of Louis XV. Immigrating to America in 1777, L'Enfant joined George Washington at Valley Forge, where he illustrated Baron von Steuben's manual Regulations, Order and Discipline for the Army of the United States, *and designed the medal for the Society of the Cincinnati. After the war, L'Enfant opened an architectural practice in New York and redesigned City Hall for the First Congress in Federal Hall. In 1791, Washington commissioned L'Enfant to design the capital city located at the confluence of the Potomac and Anacostia Rivers. Thomas Jefferson, then Secretary of State, gave L'Enfant some sketches and eleven maps of European cities, but L'Enfant had a vision for the capital city of his adapted country. High ground with favorable prospects were reserved for public spaces—one for each state—with grand avenues visually uniting the city just as the capital city was to symbolically unite the states. L'Enfant's design drawing was approved, but when printing was delayed, the surveyor Benjamin Ellicott's brother Andrew redrew the plan, missing many subtle qualities in the process. The resulting engraving included no attribution to L'Enfant.*

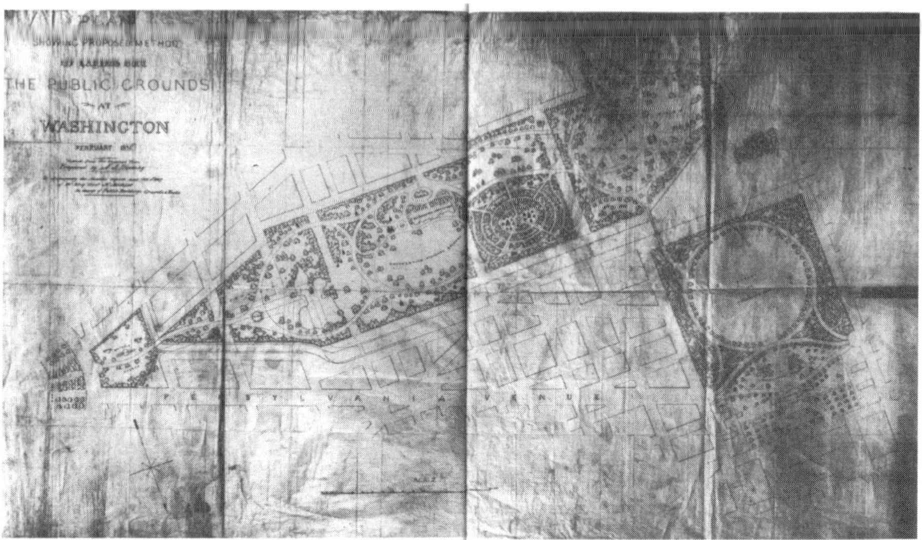

Fig. 1.36. Downing drawing, Plan showing proposed method of laying out The Public Grounds at Washington, February, 1851. (The Capitol is on the far left, the Washington Monument is in the upper right, and the White House is in the lower right.)

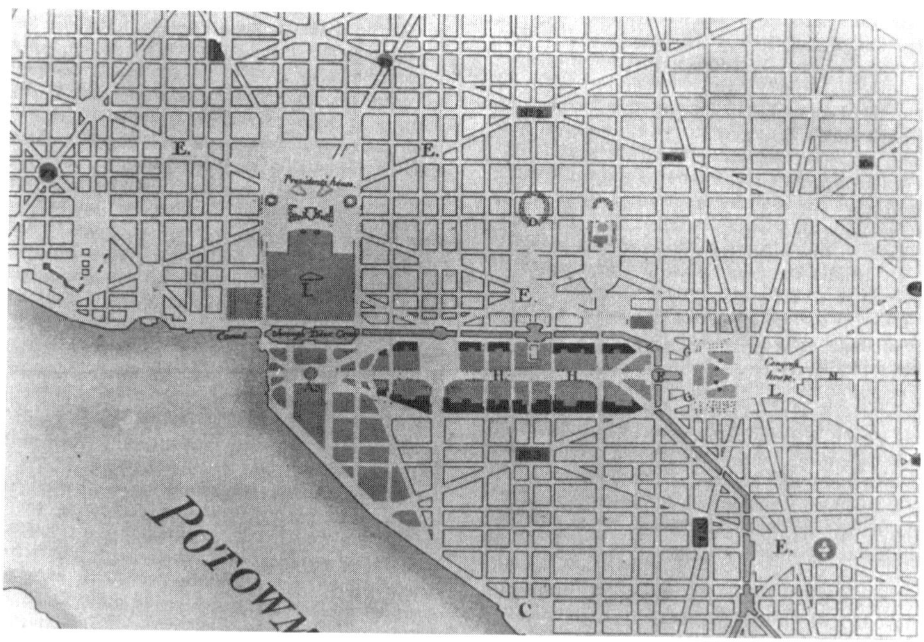

Fig. 1.37. Detail of L'Enfant map of the Federal City, 1791. (North is up. The Congress House, or Capitol, is labeled L and the Washington Monument is labeled A.)

funded, and the work of draining, clearing, and grading began in the spring. The eastern portion required additional expense to relocate the canal, which was approved in February of the following year.

In his explanatory notes to the plan, Downing explained his intent behind the design:

> 1st To form a national park, which should be an ornament to the Capital of the United States: 2nd To give an example of the natural style of Landscape Gardening which may have an influence on the general taste of the Country: 3rd To form a collection of all the trees that will grow in the climate of Washington, and, by having these trees plainly labeled with their popular and scientific names, to form a public museum of living trees and shrubs where every person visiting Washington could become familiar with the habits and growth of all the hardy trees.

Roads, some with bridges over the canal, crossed the grounds at four locations and Downing proposed lining the roads with hedges or light iron fences with gates to maintain the flowing park path lines. As for style, Monument Park had single, deciduous American trees planted on rolling lawns framing Potomac River views and punctuated with the Washington Monument obelisk, as an example of the Beautiful. The Picturesque style is found in Evergreen Garden, a closely planted regular plan designed to be especially appealing to winter experiences with a variety of rare trees and shrubs.[77] Specimen plants were part of the Smithsonian Pleasure Grounds, complementing its instructional purpose, and included all tree species that could tolerate the local climate. The only remaining evidence of this work today is the round President's Park on the south White House lawn, which has been flattened somewhat into an ellipse, and part of the Smithsonian Grounds.[78]

The design's public character was predicated on two conditions: taxation or private corporations acting in the public interest and supplying construction and operational funds, and that free access was a matter of right. Its social character was to provide a place apart from urban activity for reflection and with clean air for recreation. Downing described the park as a sylvan museum for public instruction, full of composed "natural" scenery and educational activities supporting healthful enjoyment. He believed that urban public parks should be as much as possible like the pastoral countryside with groups of trees on gently varied topography and intimate settings for people to experience some relief from the city. The curving paths united the gardens and provided a contrast to the straight lines of city blocks. These principles

Frederick Law Olmsted (1822–1903)

American writer and landscape designer, Olmsted's first and most significant design project was Central Park. Olmsted's view of urban parks as pastoral refuges from overcrowded and disease-ridden cities set a precedent that is still part of park design vocabulary. In partnership with Vaux, their other significant projects included Prospect Park and Washington Park in Brooklyn, Morningside Park in Manhattan, and the first comprehensive city-wide park, parkway, and public space system in Buffalo and later for Milwaukee, and the planned communities of Riverside, Illinois and Niagara Reservation. Olmsted started the first full-time professional landscape architecture firm in 1883 in Brookline, Massachusetts. Also significant are the grounds for the U.S. Capitol in Washington, the Biltmore Estate in Asheville, the Emerald Necklace parks in Boston, master plans for Stanford University and the University of Chicago, and the 1893 World's Columbia Exposition, which is credited with not only reintroducing Neoclassical architecture as the dominant style for civic buildings in the country, but also for the brilliant site plan. Retiring in 1895, Olmsted's two sons continued the practice until it was dissolved in 1980.

transferred to New York City when Vaux teamed in 1857 with Frederick Law Olmsted, a gentleman farmer, writer, and newly appointed superintendent of construction, on the 768-acre Central Park competition design they called the Greensward plan.[79] (Olmsted knew Vaux from social visits at Downing's home in 1851 and 1852, and Downing published Olmsted's writings on fruit and orchards in *The Horticulturist* in February, 1851.[80]) The Central Park design avoided the chief weakness of Downing's Mall design: the interrupting cross-streets. Vaux and Olmsted laid out sunken transverse roads with bridges that allowed a continuous experience above. Olmsted's understanding of site topography allowed him to develop Downing's idea of linked but distinct gardens into sweeping landscapes, created to appear as if they were naturally occurring. Vaux designed and supervised many building and bridge constructions, and included vignettes in the second edition of *Villas and Cottages* for a boat-landing, the ramble's rustic bridge, and two executed designs for shaded seats.[81]

As a landscape architect, Downing was convinced that America's main problems were the rapid growth of cities due to immigration, and continual migration as a result of worn-out farmland. Public parks provided relief to urban overcrowding, and he wrote about their virtues as offering "any breathing space for pure air, any recreation ground for healthful exercise, any pleasant roads for riding or driving, or any enjoyment of that lovely and refreshing natural beauty from which they have, in leaving the country, reluctantly expatriated themselves for so many years—perhaps for ever."[82] He also wrote about the advantage of other public institutions such as libraries, art galleries, schoolhouses, and agricultural colleges. The establishment of these public institutions, he believed, was the means for a country of restless settlers and new immigrants to become a land of cultivated taste and civilized refinement.

ON JULY 28, 1852 Andrew and Caroline Downing, along with her friend, mother, and two of her siblings, left Newburgh bound for New York on the steamboat *Henry Clay*. The boat took part in an illegal race that caused the overheated boiler to catch fire. Caroline and her brother and sister survived; Downing, Caroline's mother, and the young widow Mrs. Matilda Boyer Wadsworth of Fishkill—along with almost 80 other passengers—died. The 198-foot long boat was run ashore, but fire in the engine room forced many to jump overboard. Though the distance to shore was short, the Hudson River currents as well as the women's cumbersome fashions caused many deaths. Known to be a strong swimmer, eyewitness accounts recall Downing's repeated rescues of other passengers until he drowned.[83] Downing was buried in St. George's Cemetery in Newburgh. In 1872, his brother Charles moved his grave to the new Cedar Hill Cemetery, a few miles north, in part to attract subscribers by enhancing the reputation of this new rural cemetery. Downing's grave marker is engraved with the words, "This mortal must put on immortality. Be not dismayed for I am thy God" (Fig. 1.38).[84]

Because of the circumstances of his death, few Downing documents survived.[85] Downing's home and office had to be sold immediately to satisfy the mortgage. Friends bought the property at auction to insure a sufficient price for his widow, and resold it a year later for $18,000 to Charles C. Alger. The new owner hired Davis to expand it considerably, almost beyond recognition. Alger called it "Downing's Place, Hudson River." Davis used an engraving of his design for his letterhead. The house was demolished around 1920, with only a single terra-cotta ornamental chimney top surviving, now stored in the local historical society's basement (Fig. 1.39).[86]

Vaux maintained a practice in Newburgh until 1856 when he moved to New York City and was a founding member of the newly formed American Institute of Architects. A year later he published a collection of house designs in *Villas and Cottages* dedicated "with sincere respect, to Caroline E. Downing, and to the memory of her husband, Andrew J. Downing." In it, Vaux attributes nine designs of thirty-nine as created by Downing & Vaux, six of which were built, and four extant.[87]

In 1860, Caroline married a close neighbor and executor of Downing's estate, widower Judge John James Monell, whose first wife had written two accounts of the steamboat tragedy for *The Knickerbocker*. Vaux and Withers designed their house, called Eustatia, built in Fishkill Landing and included as Design XXV in the expanded 1873 edition of *Cottage Residences*. Even

Fig. 1.38. Andrew J. Downing and Caroline Downing Monell grave markers.

though Caroline outlived her first husband by fifty-three years, she was buried next to him when she died (see Fig. 1.38).

The outpouring of grief over Downing's death was nationwide. Horticultural societies around the country raised funds and Vaux designed a memorial urn that was installed on the Washington Mall in September of 1856, where it remained for the next one hundred and ten years. The urn was removed and stored to make way for highway construction in the 1960s. Thanks to historian David Schulyer's efforts, it was restored and installed on the Smithsonian Institution Castle grounds in 1972 where it remains today (see Fig. I.1).

Downing's legacy is based on the way he wrote about and illustrated architectural principles informing and inspiring individual owners. Aware of a scarcity of trained architects in America, Downing knew that some landowners would act as their own "clerk of the works," supplying materials and employing mechanics; however, where possible, he felt that owners should hire an architect qualified by what he had actually built in America and not strictly for his degrees and titles, as "architecture is not an art intuitively

Fig. 1.39. Chimney top from Highland Garden.

understood by all men."[88] While Downing was not about to circumvent the emerging architectural profession by giving prescriptions for model houses, he did feel that proprietors needed architects to design a specific house on a specific site as "the most effectual way of avoiding . . . disappointment and perplexity."[89] Downing's standards for architects were specific: "Unless the architect can stamp both feeling and imagination, as well as utility, upon his work, he cannot truly be called an architect."[90] With his publications, Downing hoped to assist homebuilders in forging a collaboration with architects as they learned to directing their intangible preferences with instructions and examples of appropriate architecture and landscape design. The pleasures of home building were considerable, as he wrote to John Jay Smith: it was "the only rational sort of creation that poor humans can engage in, and provided you do it wisely (which few of us do, indeed), you cannot fail to increase your happiness by it."[91]

2

DESIGN PRINCIPLES

> The villa—the country house should, above all things, manifest individuality. It should say something of the character of the family within —as much as possible of their life and history, their tastes and associations, should mould and fashion themselves upon its walls.
>
> —Downing, *The Architecture of Country Houses*[1]

IN *COTTAGE RESIDENCES* Downing outlined "certain leading principles connected to architecture" as:

> Fitness or usefulness as the beauty of utility
> Expression of Purpose as the beauty of propriety
> Expression of Style as the beauty of form and sentiment.[2]

The first principle addressed the physical necessities of shelter. Utility is the practical knowledge needed to compose the convenient arrangement of apartments that support the routines of domestic operation and provide places for contemplative—the two activities critical to satisfying Downing's idea of home. Fitness was also a matter of the mode of construction and building materials employed. The appropriate choice of exterior materials depended on scale. Cottages were to be cheerful, with crafted detail, and could be built of wood, ordinarily a less desirable material for lasting construction. Farmhouses were to have habitable attics for seasonal workers' sleeping quarters and ample garrets for storing the fruits of the field. Farmhouses could be made of wood as well, although fieldstone was preferred if it could be found on site. Villas were to express permanence and solidity, and were to be made of stone, brick, or rough brick coated with cement stucco.

The second principle, relating to purpose and propriety, directed architectural appearance and referenced associations. Downing thought that displayed attributes identified a building's purpose. In houses, specific elements such as chimneys, bay windows, and porches or verandas denoted domestic activity (Fig. 2.1). Barns, churches, and commercial buildings had elements expressing a different purpose, and required their own appropriate attributes. Appropriate color, for instance, was another way to express building purpose. Brighter colors were for shady situations, and drab colors were for locations where bright colors would be too glaring.[3] Downing recommended that barns and other outbuildings have quiet and unobtrusive color tones to denote their supportive position in the complex. Cottages were to have a mellow hue, harmonizing with the verdure landscape. A villa should be made of materials whose color displayed a dignity appropriate to its stature in the community.

In developing these first two principles of utility and propriety, Downing followed Loudon's writings closely.[4] The major departure came with the third principle of expression of style; Loudon's art of taste in the expression of some particular architectural style became for Downing more about expression of character. The expression of style as the beauty of form and sentiment is the highest in Downing's scale. Downing distinguished the leading rules that depended on proportion, symmetry, variety, harmony and unity, calling proportion "the primary law of beauty."[5] He recognized that rigid proportional formulas for the width, depth, and height of rooms was usually impossible, allowing that "economy, which obliges us, in most cases, to have all the rooms on a floor of the same height, while the rooms themselves are necessarily of different sizes, prevents us from adhering to any absolutely fixed rules of proportion."[6] Symmetry was the balance of parts. Variety added interest, often through ornament. Harmony was achieved when one feeling pervaded the whole, and unity was the consistent choice of materials, style and color.

It is useful to understand more about Loudon's thinking in order to grasp what Downing made of it. Downing considered Loudon to be the most distinguished author on landscape theory, and he appreciated Loudon's comprehensive treatment of the rural arts in his books and in his *Architectural Magazine*, the first English language periodical devoted entirely to architecture.[7] Launched in 1834, the magazine included articles on horticulture and landscape design, and domestic projects by different architects. Essays on architectural theory and criticism were also offered. John Ruskin's first book

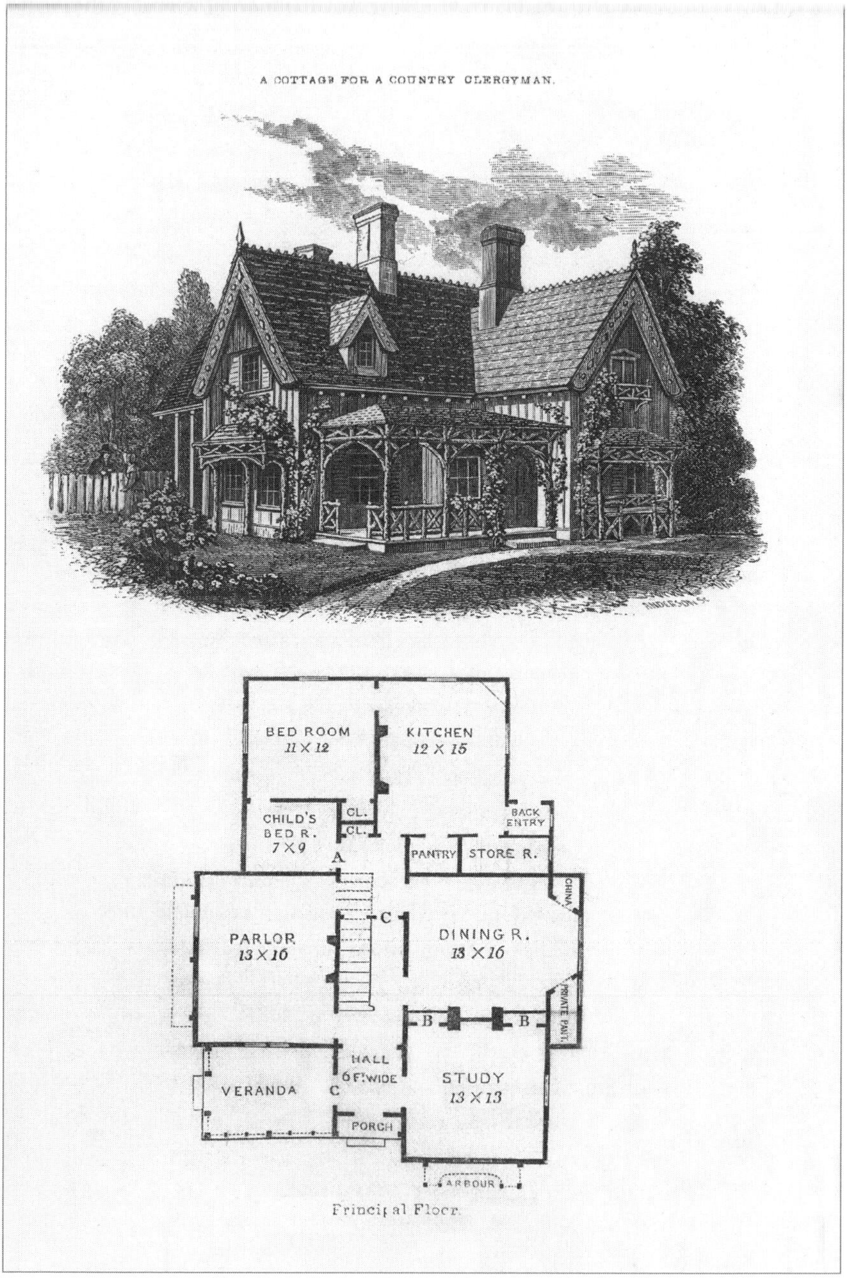

Fig. 2.1. View and Principle Floor Plan of Design XI, *CR*.

on architecture, *The Poetry of Architecture*, was published in serial form from November of 1837 to December of 1838.[8] Book reviews included Quatremère de Quincy's over 400- page volume *An Essay on the Nature, the End, and the Means of Imitation in the Fine Arts* (1823), which Loudon had translated from the French in 1837 and recommended highly: "The *Essay on Imitation* to every architect who has any pretensions to being a thinking man, and to every man of taste who has a library."[9] Intended to disseminate practical information, the magazine was also meant to direct taste, specifically "to raise the intellect and the character of those engaged in this art."[10]

Loudon's numerous publications—encyclopedias, treatises, manuals, periodicals, and books—provided architectural information from general theories of art to how to build greenhouses, lay out farms, and select manufactured furniture. With Loudon's help, readers had the information they needed to try something new in design and construction. While vernacular architecture was familiar, it was also common. The wealthy showed their worldly sophistication by favoring foreign ornament for their homes and imported exotics for their gardens. Loudon presented drawings of architectural styles as a series of ornamented "jackets" interchangeably draped over the same building shape, thereby altering its appearance (Fig. 2.2). While Loudon's motive was to improve the quality of middle- and working-classes housing, his efforts were criticized for increasing the distance between what was possible and what was appropriate.

Once style became a choice, taste became the guide for good design decisions. Cultivating taste depended on presenting principles familiar enough to be considered buildable and unique enough to attract someone who wanted something different. Loudon's publications presented a menu of styles, making design based mostly on appearance possible; however, the attraction of novelty unaided by convincing principles often led to unfortunate results. As critics have noted, Loudon "was teaching people to imitate, not to think; to copy, not to originate; to confuse ornament with design, and to learn the right patter so they could appear knowing and even authoritative about styles."[11]

Loudon's publications continued the profession's direction of shifting the architect's chief responsibility from master builder to design authority. The clerk of the works or general contractor provided technical experience and supervised construction, insuring that the building stood up. Planning a building followed one of two approaches. The first required accumulating local materials, using local labor, and following traditional methods of construction, resulting in what is known as vernacular architecture.[12] When something different was desired, reference to an authority was required. For

Fig. 2.2. Jackets of Style.

many this meant obtaining a book of plans and selecting a design. This kind of project meant transporting materials, importing and instructing workers, and questioning the taste displayed in their decisions. The reference book had to explain site selection and house location, how to lay out other structures and various cultivated grounds, and how to choose a style. It also needed to show floor plans that addressed all issues of habitation: where one worked, cooked, ate, slept, and socialized.

Freed from day-to-day involvement with the slow construction phase, architects served proprietors by providing consistent information about architectural styles and practical instructions about how to incorporate the latest technical inventions. Design needed to unify separate parts into a compatible whole. On the exterior, these parts included materials and details for masonry foundations and chimneys with ornamental tops, doors and window frames, porch posts and railings, and projecting roof overhang brackets.

On the interior, the wood doors, cabinetry, mantles, stair parts, and mouldings had to be selected to work well together. Manufactured devices were increasingly available for enhanced comfort, health, and safety, such as indoor plumbing fixtures, central heating equipment, and dumbwaiters connecting basement kitchens to dining rooms on the principal floor above.[13] Since matters of taste were not easily codified like rules of proportion and integrating mechanical equipment into house structure was new, reliance on an experienced authority was important.

Renaissance architects Leon Battista Alberti and Andrea Palladio had developed architectural principles from the single surviving treatise by Vitruvius, a first-century B.C.E. Roman architect. Vitruvius insisted that buildings have *firmitas*, *utilitas*, and *venustas*: durability and material strength or solid construction, convenient arrangement or appropriate purpose, and grace or beauty. The architect who followed Vitruvius understood the rules of proportion, the classical orders, and construction techniques. Downing appropriated these principles and framed them as a matter of good taste, adapting them for the nineteenth century.

Downing also read English writers on taste, including William Hogarth's *The Analysis of Beauty* (1753) and the Reverend Archibald Alison's *Essays on the Nature and Principles of Taste* (1790), in which the beauty of form was joined to something beyond itself. Alison considered taste to be an appreciative mental faculty with emotions responding to the perception of sublimity and beauty.[14] Downing interpreted this to mean that reading the landscape and oneself combined with the project design into a corresponding relationship between intellectual and sensory satisfaction.

If *Cottage Residences* outlined Downing's basic principles, then he further refined them in the opening chapter "On the Real Meaning of Architecture"

Marcus Vitruvius Pollio
(c. 90–20 B.C.E.)

Roman architect and engineer Vitruvius was the author of the oldest surviving and most influential book on architecture from antiquity. De architectura libri decem *or* Ten Books on Architecture, *completed before 27 B.C.E., explains the education of an architect, construction for public and domestic buildings, theaters and their acoustics, baths, harbors, and cities; and references built precedents. It codified the Orders—Tuscan, Doric, Ionic, and Corinthian—which are the column and entablature construction of Greek and Roman temples, as well as the fundamental principles of design. Known as the Vitruvian triad, building well required three conditions: commodity, firmness, and delight, which in some form are the basis of architectural theory. Rediscovered in the fifteenth century,* De architectura *was translated into Italian by Pietro Aretino and published in 1556 with illustrations drawn by Palladio.*

Leon Battista Alberti (1404–1472)

Florentine writer, painter, sculptor, mathematician and, most famously, architectural theorist and architect who exemplified the Renaissance ideal of the "complete man." Of about forty literary works, De Re Aedificatoria or On the Art of Building in Ten Books (written c. 1443–52, printed in 1485) *was the most significant. This was the first treatise on architecture and architectural principles since Vitruvius, a millennium and a half earlier. Written in Latin and with only a few small illustrations, Alberti claimed that architecture was a discipline with principles of art guiding the form and choice of materials for private, public, and sacred buildings. Sir John Soane translated the book into English in 180[illegible]. It found both an immediate audience and remains the most influential treatise on architectural theory today.*

in *The Architecture of Country Houses*.[15] The first principle, the fitness or usefulness as the beauty of utility, was now called "the Useful in Architecture." Here Downing discussed the origins of shelter, the rules of utility, quality of materials and workmanship in construction, and rules for internal convenience. Perpendicular walls, firm foundations, tight roofs, and chimneys that draw smoke properly were essential to useful buildings.

The second principle, the Expression of Purpose as the beauty of propriety, became "the Beautiful in Architecture," which discussed absolute and relative beauty. Relative beauty depended on the expression of a proprietor's character, feelings, and enjoyments, which reflected moral, social, and intellectual ideas.[16] Downing felt that absolute beauty was more likely to apply to larger houses, although it was certainly possible for cottages to achieve through intimate scale, simple form, and close correspondence with the land.

The third principle, the Expression of Style as the beauty of form and sentiment, became "the True in Architecture," which distinguished among general, local, and specific truth. General truth required a house to look like a house. For example, a Doric temple style house with invisible or disguised chimneys was a violation of general truth because chimneys were part of the domestic vocabulary associated with shelter, hearth, and home, and therefore must be expressed.

Local truth required a house design to fit its site: a vertical townhouse design for a city site, for example, should not be used in a rural setting, which had ample room to spread out horizontally. The choice of exterior color was another instance of local truth, because it increased truthful expression. Downing noted that "Sir Joshua Reynolds, who was full of artistic feeling for the union of a house with its surrounding scenery, once said, 'if you would fix upon the best colour for your house, turn up a stone, or pluck up a handful of grass by the roots, and see what is the colour of the soil where the house is to stand, and let that be your choice.'"[17]

Specific truth required that ornamentation appropriate to one scale of cottage, farmhouse, or villa not be applied to another. These different dwellings should have distinct properties to express domestic purpose and occupant activities, rather than presenting false pretenses. Cottages were more than diminutive villas, in other words, and villas were not made from cottages with multiple additions.

Before each section in the book on cottage, farmhouse, and villa design, Downing provided further explanation. The introduction to the cottage designs was titled "Examples of false taste in design," and in it Downing discouraged the building of "temple" cottages and the cocked-hat cottage with an overabundance of Gothic gables and dormers, or anything with excessive cheap ornament. Farmhouse design required less explanation, with only a short section titled "How to make it truthful and significant—Should aim mainly at expressing the life of the farmer." Finally, the third section for villas expanded on "the true meaning of the republican home."

These distinctions were intended to clear a path among the many possible directions open to architectural thinking. They were also meant to resist popular trends that resulted in all civic buildings looking like Greek temples, all libraries and churches designed in a Gothic Revival style, and Norman style-museums such as James Renwick's Smithsonian Institution, which Downing thought failed to express the truth about America or Americans (Fig. 2.3). Downing described the domestic ideal as follows: "If hospitality smiles in ample parlors; if home virtues dwell in cosy, fire-side family-rooms; if the love of the beautiful is seen in picture or statue galleries; intellectuality, in well-stocked libraries; and even a dignified love of leisure and repose, in cool and spacious verandas; we feel, at a glance, that here

Andrea Palladio
(1508–1580)

Born in Padua, Palladio was a humanist architect who worked for the landed gentry of sixteenth century Venice. Country villas (house and grounds) used the Orders to display ancient principles of propriety, order, and proportion. Many villas, churches, and civic structures survive today, of which San Giorgio Maggiore and the Redentore on the Giudecca are well known. Influenced by the Barbaro edition of Vitruvius, Palladio published a treatise of his projects both realized and unbuilt, I Quattro libri dell' architettura *or* Architecture, Divided into Four Books *(now called* The Four Books on Architecture*) in 1570. Many of his drawings were purchased by English architect Inigo Jones (designer of Covent Garden) and Thomas Howard in 1615. These drawings and their inspired followers introduced what came to be known as Palladianism to England. The style's influence was assisted by Colen Campbell's publication of a well-illustrated edition of Vitruvius by Lord Burlington and Sir Henry Wotten's unillustrated architectural manual* The Elements of Architecture (1624)*, which described the principles of Vitruvius, Alberti, and Palladio. This influence later came to America through Thomas Jefferson and the design of his home Monticello.*

Fig. 2.3. Smithsonian Institution, Washington, D. C.

we have reached the highest beauty of which Domestic Architecture is capable—that of individual expression."[18]

Individual expression combined physical attributes with personal character traits and domestic display as love of home and connoisseurship of elevated pursuits that reflected the American spirit as honest, virtuous, and likely to lead to happiness and contentment. Domestic architecture meant something more than mere shelter for modest cottages and more than money for noble villas. Refined expression of appropriate sentiments turned buildings into homes and settlements into communities.

Expression of domesticity transcended architectural style, although most of Downing's house designs are given names that identify a particular style. In describing what a country house or villa should be, Downing's expression of purpose as the beauty of propriety evolved into a principle of truth. When each element—land, person, and building—were in harmony with the other, the example of virtuous honesty became a means of elevating the entire community. The expression of style as the beauty of form and sentiment became a principle of taste independent from particular architectural styles.[19]

Choice of style was of little concern for some American immigrant communities, who maintained European ties and favored repeating traditional construction methods. Others had no such nostalgic bent, and their projects responded to site conditions and the ways in which the owners wanted to present themselves. Two things determined appropriate choice, as Downing saw it. First, understand the land. Second, define the proprietor's character so that the architecture said something about the people who lived there, beyond their social status. These basic ideas were appropriate for all economic levels because all design decisions needed reasons for scale, orientation, materials, and style choice.

Downing's emphasis on expression had its roots in Romantic aesthetic theory. While writers on this topic recognized the impossibility of defining vague emotions completely, they refused to consider these qualities as solely up to the uneducated spectator, who knew what he liked but could not say why. Systematic inquiry ought to uncover consistent principles about the role of feeling and sentiment in design. For many, this became a matter of natural and accidental associations based on informed experiences and definitions of character.

Character is the execution of moral and social values; it is a particular mark or distinguishing quality. This applies to people and to what they make. Downing's greatest contribution to design theory was connecting aesthetic sensibilities to ethical ideals. For him, the rural arts improved nature, and this affected people in ways that elevated thought and cultivated behavior.[20] In architectural associations, as contemporary critic John Archer has observed, rural arts have "the ability of a design to raise in the viewer a train of ideas illuminating the building's program."[21] Linking executed architectural principles to subsequent emotional response places individual experience central to design. George Tatum has said of the shift in perception that "artistic beauty (was no longer defined by Vitruvius, Alberti and Palladio) in terms of proportion, symmetry, and the harmonious relationship of parts—all qualities *inherent in the object*—the eighteenth century had become increasingly concerned with the *emotional reaction of the spectator.*"[22]

Nevertheless, suitability still governed tasteful design. Downing cautioned the ambitious housebuilder to be content with "the modest veranda, the bracketed roof, the latticed window, and the lovely accessories of vines and flowering shrubs," as they were part of the simple story of habitation. "The tropes and figures of architectural rhetoric which belong to the elaborate oratory of a palace or a temple" were inappropriate.[23] Even as late as the mid-nineteenth century, many Americans relied on English productions and found Downing's adaptation helpful. His instruction provided more direction than simply imitating ornamental styles. The principles guiding taste were convincing. Equating beauty with expression of character, the descriptions and illustrated examples allowed his audience to imagine what was appropriate.

ADAPTING FOREIGN INFLUENCES FOR THE AMERICAN AUDIENCE

Downing used the phrase "adapted to North America" in the titles of his first two books to draw attention to his mission of translating design principles for his American audience. His position had changed by 1845 with his *Fruits and Fruit Trees of America* and with the 1850 publication of *The Architecture of Country Houses*; by that time, he apparently considered the adaptation of foreign ideas to be counterproductive to an American culture seeking self-definition. Downing's hope was "that our domestic architecture will always be growing better, more truthful, more individual, and therefore more rational and sincere, rather than more foreign and affected."[24]

Etymologically, to "adapt" is to make suitable, to make fit. Downing identified the problem this way: "Foreign architects are finding their way to this country very plentifully. Some among them who follow rules and not principles, do us great harm by building expensive and unmeaning copies of foreign houses—as for instance, English villas, with narrow passages, disconnected rooms, and no verandas for the warm climate of the middle States. Others do us service, by studying the peculiarities of climate and mode of life, and adapting their designs to meet the peculiarities."[25]

A month before he died, Downing published an essay comparing British and American horticultural practices.[26] He estimated that only three per cent of all gardeners working in America were native-born, and therefore likely to be familiar with local conditions. Practices based on the damp and shady situation in England had to be reversed for the drier and sunnier climate typical in the country's regions with which Downing was most familiar. This difficulty in adjustment was the source of many horticultural problems due not to the selection of plant species or the plants themselves, but to poor understanding of the site situation. This required different approaches to plant placement, grouping, installation, drainage, pruning, and especially mulching.

Downing gradually came to believe that imported plants were not needed to supply pleasure grounds.[27] In this he departed from Loudon, who recommended foreign objects to elevate the common garden design to art,

Fig. 2.4. East Front of Tew Lodge, J. C. Loudon, c. 1809–1811.

especially for his Gardenesque style, which favored planting trees so that they could grow to their ideal form (Fig. 2.4). English garden suppliers had imported shrubs and trees from America since the early seventeenth century, often for American gardens on country estates where exotic plants contrasted with the indigenous to display horticultural accomplishment.[28] This is not to say that Downing—the former nursery owner—didn't admire the challenge of matching plants with local conditions. A hardy species well-established was valued for surviving transplantation and increasing the available palette for pleasure, purpose, and profit, and not simply as an unusual, attention-attracting object.

For adapting architectural principles, Downing's first consideration was still climate. Downing was clear about the need to inform people about modifications to English house forms and materials to permit construction in different climates. No architecture designed with respect to utility could escape attention to weather. Downing's second consideration was how the land form figured into the decision about style; after all, Swiss chalets were inappropriate for flat plains. Matching possible house shapes to topography limited style choice. Building locations were evaluated based on access to water, and areas with better soil were saved for gardens. Finally, Downing recognized that associations appealing to different national heritages were part of the American psyche. This was as true for recent immigrants interested in assimilation as it was for Americans whose ancestors had arrived generations ago. While Downing recognized and appreciated that foreign styles and ornamentation influenced American architecture, he also believed that "the general composition of the design and the arrangement of the plan, of course, belong wholly to our own habits in domestic life, and have nothing to do with houses abroad."[29] Clearly, his intent was to adjust forms and materials to suit local and cultural circumstances. If certain architectural styles were part of an American heritage of European traditions and the expression of style was an architectural principle, then adaptation of style was part of developing inspiring designs.

Downing resisted thinking of style as a matter of a few ornaments tacked on in a superficial rendition of an original version. The Second Empire style with its mansard roofs and the Queen Anne style with its flimsy fretwork held little attraction for him. He was interested in the entire production, from floor plan arrangement to material choice, reflecting the best traits of the family's character and giving "some *meaning* in its beauty, considered in relation to their own position, character, and daily lives."[30] This approach to architecture was not the exclusive domain of the wealthy, nor out of reach for the poor. Architectural principles were even more important to those of modest means, who had to rely on a few simple elements to convey a sense of home. Downing began *The Architecture of Country Houses* with the clear statement:

> There are three excellent reasons why my countrymen should have good houses. The first, is because a good house (and by this I mean a fitting, tasteful, and significant dwelling) is a powerful means of civilization. The second reason is, because the *individual home* has a great social value for a people. It is the solitude and freedom of the family home in the country which constantly preserves the purity of the nation, and invigorates its intellectual powers. The third reason is, because there is a moral influence in a country home . . . where the family hearth is made a central point of the Beautiful and the Good.[31]

Letters from European visitors and comments from Thomas Jefferson returning from visits to the Continent noted the state of American architecture with dismay. Charles Dickens wrote his *American Notes* in 1842, which, according to at least one critic, reads at times "like a catalogue of American vulgarities."[32] Dickens wrote about the undeniable distance between dreams of opportunity and the realities of poverty. Seven years later, with the publication of *The Life and Adventures of Martin Chuzzlewit,* Dickins was also critical of American problems with social class distinction, land ownership, slavery, and a general busyness, as well as the lack of educational institutions, culture, and social graces. Downing took exception to these sorts of depictions and wrote about America's vitality as "the moving and breathing of a robust young giant, compared with the crippled and feeble motions of an exhausted old man" that was Europe.[33]

Nevertheless, Downing did think Americans suffered from a poverty of ideas and a dormant sense of the enjoyment to be found in orderly, tasteful, and agreeable dwellings and villages. Downing believed the American national character had two fundamental qualities: that of imitation and that of progress.[34] He wanted Americans to think about improving their houses and towns because of community pride and a natural competitiveness, going so far as to write about how town life is improved when pigs were not allowed to roam the streets. As he replied to one complaining letter writer in a full essay about the improvement of country villages, he should become an "apostle of taste" by planting trees along town streets as a first step toward civic improvement, setting an example for others to follow.[35]

Observing that many people moved from their place of birth to find and cultivate land and to build their homes, Downing termed this spirit of unrest an Anglo-American love of change, which he hoped would evolve into a love of home.[36] The regions for settlement in North America were diverse, ranging from the expanding East Coast to the Great Lakes region, to the Ohio Valley and the West Coast.[37] New communities found that two shared interests transcended diverse ethnic backgrounds, economic status, and social class: the reasonable expectation of personal safety, and access to education for their children. The Homestead Act of 1862 promoted land ownership that supported these common goals of settlement and cultivation. Owning land in particular "seemed to nearly all Americans the key to happiness."[38] In pursuit of a new life, immigrants without money usually worked on transportation projects, in mills or factories, or provided domestic service. Those with money had the chance to buy inexpensive rural land, and start farms and businesses of their own. Many, even those who could no longer be considered immigrants, heeded the call to go west, to start over, to make something of themselves in this land of opportunity, and then to settle down. Advancement was considered a matter of working hard and seizing opportunity, and not a result of an unearned accident of birth and primogeniture inheritance.[39]

Downing believed that all Americans had the potential to become homeowners with well-designed houses and grounds. Tasteful homes led to a cultured community of villages with noble civic buildings and public parks. Indeed, properly instructed, all men could become gentlemen, as Downing believed he had done. In this, America followed the newly developing middle classes in England, where a gentleman was "a social type unknown before the nineteenth century."[40] Attitudes about self-improvement and how this related to land ownership were forward-thinking. As one foreign observer noted, "the Americans love their country, not, indeed, as it is, but as it will be. They do not love the land of their fathers; but they are sincerely attached to that which their children are destined to inherent. They live in the future, and make their country as they go on."[41]

It was in the making of their country that information from an authority who understood everything from fruit tree species to domestic design principles was wanted. Once land was purchased, considerations of climate and geography, available materials and labor, family size, number of likely servants and seasonal workers, and cultural and historical associations were all considered in terms of design. For the grounds, new homesteads required trees for orchards, cuttings for vineyards, and seeds for crops and kitchen gardens. Trees, shrubs, and flowers for pleasure grounds also became important as security and prosperity increased. Newly available printed catalogues presented choices with reasonably priced manufactured products for the home, including ready-made furniture, wallpaper, curtains, and mantles (Fig. 2.5). Downing offered guidance to those concerned about practicality and taste.

"The American cottager is no peasant," Downing proclaimed.[42] Redefining the cottage from the uneducated poor's mean habitat, Downing instead wanted cottages to be small and simple dwellings with suitable accommodation and appropriate expression. He felt that the true philosophy of living in America was to be found in moderate desires, moderate establishments, and moderate expenditures. If successful, Downing's principles would guide an inescapable bond between home, family, and land without regard to economic status. Every American—especially every worker—could thus acquire the refined pleasures of life found in an appreciation of the beautiful in nature and in the ability to improve a home he owned, and, with village schools, the opportunity to educate his children. The ability to adapt to new circumstances was a distinct advantage, as if people, just like certain species of fruit trees, were appreciated for their "capacity of adaptation that fits them for soils and exposures of almost every character."[43] To a degree, adaptation

Fig. 194 shows one of these sets. It consists of

1. A Dressing Bureau. 2. A small Table.
3. A Wash Sink. 4. A French Bedstead.
5. Four Cottage Chairs.

Fig. 2.5. Catalogue of furniture.

meant flexibility and freedom, and good taste meant the skill to make suitable choices.

Downing concluded his chapter "Landscape or Rural Architecture" in *A Treatise on the Theory and Practice of Landscape Gardening* with a footnote addressed "to readers who desire to cultivate a taste for rural architecture," which recommended several English sources on the topic.[44] Among these was Loudon's *Encyclopedia of Cottage, Farm, and Villa Architecture*, which featured over 1,300 pages, 100 lithographs, 2,000 wood engravings, and the work of fifty architects.[45] Peter F. Robinson's *Rural Architecture* and *Designs for Ornamental Villas* were also noted; both books included scenic views emphasizing Robinson's painterly conception of design, and the latter is credited with the popularization of the Swiss and Tudor styles.[46] Residential architect Robert Lugar (who had earlier published *The Country Gentle-*

man's Architect) was recommended for his *Villa Architecture*.[47] Downing also directed readers to Francis Goodwin's *Rural Architecture*, Thomas F. Hunt's *Picturesque Domestic Architecture* and *Exemplars of Tudor Architecture*, and Augustus C. Pugin's *Examples of Gothic Architecture* as valuable sources.[48]

These English authorities were important as illustrated examples of domestic architectural styles. In particular, they are a collection of the picturesque movement in English architecture; taken as a whole, however, Downing saw problems adapting their designs for America. Most English house plan designs were too large for Downing's purposes. Many smaller cottages were designed not to stand alone, but as accessory structures, entrance gatehouses, or the domain for peasants, groundskeepers, and other large estate staff. Consequently, their appearance was more likely to reflect the character of the landlord and his mansion than the tenant occupant. Loudon had noted this problem and included independent cottage designs in his 1840 publication "Cottage Economy." This essay, probably more than any other, popularized the suburban house as a domestic ideal. Loudon praised the "sense of property, the possession of a comfortable house, and the social affections and local attachments thereby produced."[49]

Clearly Downing identified an underserved market for publications that showed affordable, owner-built cottages for rural or suburban areas. His books go further and include a range of house sizes, materials, and costs, and consider possible climatic and geographic conditions. Explanations were offered on how one would decide in which style to build, and cautions were given about building more than a family's future generations could maintain.

An example is Downing's adaptation of English architect Peter Robinson's Design No. 19 (Fig. 2.6) for his brother's house, published as "a Cottage in the Pointed or Tudor Style" (see Fig. 1.12). The floor plans resemble each other in several distinct ways. Robinson's front rooms have a center hall between a staircase hall and library. Room purpose is similar, although Downing used different names for the eating and drawing rooms. An umbrage or awning extends these apartments toward distant views. One obvious difference between the two floor plans was Downing's addition of openings between rooms. The opening between the principal apartments had pocket doors so that the rooms could be "thrown into one" for social occasions. Robinson's design had doors opening only onto the hall, and they were likely to be hinged in the direction to reduce drafts—understandable, given England's climate. Downing's plan had more doors and larger openings to increase air circulation. There were also two bedrooms in the attic for

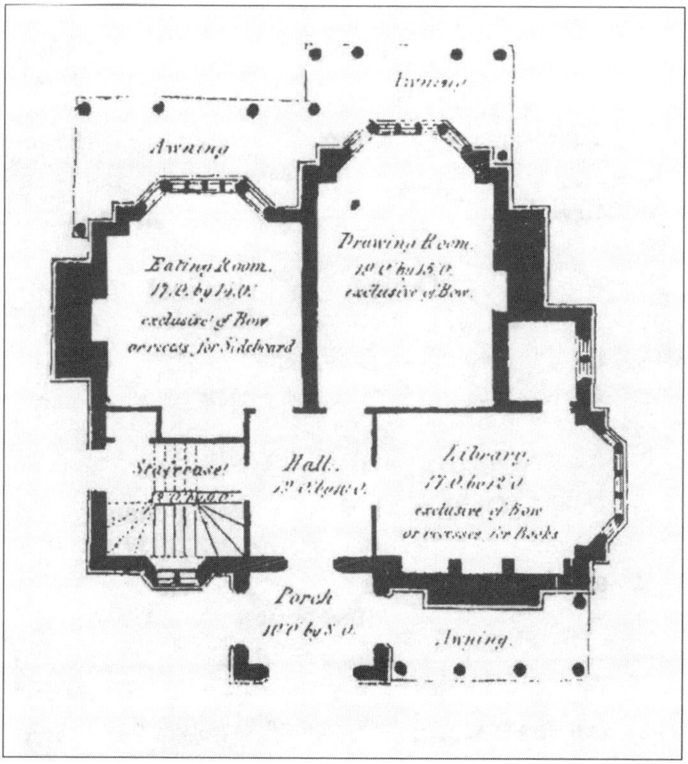

Fig. 2.6. Principal Floor Plan, Design No. 19.

servants and one in the cellar. Robinson's gentleman's cottage required five bedrooms in the attic for servants.

On the exterior, the designs appear very different. For Robinson, the covered open awning areas were meant to provide shelter protecting firewood and livestock (Fig. 2.7). Robinson's awning roofs were made of flimsy material such as canvas, with thatch for the steeper main roofs. For Downing, an umbrage was a shady sitting place for people to enjoy a fine view. Downing's umbrage roof was made of lead or tin, which worked well for low roof pitches, and the main roof was shingles. Its steep pitch was suitable for climates with heavy snow. As he put it, "In a cottage or villa of this style in England, the veranda would be useless, for the damp climate, so unlike ours, demands sun and air rather than shelter and shade."[50]

Other Downing adaptations included moving fireplaces and chimneys to interior walls where heat is more efficiently held within the house, and a fireplace can draw better.[51] As a result, Downing's rooms had windows on two

Fig. 2.7. View of Design No. 19.

exterior walls for cross ventilation, a desired amenity for warmer climates. Thatch as an English roofing material was more prone to catching fire, and this made the chimney perimeter location more desirable.[52] Downing's simplified roof plan also eliminated the long valley between the gable-end roofs over Robinson's eating and drawing rooms, something of paramount importance in a climate with snow and ice. In both designs, the projecting balcony or oriel window provided shelter over the door and drew attention to the entrance.

In the landscape, ideas of adaptation were partly about how something new was made to fit into the existing situation. Illustration techniques had begun with Humphry Repton who employed a method of "before and after" views in at least 114 red books with maps and sketches of improvements to country estates between 1788 and 1814.[53] Loudon's *Treatise on Forming, Improving and Managing Country Residences* (1806) also had numerous images of rural landscapes with "lift-up slides" comparing existing condition to proposed improvements. Downing used a similar technique in two drawings to show possible improvements (Figs. 2.8 and 2.9). Changes shown include making the straight and direct road into a sweeping curve with a hidden fence, trees in clumps, and the addition of a broad veranda, more dramatic roof lines, and expressive verge-boards and chimney tops to the house.

Fig. 2.8. View of a Country Residence, as frequently seen.

Fig. 2.9. View of the Same Residence, improved.

Another Downing before and after illustration (Fig. 2.10) shows a cultivated scene with curving drive, rustic seat, and planted beds. The house has been changed to include a habitable veranda, attic gable window, ornamental details, and elaborate chimney tops. The overall feeling has shifted from adequate to hospitable without increasing the size of the house.

Downing's designs were also animated by the inclusion of human figures. For example, Design II in *The Architecture of Country Houses* for a small bracketed cottage is shown in a rural setting (Fig. 2.11). A man is leaving the house with a tool over his shoulder, and a woman sits under a vine-covered arbor contemplating the view. Downing also includes an image of the same cottage, unadorned, and lacking what he called *feeling* (Fig. 2.12). He instructed his reader that it is possible to convey a sense of refinement and taste, saying that

FIG. 2. VIEW OF A COMMON COUNTRY HOUSE.

FIG. 3. VIEW OF THE SAME IMPROVED.

Fig. 2.10. View of a Common Country House and View of the Same Improved.

Fig. 2.11. View of Design II, *ACH.*

Fig. 2.12. View of Design II, *ACH,* unimproved.

"something of a love for the beautiful, in the inmates, is always suggested by a vine covered cottage, because mere utility would never lead any person to plant flowering vines; and much of positive beauty is always conferred upon simple cottage forms by the graceful growth of vines, through the rural and domestic expression they give to the cottage."[54]

The first advice Downing offered to someone about to build was to find land with a "*natural wood*, and where nature offers the greatest number of good features ready for a basis upon which to commence improvements."[55] This attitude reflected Downing's experience as a landscape designer and his familiarity with clients who underestimated the effort and cost of land improvement. A superior site was "ready" or appropriate for house construction. Such land was likely to promote architecture that corresponded more to the immediate situation and less to foreign ideas. Downing understood that a sense of truthfulness guided improvement in material choice and practical forms—a simplicity espoused in America by Ralph Waldo Emerson and by John Ruskin in England. This early modernist approach, complete with an appreciation for nature as the source of emotive fulfillment, found form in organic arrangement and detail, and merits closer attention.

TRUTHFUL ARCHITECTURE

Downing's interest in understanding truth as an interpreted reality came from an appreciation for scientific advances "observing and recording more accurately the phenomenal aspects of the natural world," and the ways in which this translated into design.[56] If truthful attributes of domestic occupation were to be expressed in architecture, then images of ideal family groups at leisure, ignoring the depiction of the labor that awarded such play, showed something of Downing's idea of the tasteful life. While some have criticized this depiction as the "blissful masculine indifference to household workings"—and indeed we are speaking about male artistic projections—they reveal more about human progress than domestic gender roles.[57] It was generally true at the time that while husbands worried more about house costs and wives about convenient layouts, everyone participated in daily activities. Downing's moralized landscape represented a social agenda he meant to encourage and inform.

For a thorough comprehension of truth and expression, it is useful again to turn to both Loudon and Ruskin as underlying sources. Loudon said of Ruskin's *The Poetry of Architecture* that "this important series of articles treats function, expression, and composition in vernacular architecture," in association with natural scenery and National character.[58] Loudon further qualified their intent by noting that:

> These essays will afford little pleasure to the mere builder, or to the architect who has no principle of guidance but precedent; but for such readers they were never intended. They are addressed to the young and unprejudiced artist; and their great object is to induce him to think and to exercise his reason. . . . There are some, we trust, of the rising generation, who are able to free themselves from the trammels and architectural bigotry of Vitruvius and his followers; and it is to such alone that we look forward for any real improvement in architecture as an art of design and taste.[59]

The articles, illustrated with Ruskin drawings, reviewed cottage and villa architecture in European countries and emphasized the associational qualities based on regionalism. The essay opened stating that "the Science of Architecture . . . is not merely a science of the rule and compass . . . or of fair proportion: it is, or ought to be, a science of *feeling* more than of *rule*, a ministry to the *mind*, more than to the *eye*."[60]

Ruskin originally meant the multivolume *Modern Painters* to be a pamphlet responding to critical attacks on J. M. W. Turner's landscape paintings.[61] He considered Turner the father of modern art for painting subjects taken from contemporary life, for his scientific use of color, and for his understanding of visual perception. Turner's paintings are considered to be more "true" than real, as he painted the nature of light and other qualities intrinsic to natural phenomenon (Fig. 2.13). The public controversy stemmed from claims that Turner misrepresented and surpassed truth with his interpretation of society and his failure to present factual accounts of nature. Turner's use of color required, as Ruskin noted, the observer's "*innocence of the eye* . . . sort of a childish perception," allowing the representation of things to have a diminished significance and to be valued as intuitive expression.[62]

Volume I of Ruskin's *Modern Painters* was published in England in 1843. According to scholar Judith Major, Volume II, published in 1846, had more influence on Downing because it provided an alternative to the *beau idèal*, allowing him to recommend a native tree or humble cottage as worthy of aesthetic consideration since they were appropriate and truthful.[63] Ruskin considered the communion between building and spectator to be truthful when the architecture had propriety, and thereby accurately represented the true character of the inhabitant, his virtues, occupation, and history. This is

Fig. 2.13. *Lucerne from the Lake*, Joseph Mallord William Turner, 1845.

a logical extension of Ruskin's belief that the artist revealed his moral character in his art, including the decisions necessary for its production. Hence, morally considered architecture belonged to the landscape through appropriate building position, scale, and form, and the choice of material. In this way architectural decisions submit to the landscape as a necessary condition of belonging. As defined by philosopher Eugéne Minkowski, "I *belong to* . . . differs from *having* in that it does not center the whole universe around me but on the contrary makes me enter into that universe."[64]

Downing referred to the people who occupied his houses as proprietors. In the mid-nineteenth century, "propriety" was defined as having a right of ownership, although not necessarily possession. A proprietor understood that changes had a larger consequence than immediate use. For better or worse, what was made belonged to the world. Further definitions of "propriety" include "fitness, suitableness, and consonance."[65] In a moral sense, one had to conform to social expectations; in matters of expression, one had to be proper. Henry Ward Beecher, Downing's contemporary and frequent contributor to *The Horticulturist*, put it well: "A man who builds a noble house does it for the whole neighborhood, not for himself alone. He who surrounds his children with books, refines their thoughts by early familiarity with art, is training them for the State."[66]

Ruskin claimed that art was a moral critique of society and reflected the country's character. Paintings were more than pleasant images; they revealed the world as it could be known. This effect required people to notice, to respond emotionally, and to take ownership of the natural world as a palette for composition—and, by extension, their place in it. Critical of the snobbery of taste, Oscar Wilde wrote an account of London fog, "where the cultured catch an effect, the uncultured catch cold."[67] Nineteenth-century England saw a rise in the importance of landscape painting with scenes composed more as ordered projections than photographic records. In America, this occurred later with the Hudson River School landscape painters in particular, although Downing's depictions reinforced the idea of landscape as an occupied scene.[68]

Downing read Ruskin's *The Seven Lamps of Architecture*, published in London and New York in 1849.[69] In the preface, Ruskin said that his book was an expansion of his thinking about beauty later published in Volume III of *Modern Painters*. Some consider Ruskin the most popular writer on architectural thinking in America, although his work actually had little influence on what was built.[70] Before the first American edition of Volume I in 1847, Ruskin's name and writings were virtually unknown to American readers; by 1855, he felt that he had a more significant audience for his ideas in America than in England.[71] This is due in part to Downing, who, according to Vaux, "was, certainly, the principal spokesman for Ruskin's architectural ideas in the United States."[72]

Taking the position that good architecture did not depend on building size or owner wealth, Ruskin insisted that what led to the "good life" was not only virtuous behavior, but also design expressing this behavior. Ruskin witnessed a new English aristocracy arising from industrial capitalism capable of copying the outward appearance, but lacking the intellectual subtleties of the hereditary wellborn. His subsequent criticism naïvely generalizes that those of noble birth had a natural tendency to execute their duty to alleviate the sufferings of the less fortunate, even if their overall circumstance was meant to remain unchanged.[73] Ruskin also generalized that successful corporations were unconcerned about the social consequences resulting from their exploiting industries. Progress meant that newly industrialized societies had new methods for compensating relief. For instance, a public park brought the benefits of the country into the city for those who had no time or money for holiday excursions.

One area in which Downing differed from Ruskin was in thinking about building materials. Ruskin insisted on using traditional building materials

Fig. 2.14. The Conservatory and Flower Garden at Montgomery Place.

such as wood, stone, and clay; Loudon, on the other hand, "recognized the beauty of glass and iron [made affordable with recent tax eliminations, as] materials which suggested new, equally 'truthful,' but lighter, more elegant construction."[74] Downing agreed, and wrote about greenhouse construction and the advantages for plant cultivation numerous times, and published letters in *The Horticulturist's* domestic notices section about his readers' successful experiments (Fig. 2.14). England's glass greenhouses created artificial micro-environments for exotic plants collected on global expeditions, helping delicate plants survive the winter. The resulting gardens could then contain unusual plants that could either be seen as a display of England's cultural advancement or as diluting the vernacular landscape character. Technical advances such as this were welcomed for the comfort and convenience they offered, and in time became absorbed into an expanded cultural definition.

In response to life in newly industrialized cities, Ruskin felt that the social pressure for civic virtue translated into an abhorrence of machine-made architectural ornament because the result failed to reflect a love of work necessary for truthfulness. Handmade work freed the craftsman; machine-made ornament made people servile and turned their labor into a commodity. Ruskin declared such ornament was a lie, as it no longer was able to express the purpose of the building, its inhabitants, or its making.[75] Fundamentally, true architectural structure was to be seen, and materials were never to be finished to look like other materials. Ruskin insisted that "We may not be able to command good, or beautiful, or inventive, architecture; but we *can* command an honest architecture: the meagerness of poverty may be pardoned, the sternness of utility respected; but what is there but scorn for the meanness of deception?"[76]

In 1829, the election of Andrew Jackson to the presidency ushered in the Age of the Common Man, when "taste became everybody's business and not just the business of the cultured few."[77] Downing, as a tastemaker, staked his principles on issues of propriety less as a check on civic virtue, and more as a means of promoting and elevating taste. He was well aware of population increases, the availability of inexpensive land, and the enterprising quality of American character. He worried less about the dues that the ambitious capitalist owed society than wasteful and inappropriate houses that failed to support health or happiness. His anticipation of problems surfaced with his caution about building in an ostentatious manner. Linking social behavior with truthful architecture, he claimed that "uncouth, mean, ragged, dirty houses, constituting the body of any town, will regularly be accompanied by coarse, groveling manners. The dress, the furniture, the mode of living, and the manners, will all correspond with the appearance of the buildings, and will universally be, in every such case, of a vulgar and debased nature. We would encourage a taste for beautiful and appropriate architecture, as a means of promoting public virtue and the general good."[78]

For Downing "truthful" was equivalent to understanding what was "significant" or "meaningful." For something to have meaning, it must designate or refer to something else. This interest in meaning was not a literal interpretation of domestic objects; Downing's domestic elements are not meant to stand for or represent something abstractly, but to be clear architectural expression. This was less a nod to Europe and more an exercise of "studying the characteristics of the farmer's life, and expressing, first of all, in the forms of his dwelling, the peculiar wants and comforts of that life." Architecture could be more than useful and beautiful; it must also be "truthful or significant. The intellect must approve what the senses relish and the heart loves."[79]

Two important points can be determined based on Ruskin's position about truth and its impact on Downing's architectural principles. First, no architecture is complete if it is untruthful. For Downing, utility was satisfied with appropriate shelter, and beauty was found in things and aroused sentiments. Truthful expression came from honest design. Only then could the formal expression of the proprietor's character and building on a specific site be linked together. "Domestic Architecture is only perfect when it is composed so as to express the utmost beauty and truth in the life of the individual," Downing concluded.[80] In this way, the inhabitant became the proprietor.

The second point addresses how this was achieved. Downing wrote that "every feature . . . which denotes domestic life, becomes a valuable truth in Domestic Architecture. Windows, doors, and chimneys . . . belong to or distinguish a dwelling-house from all other buildings. . . . Verandas, piazzas, bay-windows, etc., are the most valuable general truths in Domestic Architecture; they express domestic habitation more strongly because they are chiefly confined to our own dwellings."[81]

It is important to observe that Downing used the word "denotes," defined as "to mark, to signify by a visible sign, and to indicate," and not "represents," defined as "to show or exhibit by resemblance." Downing's principles of expression were not abstract references, but based on real associations. Democracy represented in Greek temple design may be appropriate for civic architecture, but attributes of dwelling distinguished homes.

These marked elements comprised an architectural vocabulary that satisfied the senses and the mind because they remained faithful to the principle of truth for dwelling in the house and the grounds. Based on principles, taste guided architectural form, material, and style choice. Ruskin was explicit when he declared that "taste is not only a part and an index of morality—it is the ONLY morality."[82] This applied to what was called the *paysage moralisé* or the truthful landscape.

TRUTHFUL LANDSCAPES

An appreciation for the effects of heightened sensibility guided the landscape painters and poets of the eighteenth century whose work described the landscape, the seasons, the wilderness, and the magnificence of rural America. Painters in particular composed the world as a picture; that is, a fiction of elements. James Jackson Jarves, the Hudson River School art critic, noted that their paintings had general truth combining correct detail in a false scene, but no sense of place or rather only idealized, fabricated places suitable for ideological propaganda.[83] Downing's writings argued for improvements made in a harmonious and truthful way. Richard Brown's drawing of various architectural styles and their appropriate situation and scenery illustrates this idea (Fig. 2.15).

Site development has certain attributes when it follows practical approaches. Rows of trees and shrubs planted on leveled land in a more forceful geometry require more land cutting and filling than arrangements follow-

Fig. 2.15. *Norman, Tudor, Grecian & Roman Residences: Their Appropriate Situation & Scenery*, Richard Brown, 1842.

ing natural contours. For Loudon, rigid geometric patterns with long vistas punctuated with terminating objects characterized the Ancient, Roman, Geometric, Regular, or Architectural style. Loudon's other approach was called Modern, English, Natural, Irregular, or the Landscape style, which Downing considered a more truthful way to improve the land.[84] Downing further distinguished Loudon's Modern style as either Beautiful or Picturesque. The Beautiful had round-shaped deciduous trees, often with branches drooping to the ground, smooth bark and luxuriant foliage, planted singly so their full form was visible. All was to be kept neatly trimmed and in good order. The other approach, the Sublime modified to be buildable, became the Picturesque. It had irregular outlines, wild and bold evergreens with pointed, spiry shapes and rough textures, planted closely in thickets and clumps (Fig. 2.16).

Improvements in harmony with existing situations resulted in more truthful construction because they followed nature more closely. Winding roads located according to land shape were lined with trees planted to conceal or to frame favorable views. The sequential experience of due concealment and revealed prospects created surprise and delight in the unfolding scene, felt more strongly because it seemed to occur naturally. In this way, design oriented the spectator, making prospects noticeable and presenting aspects of

FIG. 13.—Exan]le of the Beautiful in Landscape Gardening.

FIG. 16.—Example of the Picturesque in Landscape Gardening

Fig. 2.16. Examples of the Beautiful and Picturesque in Landscape Gardening.

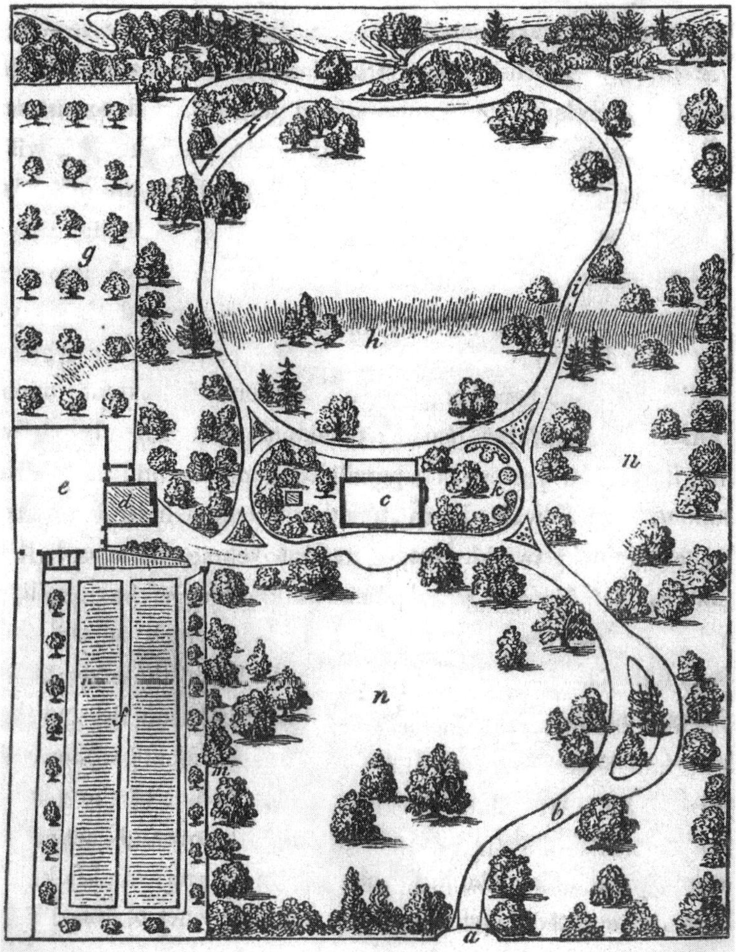

Fig. 2.17. Plan of the Grounds of Design III, *CR*. A diagonal approach "in the picturesque manner" (b) is planted to conceal a view of the house from the road and to allow it to burst into view at the most favorable moment.

the landscape to the best advantage.[85] An example is Design III from *Cottage Residences* (Fig. 2.17). Richard Brown, an English architect and writer Downing studied, put it well when he said that "where there is no diversity in the line of the road nor change of object, the mind becomes wearied of the sameness; and the grandeur of the mansion, which should burst upon the view in all its impressive magnificence, is lost." There is a lack of truthfulness when "a straight road . . . leads up to the house, which is ever in view; first in semblance of a cottage, then as a respectable house, and, finally, as a magnificent and elegant mansion, which is its true character."[86] Seen in this way, the approach unified the sight of house and the feel of the grounds.[87]

This correspondence is readily shown in many designs in *Cottage Residences*. Pleasure grounds have meandering paths gently veering in response to topography or to set up a view. Productive and pleasure grounds were concealed from each other with careful positioning and thick belts of arbor-vitae shrubs. Pleasure grounds had curving shapes with soft borders while productive kitchen gardens, orchards, vineyards, and plowed fields have straight rows reflecting their practical purpose. Downing credited Ruskin for suggesting the power of Hogarth's claim that the curve is the line of beauty because "it expresses in its varying tendencies, the infinite."[88] This was also a method of making a smaller suburban site appear to have a greater extent and capacity for pleasure while productive grounds were kept efficient.

Downing concluded his chapter on rural architecture in *A Treatise on the Theory and Practice of Landscape Gardening* with a confirmation of Repton's requirement that if the property were sufficiently large, neither the house nor the entrance be visible to each other.[89] He suggested that careful plant arrangement could conceal the two from each other without relying on distance, which was a practical suggestion since the very first caution Downing gave homebuilders was to keep the house close to the street for economic road construction and maintenance, and ease of access during bad weather. Proximity to what Downing called the "nervous hand of commerce" was also to be concealed. The effect of undisturbed and isolated nature occurred more forcefully when views of road and town were obscured.[90]

One exception to the modern style for pleasure grounds was Downing's Design VIII, "A Villa in the Italian Style." The arrangement of the grounds shows an attached geometric flower garden (shown as *e*) as an extension of a large terrace (*f*) (Fig. 2.18). Historian John Dixon Hunt notes that Repton influenced Ruskin who praised the use of terraces for Italian villas as a "necessary link between nature and art."[91] Downing qualified its inclusion by noting that "we are not admirers of geometric or formal flower-gardens like this, considered by themselves, and merely as flower-gardens, because we think a natural arrangement is more replete with beauty and grace . . . but it is a garden of architectural and floral beauty combined; it is as much an accessory of the building as a portion of the grounds, and therefore it very properly exhibits much of the regularity and symmetry of architectural forms and compositions."[92]

After gardens and fields were located depending on soils, slopes, light, and shade, house placement was the next opportunity for truthful considerations of fit.[93] Downing's published designs showed the house in perspective,

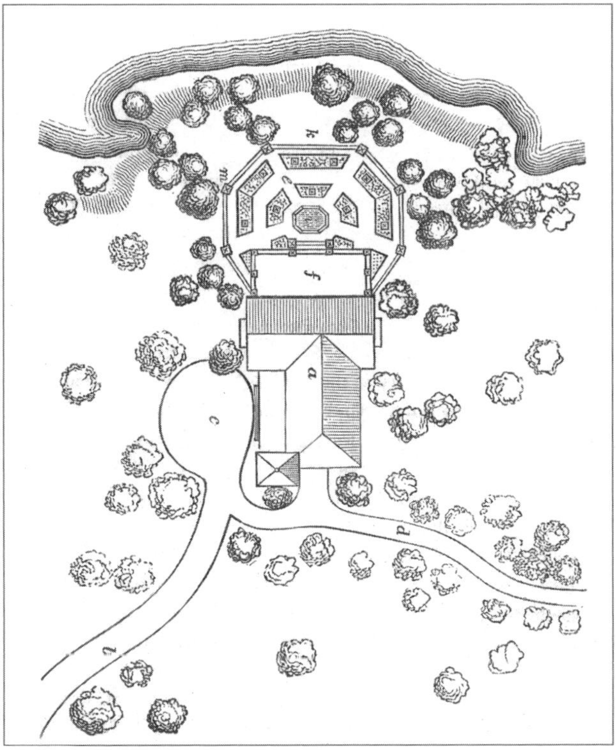

Fig. 2.18. Plan of the Grounds of Design VIII, *CR*.

Fig. 2.19. Richard Payne Knight, Downton Castle, Herefordshire, England.

exposing the front and side elevations simultaneously with foreground and background in complementary style. "Our every day comfort is so entirely dependent on a convenient arrangement of the rooms, or plan of the interior, that this is universally acknowledged to be the most important consideration," Downing said. "To have the principal rooms or apartments situated on the most favorable side of the house with regard to aspect, in order that they may be light, warm, or airy, and, in respect to view, that they may command the finest prospects, are desiderata in every kind of dwelling."[94]

Loudon considered Downton Castle near Wales to be the first and perfect example of uniting house to grounds where "the *genius loci* had been so happily humoured." Richard Payne Knight's mansion, built from 1774 to 1778, had a deliberately designed irregular floor plan oriented to outside views (Fig. 2.19). The estate grounds were laid out as a Claudian landscape, with landscape painter Thomas Hearne hired to record the scenes.[95]

Downing described the *Cottage Residence* ground plan designs with some comment about the prospective view. A house with a bay window provided a framed view or prospect, where obscured peripheral vision focused the intended picture as a planned composition in sharper detail. In this way, architecture helped to construct the visual connection between spectator and landscape. The idea of "subjective vision" was part of nineteenth-century cultural discussions, most often in the context of Romanticism, where the shift was one "from conceptions of imitation to ones of expression, from the metaphor of the mirror to that of the lamp."[96] Truth was possible in landscape design with well-received aspects and well-directed prospects. An oriented house belonged to the land visually, and conversely, composed grounds anchored the house as it appeared. Downing's design principles now had to be made physical, putting theory into practice.

3

HOUSE AND GROUNDS

> The relation between a country house and its "surroundings" has led me to consider, under the term residences, both the architectural and the gardening designs. To constitute an agreeable whole, these should indeed have a harmonious correspondence, one with the other.
>
> —Downing, *Cottage Residences*[1]

DESIGN PRINCIPLES about taste and improvement may be described and explained, but unless they are illustrated with examples putting theories into practice, the ideas remain remote for most readers. Downing's mission gained effectiveness because his published house drawings and accompanied text systematically introduced ideas about housing design and land cultivation. The examples helped his audience understand why something as simple as planting a vine to grow over a doorway was worthwhile and important to creating a feeling of home.

Downing thought that houses did two things: they supported routines of domestic operation and provided a place for contemplation. The intent of his design principles was that an encouraged desire for settlement would lead to cultivation. Remaining in one location allowed productive agricultural and horticultural practices that depended on permanent investment of person to place. Recognizing rapid population increases and the resulting unrest, Downing felt that a love of change was an American strength so long as it became satisfied with settlement eventually and did not turn into a blind passion for novelty. Once land was productive and improvements well

Fig. 3.1. Anglo Grecian Villa, William H. Ranlett.

executed, living above the survival level was possible, and leisure activities and refined pursuits became likely.

Downing's understanding of his audience's interests becomes clear if his work is compared to William Ranlett's *The Architect, a Series of Original Designs, for Domestic and Ornamental Cottages and Villas; Connected with Landscape Gardening, Adapted to the United States*, an impressive two-volume set of fifty-three designs in twenty-one styles, published in New York in 1848. Ranlett's "original and rural" houses in this portfolio of prospective projects, intended for all economic classes, had construction prices between $900 and $12,000, but these large and well-illustrated books cost more than most middle-class families could afford (Fig. 3.1). Its vast range of choices were also unaided by a strategy for selection, and would likely confuse more than help prospective homebuilders. Ranlett's lithograph illustrations included the usual plans and elevations, isometric views of floor plans, construction-ready framing and wall sections, large-scale details, and site plans with site profiles. Also included were specifications for twenty-one trades, cost estimates for masons, carpenters, and painters, and sample contract forms. Commentary throughout the volumes concentrated on the "moral

Fig. 3.2. Alexander Jackson Davis, Highwood for James A. Hillhouse, New Haven, Connecticut, 1829.

aspect" of architecture. In contrast, Downing's expanded fourth edition of *Cottage Residences,* published four years after Ranlett's book, contained fourteen house designs in six styles, half with estimated costs of less than $5,000, and Downing's *Architecture of Country Houses* had twenty-three designs with estimated costs of less than $2,600.

The strategy for selecting house size and style began with an argument against what Downing saw frequently constructed in Newburgh and elsewhere in New England.[2] Downing particularly disliked the popular Greek Revival style (Fig. 3.2). For domestic architecture, Downing argued against imitating the Vitruvian orders with columns, pediment, and entablature as seen in ancient Roman and Greek architecture, insisting that "Churches, banks, and court-houses, one could very well bear to see *Vitruvianized.* Their simple uses and respectable size bore well the honors which the destiny of the day forced upon them. But to see the five orders applied to every other building, from the rich merchant's mansion to the smallest and meanest of all edifices, was a spectacle which made even the warmest admirers of Vitruvius sad, and would have made a true Greek believe that the gods who preside over beauty and harmony, had for ever abandoned the new world!"[3]

Fig. 3.3. Grecian Residence.

The first house illustrated in *A Treatise on the Theory and Practice of Landscape Gardening* was an example of the Greek Revival style (Fig. 3.3).[4] Conceding the appropriate application for civic buildings or palaces where "it is evident that ample accommodations may be obtained in any style," and that the Greek Revival style had associations with the ideals of democracy, as Downing pointed out, even the Greeks did not live in temple-like houses.[5] "Thus, if we talk pure Greek," he said, "and build a Grecian temple for a dwelling, we shall be little understood, or perhaps only laughed at by our neighbors."[6]

His chief complaint was that the rigid form of the Greek Revival style was unresponsive to varying topography. The covered portico, "so high as neither to afford an agreeable promenade, nor a sufficient shelter from the sun and rain," did not serve as the useful porch Downing thought expressed qualities of leisure and repose.[7] The suppressed appearance of chimneys also failed to comply with his principle of expression. Greek temples did not have chimneys because they were not heated with fireplaces, and therefore Greek Revival style houses had to minimize the presence of their chimneys in every possible way in order to remain close to the appearance of a Greek temple. Even the painted white color offended Downing, who considered it too glaring to blend into a verdant landscape. But his greatest criticism was that the building form and subsequent floor plan with a single dominating room lacked flexibility, and its capacity for domestic occupation was limited because various activities had practical room sizes and preferred adjacencies.

One architectural historian noted that "the Greek Revival . . . bore within it the seeds of its own destruction. Just because of its relative fixity of ideals, its essentially imitative character, it had less capacity for indefinite growth."[8] Downing believed that the style was more appropriate for urban, level, and rectangular sites, often with a single street façade, rather than rural locations where buildings were exposed on all sides. In the country, topography was more often varied. A Greek Revival house had to sit as an isolated form perched on the land, requiring the natural terrain to be flattened into a platform. As explained by historian Vincent Scully, "in Greek Revival architecture, site, planning, materials, and construction were essentially secondary, or were at least dominated by the abstract cube and its placement in space. It was an architecture which was applied from without; it did not grow from within or depend upon peculiarly American conditions."[9]

This concept was unacceptable for Downing. "We have no more patience with those architects who give us copies of the temple of Theseus, with its high, severe colonnades, for dwellings, than with a friend who should describe his wife and children to us in the lofty rhythm of Ossian," he said.[10] Downing's response was to design houses with floor plans that I identify as either subdivided or assembled. Downing distinguished two basic kinds of architectural form: the horizontal and the vertical. Horizontal forms were the "rational, logical, sensible idea, bounded by the regular horizontal line of classical architecture" (Fig. 3.4). Vertical forms, by contrast, were the "more poetic, aspiring, imaginative idea embodied in the upward lines of pointed architecture" (Fig. 3.5).[11] Downing followed the same approach in his landscape design where the useful is manifest in the regularity of productive grounds and plowed fields, and the beautiful in the irregularity of pleasure gardens with curved paths and planted beds. The house designs can be identified as either a horizontal and regular form with a subdivided floor plan, or a vertical and irregular form with an assembled floor plan.

The subdivided floor plans in regular forms are often symmetrical, displaying balance and unity. Their distinct advantage is simpler and more economic construction, and an appealing predictability for a proprietor whose common sense was his chief characteristic. Their main disadvantage is an inability to expand where an addition would throw off the orderly composition of the existing structure.

Downing's assembled floor plans in irregular forms are often asymmetrical. They have the advantage of being able to group different size rooms,

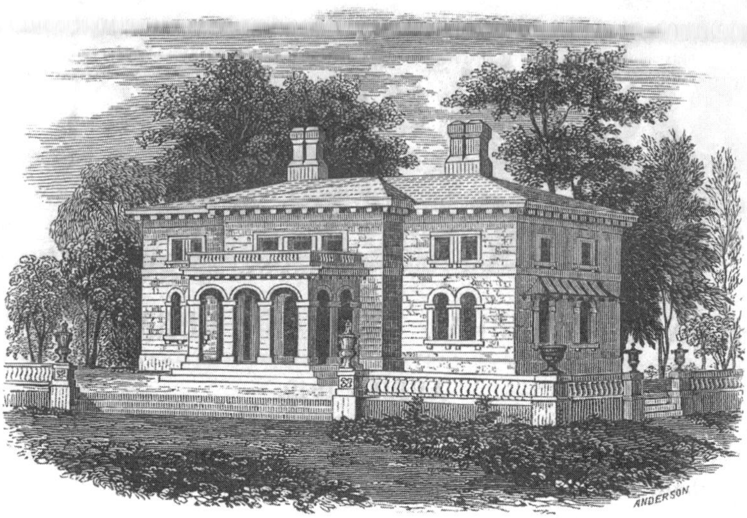

Fig. 3.4. Italian Villa.

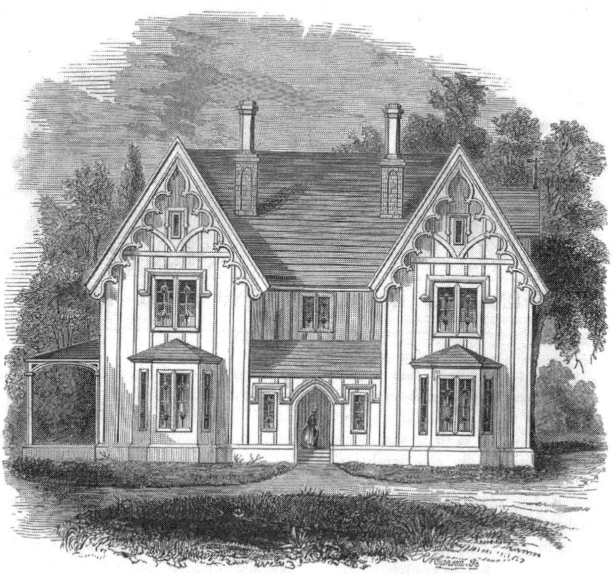

Fig. 3.5. English Cottage.

so long as they are joined in some coherent way. The disadvantage comes with finding the correct strategy to organize the disparate parts. For Downing's larger plans, corridors often provided the ordering device. Assembled arrangements were more likely to better accommodate the various demands of dwelling. The exterior often had a variety of ridge heights and slope directions. The resulting variety appealed to a proprietor with either a character of sentiment and feeling, or of imagination.

Besides his own house, Downing published designs for forty-nine houses or house-like buildings such as gate lodges, of which ten were designed with Calvert Vaux to some degree. Of the house designs published in Downing's two architecture books, ten cottages had subdivided and six had assembled floor plans.[12] Farmhouses had an equal number of subdivided and assembled plans at four each. Four villas had subdivided plans and nine assembled. In general, the smaller and simpler cottage floor plan tended to be subdivided, and villas tended to be assembled.

It is not always obvious if larger houses have subdivided or assembled floor plans. Some assembled floor plans are a collection of subdivided blocks. There is a practical structural reason for this. The length of wood joists spanning between load-bearing walls usually limits room dimensions to no more than twenty feet.[13] Cellar floor plans verify this, showing masonry walls located to support the simple span-framing above. When houses were more than one span deep, the load-bearing perimeter walls could be combined as distinct blocks. The difference between the subdivided and assembled floor plan becomes clearer when the roof plan is examined. The expression of a subdivided house as a block is usually reinforced tectonically with a single roof form. The newly imported French Second Empire mansard-type roof with an almost flat central portion was often used for the subdivided house whose floor plan was too big for a simply framed pitch roof (Fig. 3.6). It is also evident that this house has a subdivided floor plan because room sizes have been adjusted to fit into the whole composition. On the exterior, gables cover the projections below.

Some historians have seen Downing's unique contribution to domestic architecture to be the promotion of a modified Italianate style with an assembled floor plan breaking the tradition of a rectangular footprint such as is found in the center hall Colonial style. One influential book from England was architect Charles Parker's *Villa Rustica,* published in a series from 1832 to 1841. The book contained drawings of rural Italian vernacular houses set into the scenery, along with suggestions of how these plans might be adapted to the English country house. It appealed to those who enjoyed and wanted to

DESIGN No. 20.—(D. & V.)

PERSPECTIVE VIEW.

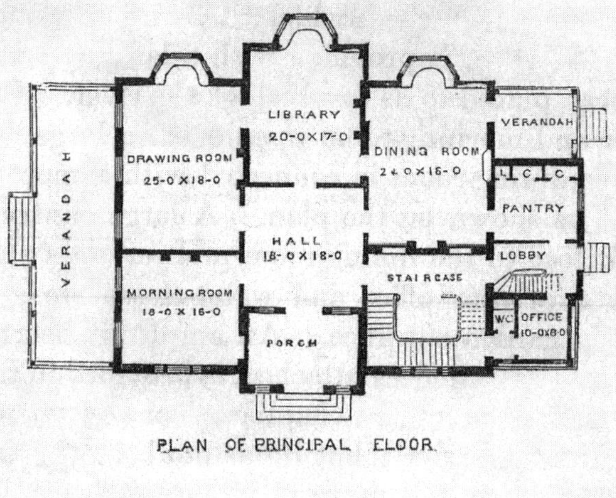

PLAN OF PRINCIPAL FLOOR

Fig. 3.6. View and Plan of Principal Floor of Design No. 20.

display their associations to Rome. These irregular plans served as examples of how house and landscape fit together, and implied that they should.

Downing offered Design VI in *Cottage Residences* (see Fig. 3.10).[14] Historian Jane Davies has concluded that "the house shape was Downing's concept, a new pattern in America: a deliberately L-shaped house, with the angle toward the front, and, moreover, a tower in the angle."[15] The tower contributed to its quality, expressing the presence of desirable prospects and offering a varied form not found in unified subdivided plans.

There were other irregular house shapes in *Cottage Residences* and *The Architecture of Country Houses.* There are seven L-shaped plans of Downing's design (see Fig. 1.10), plus two by G. J. Penchard and Richard Upjohn and six T-shaped (with one by Davis) (Fig. 3.7). Downing also includes one H-shaped (plus two by Gervase Wheeler), and two with a cross-shaped (+) plan (with five by others) (see Fig. 5.3).[16]

One distinct advantage to the assembled floor plan was its ability to fit more readily into irregular land shapes. New construction usually required clearing forests for fields and buildings, but with varied plans, leveling the land was less necessary. The house had a means to yield to land shape, instead of the other way around. Distinguishing subdivided and assembled floor plan design and the ways in which each matched distinct proprietor and landscape characteristics is a way to understand Downing's design examples beyond categorizing size and style. The follow sections examine this in greater detail.

A REGULAR HOUSE WITH A SUBDIVIDED FLOOR PLAN

Subdivided floor plans with regular forms had the advantage of simplicity of construction. Downing repeatedly emphasized economic considerations throughout his writings: "As the most economical form for a cottage is a square, and next to that a parallelogram, it is evident that all irregular cottages are more costly than regular ones."[17] The economy of regularity in form meant simple framing and easier construction. The regular form lent itself to a subdivided floor plan with principal rooms fitting within the shell and with supporting rooms often squeezed into partitioned-off, leftover areas (Fig. 3.8). By definition, a technique of subdivision cuts a floor plan into smaller and smaller parts, with the consequence that some rooms take priority over others. For instance, there is only one southeast corner in a rectangular floor plan, which works well for a morning room, but this eliminates the possibility

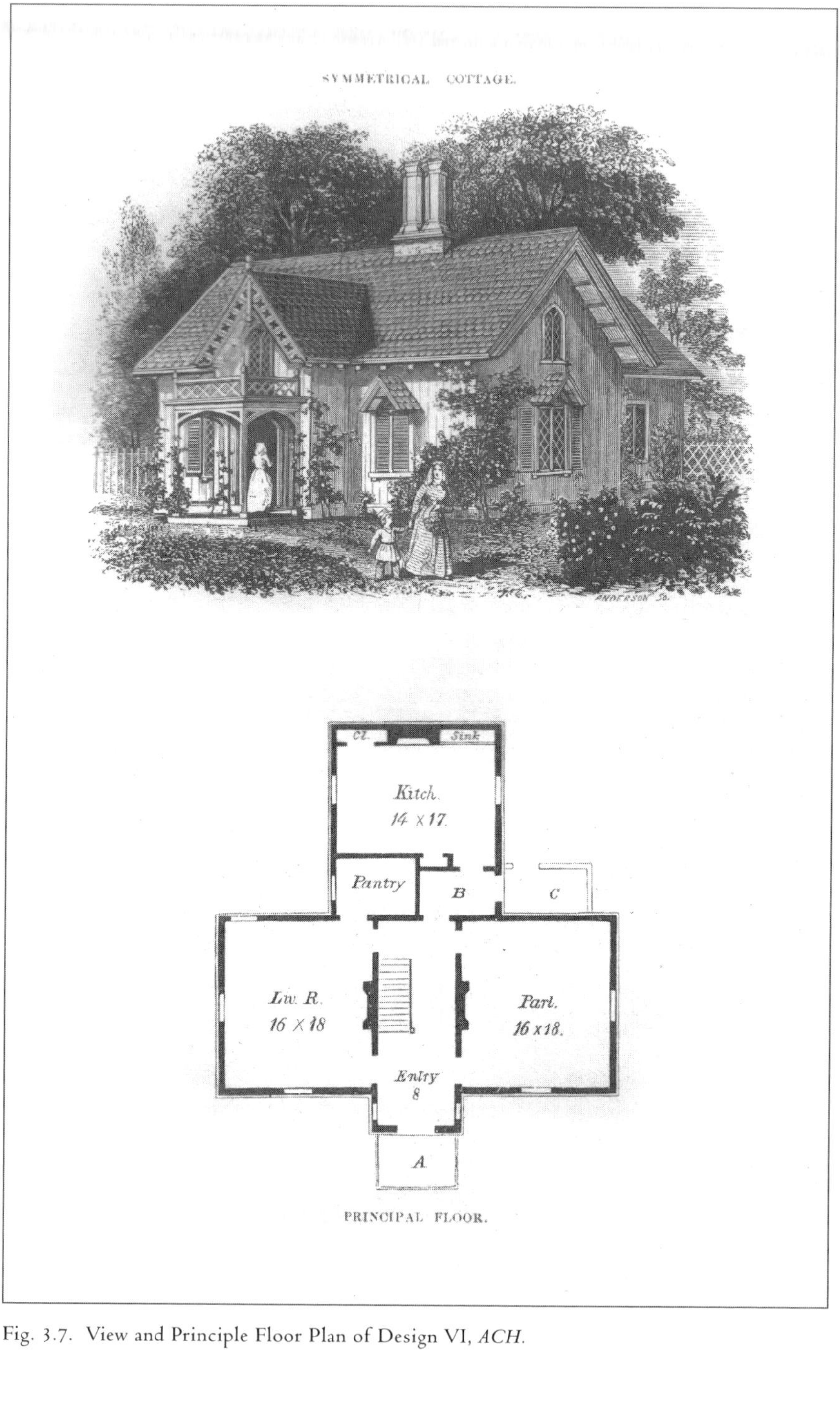

Fig. 3.7. View and Principle Floor Plan of Design VI, *ACH.*

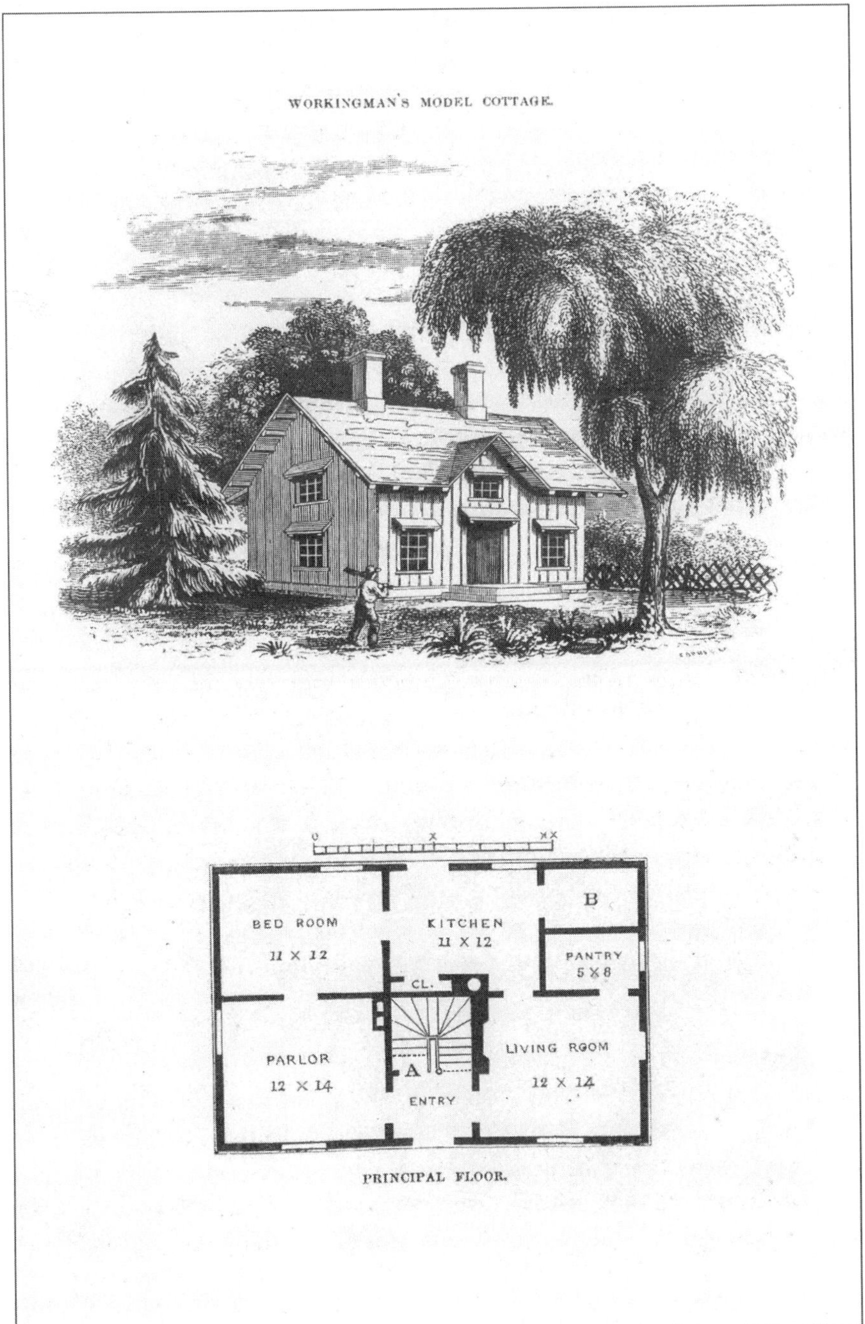

Fig. 3.8. View and Principle Floor Plan of Design V, *ACH*, a subdivided floor plan.

of another space having the same aspect. In construction, rooms made with interior wood frame and plaster subdividing partitions were less expensive to build than exterior masonry load-bearing walls that were also charged with waterproofing responsibilities.[18]

The subdivided floor plan fits together like a puzzle, where edges are clearly determined and the overall form is recognizable as a distinct shape. A probable scenario for designing begins with identifying what room was most important: perhaps a library facing the drive to see approaching business associates, or a parlor and veranda open to a river view, or kitchen offices convenient to orchards, vegetable gardens, and livestock yards. That privileged room has first priority with consideration to aspect, prospect, and situation. The less important rooms are subordinate to the main room and would be located in the remaining space.[19]

In the landscape, once the "geometric" field is cleared and leveled, it is easier to plow, cultivate, and harvest; as this is done every season, the logical advantage is unassailable. It is also easier to calculate its size and production quantity, and to assess taxes. Therefore, the appeal of regular form to common sense came from an ease of forecast, rather than an appeal to the mysterious unknown.

Downing directed readers whose practical requirements were their chief concern to building blocks executed in a variety of styles while retaining the simpler, more economic approach to design and construction. His design names specify this character, designating one design as "regular," four "symmetrical," one "square," and one "cubical."

Thick, load-bearing masonry walls and thinner wood subdividing partitions are apparent on Downing's floor plans. Design II in *Cottage Residences* is an example of a subdivided floor plan (see Fig. 1.11). The interior composition has a center-bearing wall where Downing located the fireplaces, and subdividing partitions to separate the rooms. On the exterior, the block form appearance was reduced with a broad veranda and a hipped roof with central gable and verge board edges, and large roof overhangs supported on ornamental brackets that cast deep shadows upon the walls. The grounds are divided between the pleasure grounds and productive gardens (Fig. 3.9). There is a direct, logical correspondence between the front library and parlor rooms, the umbrage, and the gardens to the front, as well as the kitchen and adjacent laundry-drying plots (shown as *g*), the outhouse, and stable (*c*), which are close to the vegetable garden (*h*), grapevine arbor (*j*) and fruit trees (*k*) in the back.

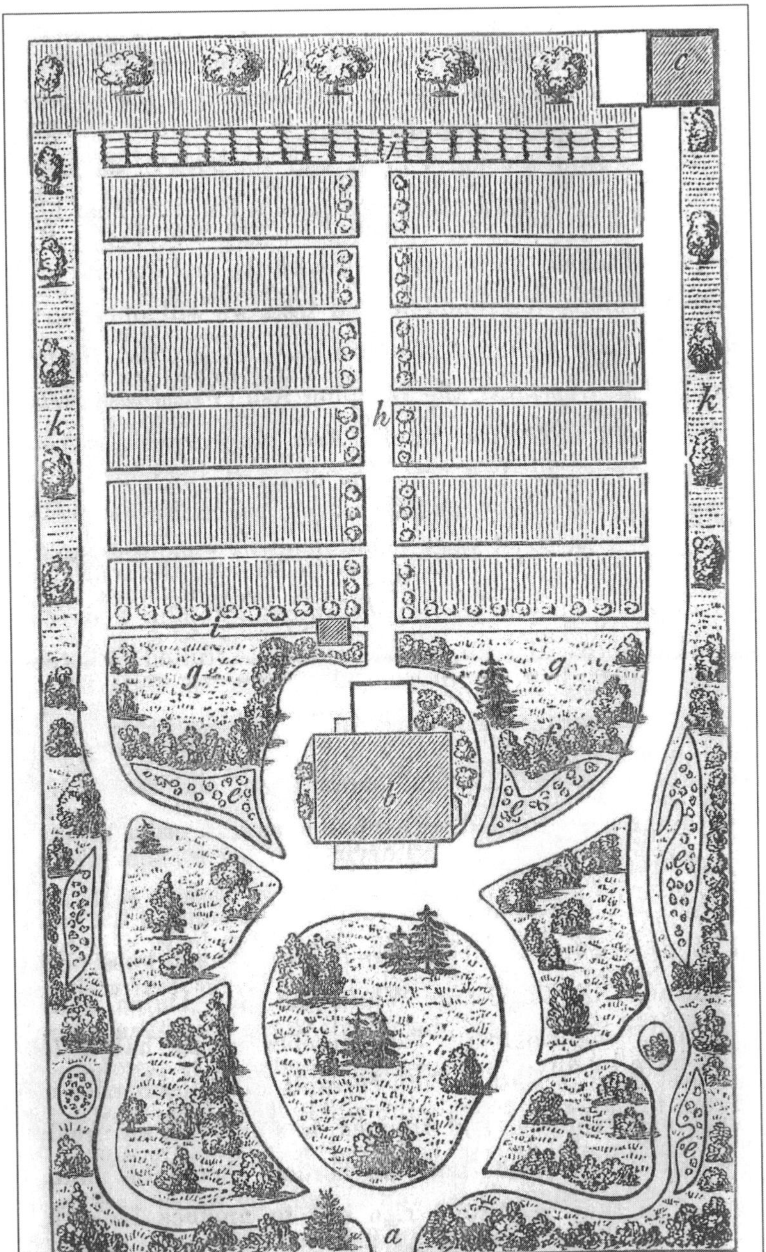

Fig. 3.9. Plan of the Grounds of Design II, *CR,* a subdivided site plan.

AN IRREGULAR HOUSE WITH AN ASSEMBLED FLOOR PLAN

There is a difference between the words "assemble" and "add." Assemble comes from the Latin *convocare,* "to call together," and add comes from *addere,* "to join or unite." Adding joins things that may have nothing in common. Assembling fits together distinct things, suggesting they have something in common or are similar in some way.

In the assembled floor plan, rooms are designed with individual qualities given priority. Apartments are sized and arranged to suit their necessities first. Each room is therefore less a subset of the whole and more a distinct place with a relationship to the whole. Downing noted that the internal motive for domestic life "requires apartments of various dimensions, some large and others smaller, which, to be conveniently, *must* often be irregularly placed, with perhaps openings or windows of different sizes or dimensions."[20] Irregular floor plans respond in different ways to external motives such as more complex land forms, and favorable or unfavorable prospects. Uvedale Price had written on the picturesque in 1794 that "if the owner of such a spot, instead of making a regular front and sides were to insist on having the windows turned towards the points where objects were most happily arranged, the architect would be forced into inventing a number of picturesque forms and combinations which otherwise might never have occurred to him; and would be obliged to do what has so seldom been done—accommodate his building to the scenery not make that give way to the building."[21] An assembled floor plan has the advantage of multiplicity, and more readily adjusts to the distinctions of the individual site and situation. Both subdivided and assembled house plans have an orientation, but only the assembled plan can actually address the full capabilities of the site.

Design VI of *Cottage Residences* gives an indication of the individuality of the room design and the comprehensive site consideration (Fig. 3.10). The consequence of an assembled floor plans is evident in the number of exterior areas included in the design (Fig. 3.11). Downing has a porch and terrace on the front facing the driveway (shown as *b*), a broad veranda on the side facing an oval lawn *(m)* and the river, and another porch facing the ornamental garden beds (*l*) to the rear. Three sides of the chamber floor have balconies, two of which are over projecting bays. The site plan is a composition of assembled elements with an elevated distinction between the cultivated and uncultivated grounds. Downing says, "the oval area of lawn, *m*, and

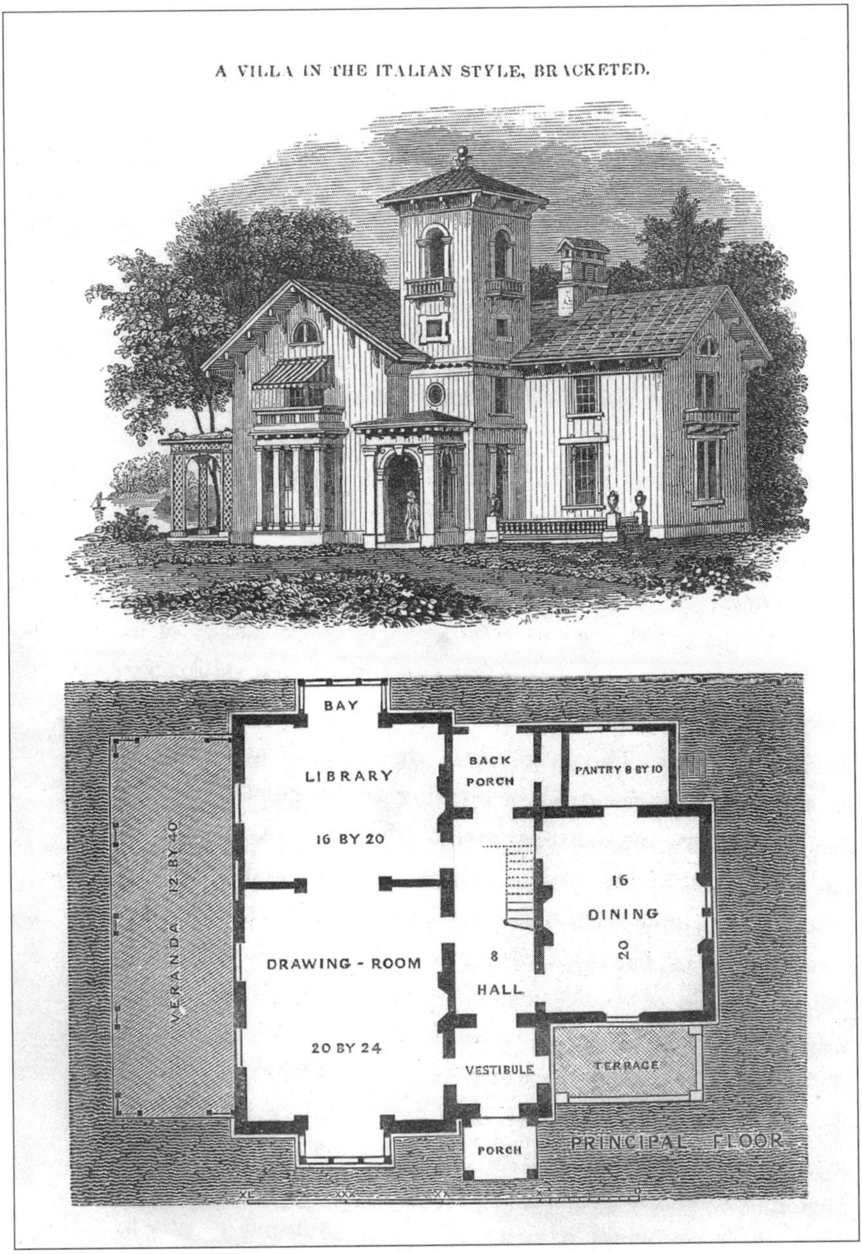

Fig. 3.10. View and Principal Floor Plan of Design VI, *CR*, an assembled floor plan.

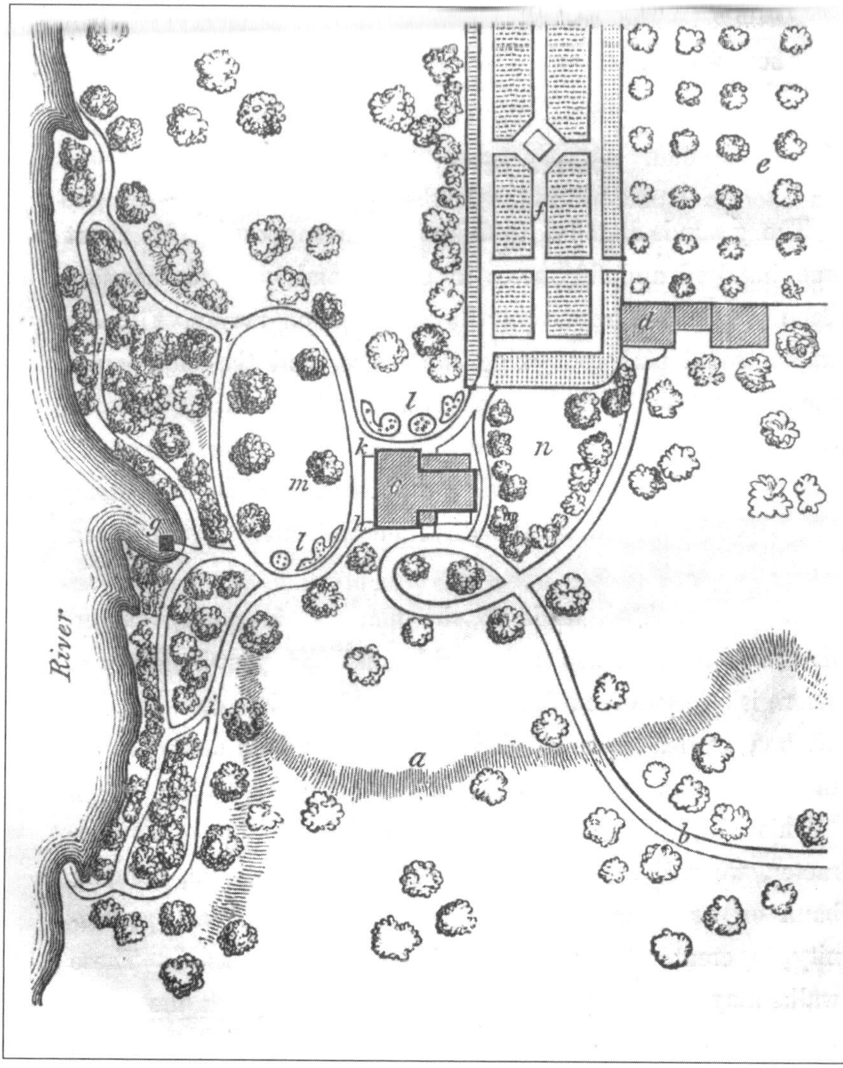

Fig. 3.11. Plan of the Grounds of Design VI, *CR,* an assembled site plan.

the space between the porch and where the ground descends at *a*, should be kept constantly mown, and in the highest order, so as to heighten, and render more forcible by contrast, the wilder and more picturesque beauty of the sylvan walks *i*."[22]

There are other innovations in floor plan design present in Downing's work. In *Cottage Residences,* Downing always arranges the principle floor plan with a center hall and flanking rooms. Eight years later in *The Architecture of Country Houses,* seventeen designs have center halls but nine do not, indicating that Downing became more comfortable with L- and T-shaped plans for assembled designs and the greater flexibility they allowed. Vaux appreciated these changes for "the advantages of a studied irregularity and broadly conceived picturesqueness in arranging country houses."[23]

Assembled floor plans allow the house design to be put together from the inside responding to individual room requirements, and from the exterior responding to its situation. For Downing, this allowed an irregular or a modern approach to house design and a more natural landscape design. The result enhanced a sense of fit and belonging to the land as each room more closely corresponded to its intended purpose and was positioned more favorably in terms of the site. The house responded to qualities of aspect while the architecture framed prospects or views.

Assembled floor plans led to interior rooms and exterior spaces with a poetic quality less possible in subdivided floor plans. If a proprietor thought he was a person with cultivated sensibilities or a heightened sense of imagination, the assembled plan offered more possibilities. Downing identified "two distinct classes of taste in rural art; first, the poetic or northern taste, based on a deep instinctive feeling for nature; and second, the artistic or symmetric taste, based on a perception of the Beautiful, as embodied in works of art."[24] (His slight by omission of any reference to southern taste may have been a political comment.) These characteristics were alternatives to design where practicality was paramount. In seeing the value of linking the proprietor's character to the house floor plan design, and suppressing or capitalizing on its potential relationship to the land, Downing was unique.

LINKING A PROPRIETOR'S CHARACTER TO ARCHITECTURE AND LANDSCAPE

Edmund Burke's *Philosophical Enquiry into the Origin of our Ideas of the Sublime and Beautiful* was first published in 1757. Two years later Burke published a second edition adding an essay on taste, where he stated "I mean by the word Taste no more than those faculties of the mind which are affected with, or which form a judgment of the works of imagination and the elegant arts." Making this a subjective activity, taste was improved "by extending our knowledge, by a steady attention to our object, and by frequent exercise," treating the deficient parts of an object with the character of the whole

Edmund Burke
(1729–1797)

Born in Ireland in 1729 and educated at Trinity College, Burke went to London to study law, but found his purpose in writing and public service. Burke's Natural Society *and* Philosophical Enquiry into the Origin of Our Ideas on the Sublime and the Beautiful *(both 1756) were well received. Burke's position on the sublime and the beautiful helped shift English aesthetic taste from classical formalism, where clarity was the chief intent of great art, to a more romantic formulation where obscurity was valued because it stretched the imagination in its perception of the unbounded and indistinct. Burke was Hazlitt's favorite author, and it is likely that Downing was familiar with Burke's aesthetic philosophy as well. Burke was involved in politics until he died in 1797.*

in mind.[25] Keeping the character of the whole in mind, Downing helped narrow the choices to what was appropriate given the particular characteristics of proprietor, house, and grounds. His intent was to raise the satisfaction and enjoyment possible when decisions reflected sound principles and recognized these relationships. Downing's interpretation of this connected and interdependent relationship can also be expressed as the following equation: when the proprietor's character plus a chosen architectural style is matched to a specific landscape, it results in a practical, romantic or picturesque composition in what Downing called a "harmonious union."[26]

The practical house and garden was for the man with common sense whose rational analysis gave priority to construction economy, with little interest in artful displays. Geometry and symmetry governed house design and resulted in regular forms, usually with subdivided floor plans. Highly refined materials and orderly lines gave weight to this design approach. Downing favored the American Bracketed mode and included ten designs in this style reflecting his endorsement for what he hoped would become the new American style. Other designs meant to appeal to practical sensibilities included two designs in the Anglo-Italian or Tuscan style, and one in the Classical (by Davis). The ideal landscape was a gentle plain. Pleasure grounds might include urns and statues set on pedestals that served as terminating objects to long vistas. The grounds had cut flower beds with arabesque borders, and single stately trees on turf lawns. Downing's very first house in *Cottage Residences,* a design for a Suburban Cottage for a Small Family, is an example of his ideal notion of refined simplicity (Figs. 3.12 and 3.13). For the proprietor with common sense who valued regularity and economy, this house design provided a simplified American bracketed style on a flat site with no

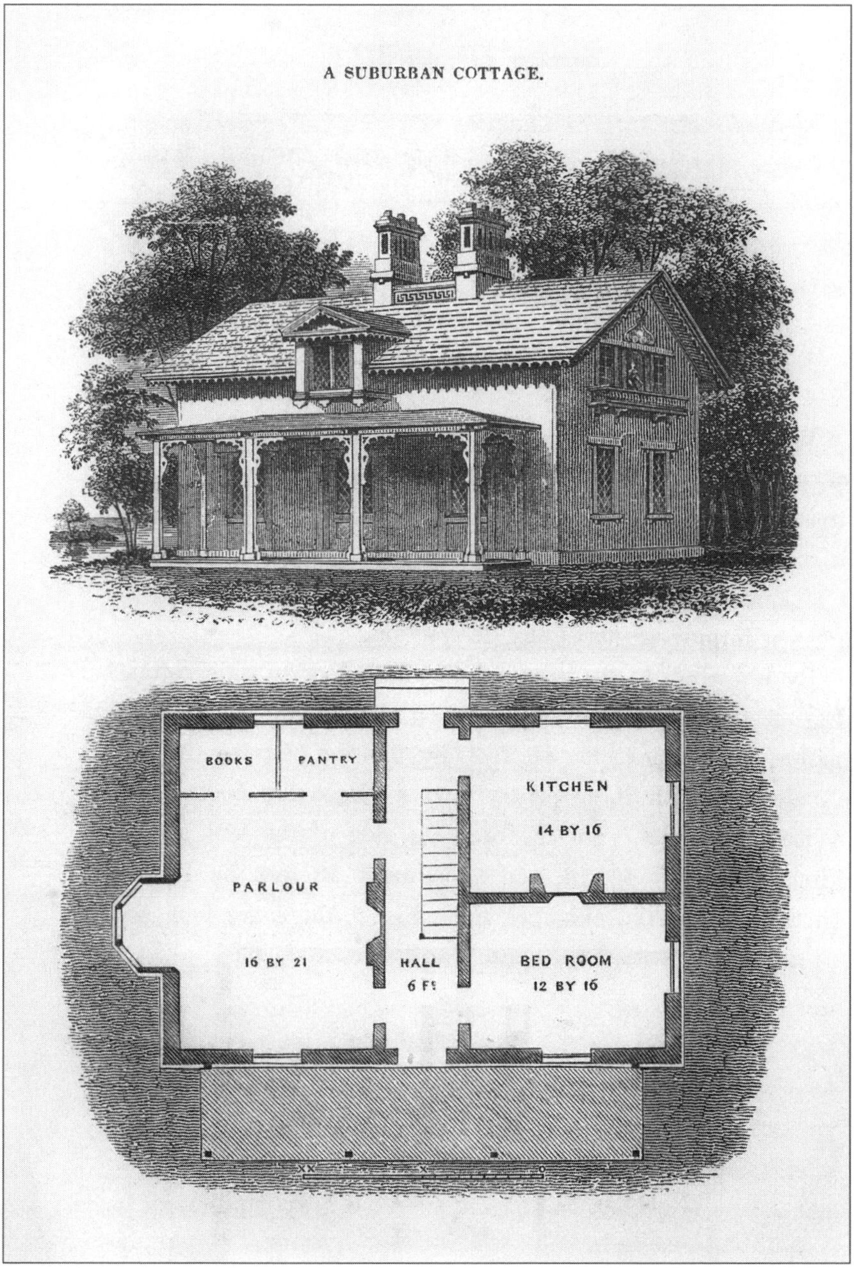

Fig. 3.12. View and Principal Floor Plan of Design I, *CR.*

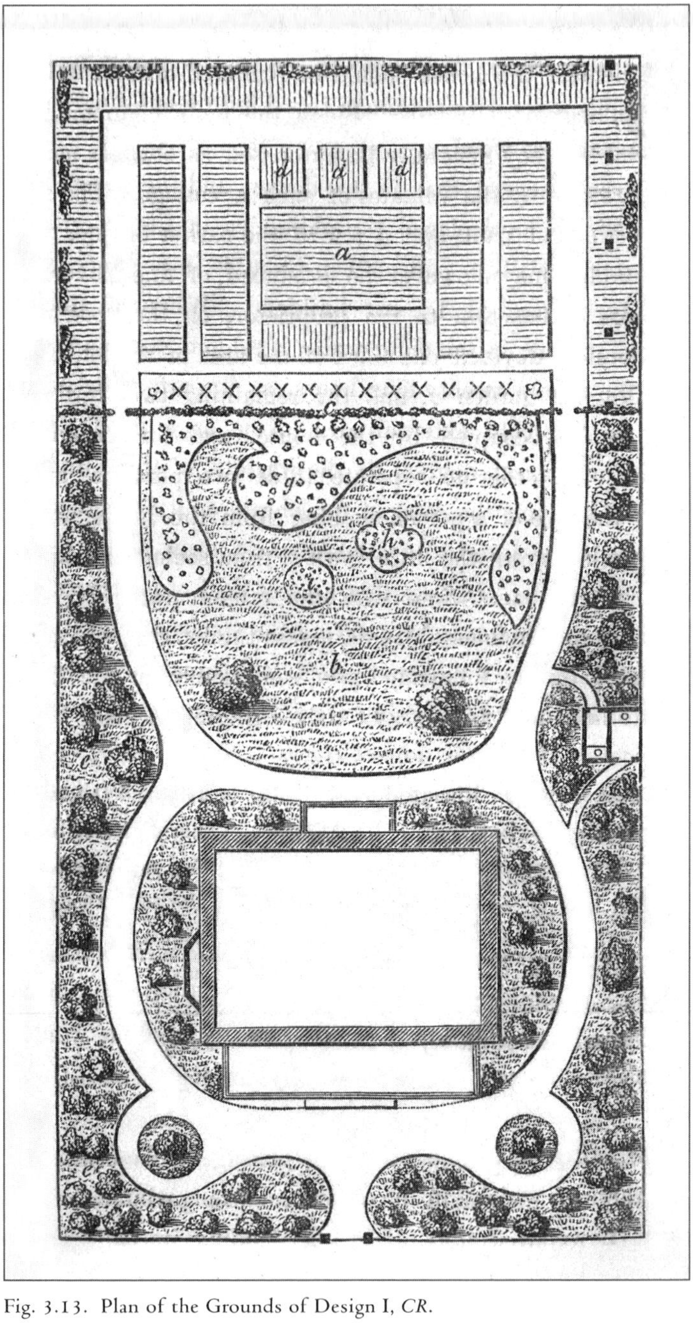

Fig. 3.13. Plan of the Grounds of Design I, *CR*.

distinguishing features, improved with thickly planted borders, flower beds in lawn, and kitchen gardens.

Downing also offered other designs for those with a greater interest in the beauty of effect than in the rationality of regularity. The man of sentiment and feeling favored the irregular house and garden designs, which appealed to the senses. The design's description was romantic: "something in its aspect which the heart can fasten upon and become attached to, as naturally as the ivy attaches itself to the antique wall, preserving its memories from decay."[27] It followed Burke's definition of the beautiful typified by spatial intimacy and gradual variation in material. The English or Rural Gothic styles were preferred by people of sentiment, and Downing supplied eight designs. Designs in the Rustic Pointed, Elizabethan, and Romanesque style were also included. The ideal site was a fertile valley. An appropriate site for Design VIII in *Cottage Residences,* a Villa in the Italian Style, was a "romantic vale, or sylvan nook . . . and equally appropriate for an open smiling plain, diversified by hill and dale, and sprinkled with groups and masses of trees" (Fig. 3.14, and see Fig. 2.18).[28] For those who valued expression in irregularity, these designs included recesses and projections as well as a prospect tower to give the composition verticality, and an interior arrangement oriented to an approach (shown as *b*) and a terrace with a river view.

The man of imagination who appreciated boldness and originality favored the picturesque house and garden, also governed by irregular form. The design followed Price's definition of the picturesque, guiding a sense of contrast with attention to intricacy and variety. Downing included four designs each in the modern Italianate and Pointed Tudor styles, as well as two examples of the Swiss and one each in the Norman and Rhine styles. The house by Albany architect G. J. Penchard, Esq., included as Design X in *The Architecture of Country Houses,* was a Swiss cottage, a style Downing considered to be "the most picturesque of all dwellings built of wood" (Fig. 3.15).[29] Ideal landscapes were the sides or under the brow of steep mountains and rocky passes. For Design VII of *Cottage Residences,* an irregular cottage in the Old English style, Downing noted that "the situation for this cottage may be in a richly wooded plain, or a sequestered valley" (Figs. 3.16 and 3.17).[30] These irregular designs utilized partial concealment and an internal arrangement directed toward many created scenes in the landscape. Walking through the grounds, one would have numerous experiences of buildings and gardens first concealed and then opened to view, taking advantage of the diverse topography, clearings, and forest.

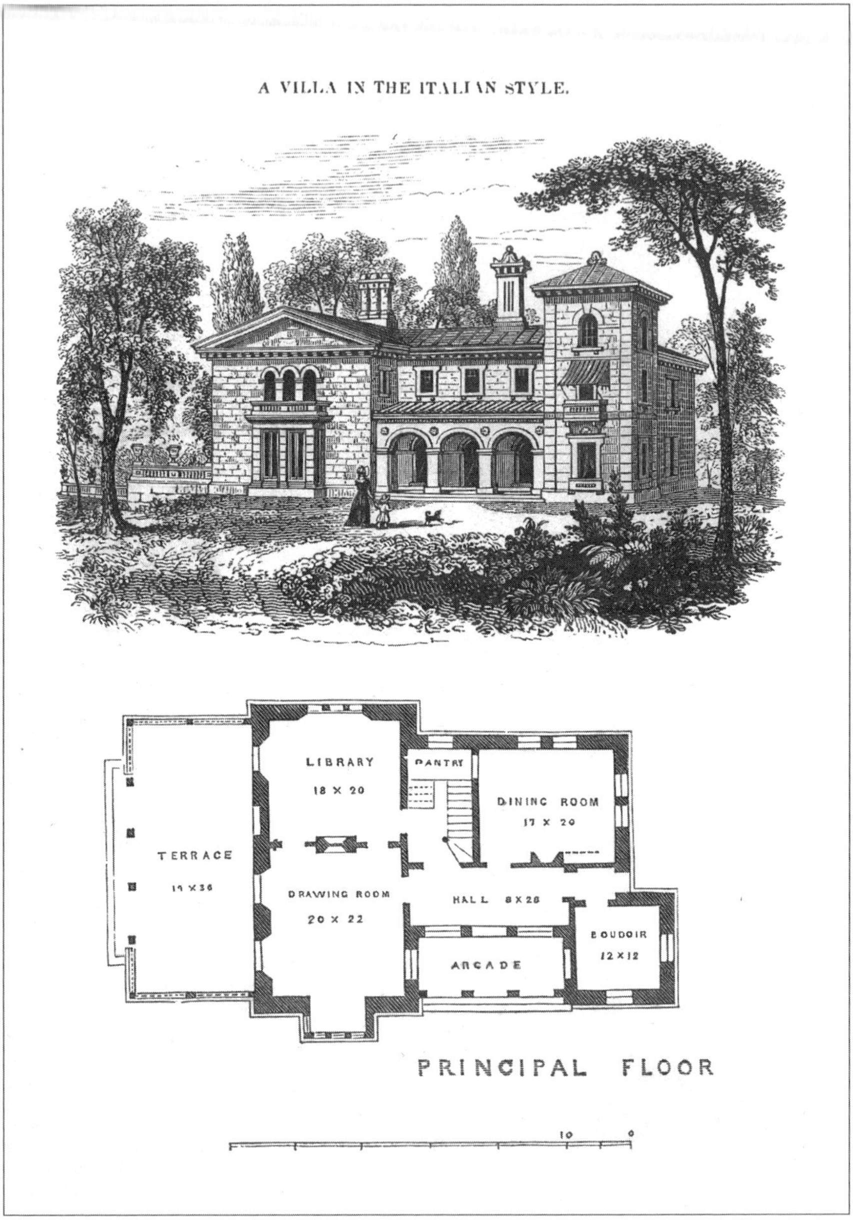

Fig. 3.14. View and Principal Floor Plan of Design VIII, *CR*.

A SWISS COTTAGE.

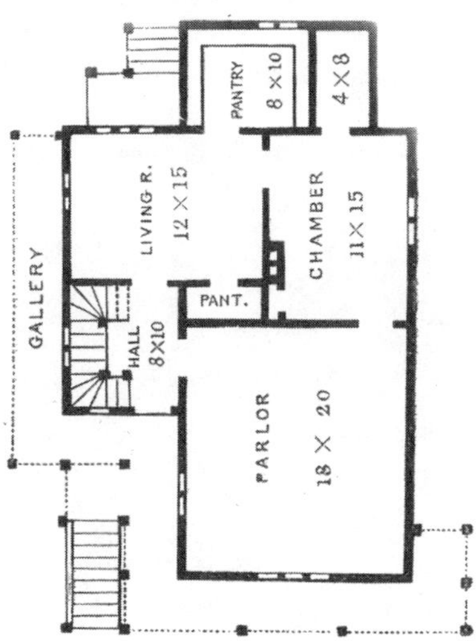

PRINCIPAL FLOOR.

Fig. 3.15. View and Principal Floor Plan of Design X, *ACH.*

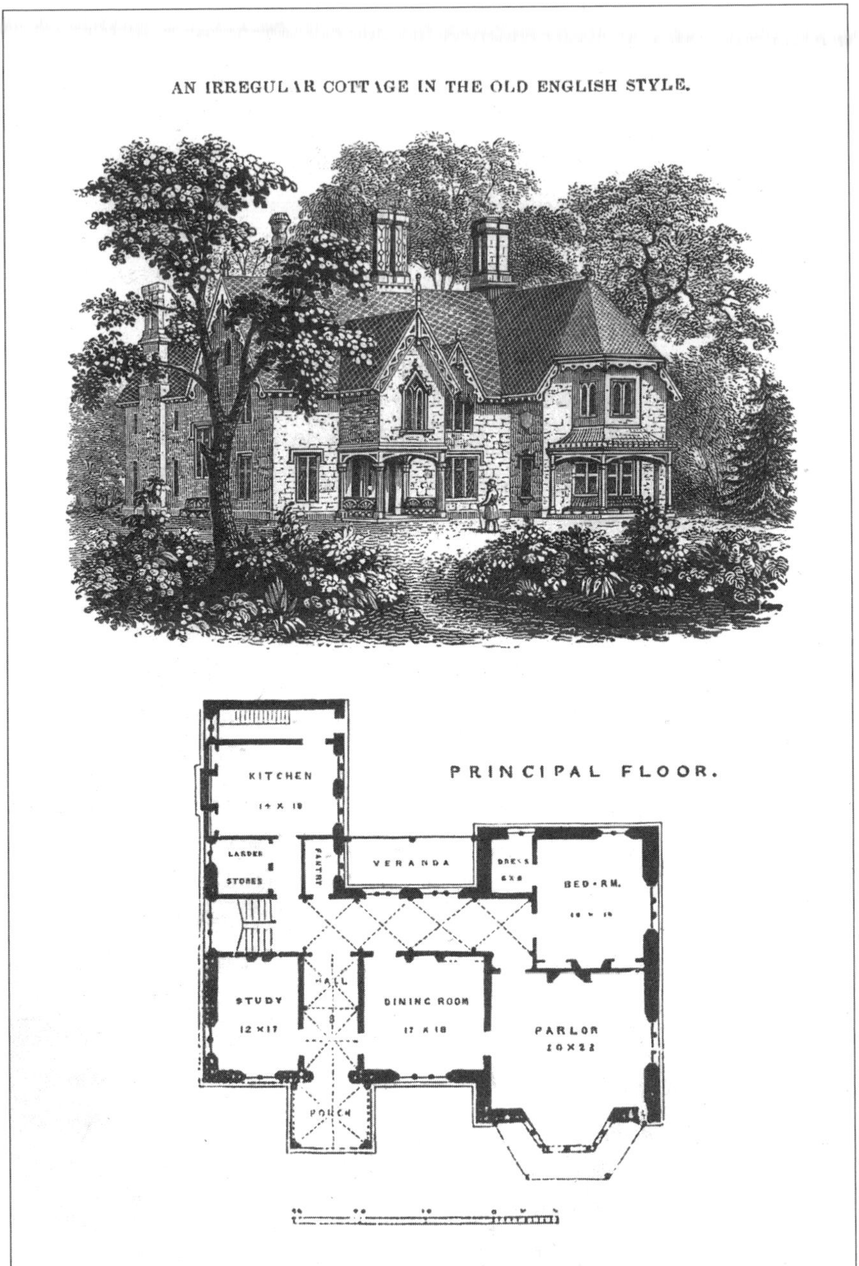

Fig. 3.16. View and Principal Floor Plan of Design VII, *CR*.

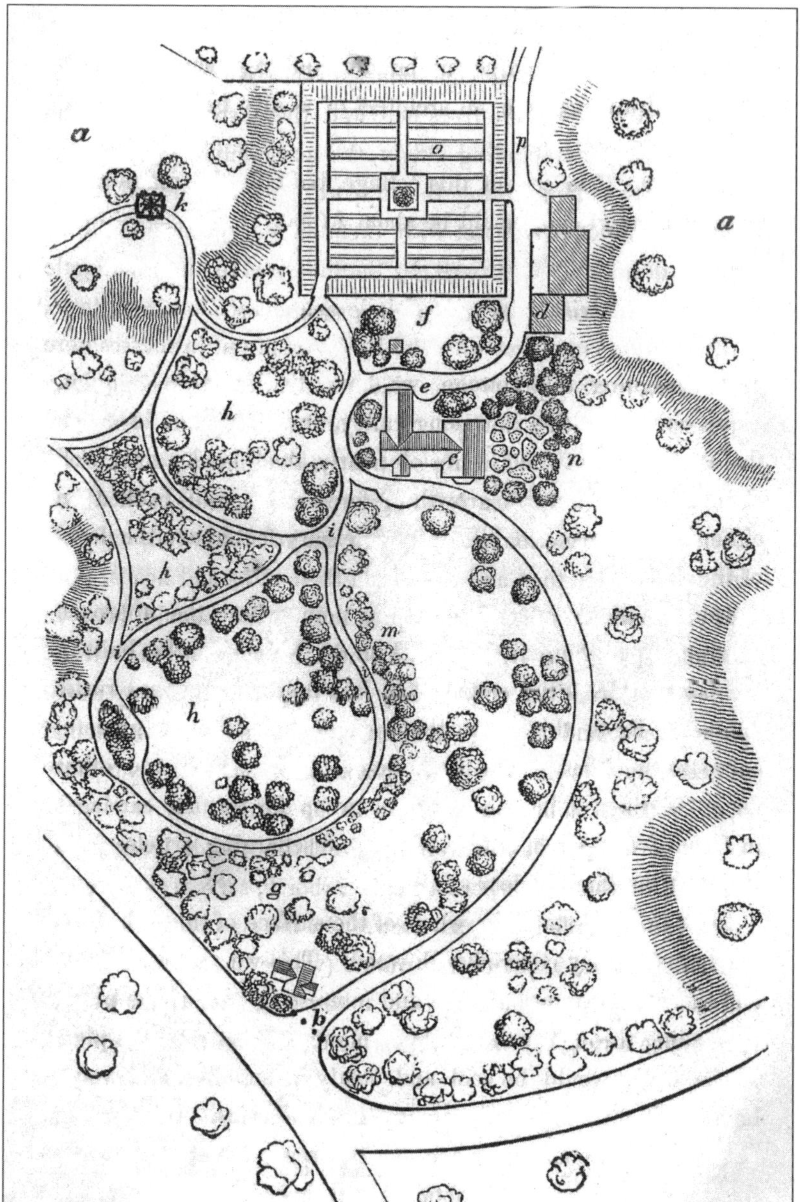

Fig. 3.17. Plan of the Grounds of Design VII, *CR*.

Through Downing's guidance, a housebuilder would first consider his own character, then find a building site or a location within his property that corresponded to his nature, and only then select the appropriate architectural style. This procedure, Downing argued, led to a harmonious union between people and dwelling in both house and grounds. Sensitivity to aspect and prospect established a visual relationship between the spectator and the world. A deeper physical relationship came from folding together the visual appearances of house and grounds where each remains distinctly expressed, yet mutually supported. Now the question becomes understanding why Downing's designs expressed attributes of dwelling that resonate with human understanding and sensibilities. As the next chapter proposes, including elements such as bay windows, verandas, ornamental chimney tops, and projecting roof overhangs appeals to transcendent human tendencies, and this accounts for the enduring relevance of Downing's work.

4

ORIGINAL FORMS OF DWELLING

> What this habitation shall be, depends partly on the habits of the man, partly on the climate in which he lives. If he is a shepherd and leads a wandering life, he pitches a tent. If he is a hunter, he builds a rude hut of logs or skins. If he is a tiller of the soil, he constructs a dwelling of timber or stones, or lodges in the caverns of the rocky hill sides.
>
> —Downing, *The Architecture of Country House*[1]

DOWNING KNEW his audience. The small homesteader needed a functional and pleasant suburban cottage or farmhouse, and the wealthy enjoyed country villas. This appreciation becomes obvious when comparing Downing's Cottage for a Working-Man (Fig. 4.1) with Alexander Jackson Davis's published vision of the rural American cottage as a log temple with columns and engaged pilasters (Fig. 4.2). Davis claimed that his "American cottage" was made in "a classical form with propriety and the closest attention to economy."[2] Downing emphasized economy, materials, workmanship, and convenience as the means to elevate primitive shelter to permanent architecture. His audience was not looking for idealized log temples, but for designs that helped them imagine the life they desired and thought possible to achieve.

Downing's architectural principles found traction in linking the characters of the proprietor to the land and its improvement. He argued that this consistently applied to fitting architecture to landscape, especially important for house construction. Downing's first principle—fitness or usefulness as shelter—meant that the practical needs of shelter and accommodating

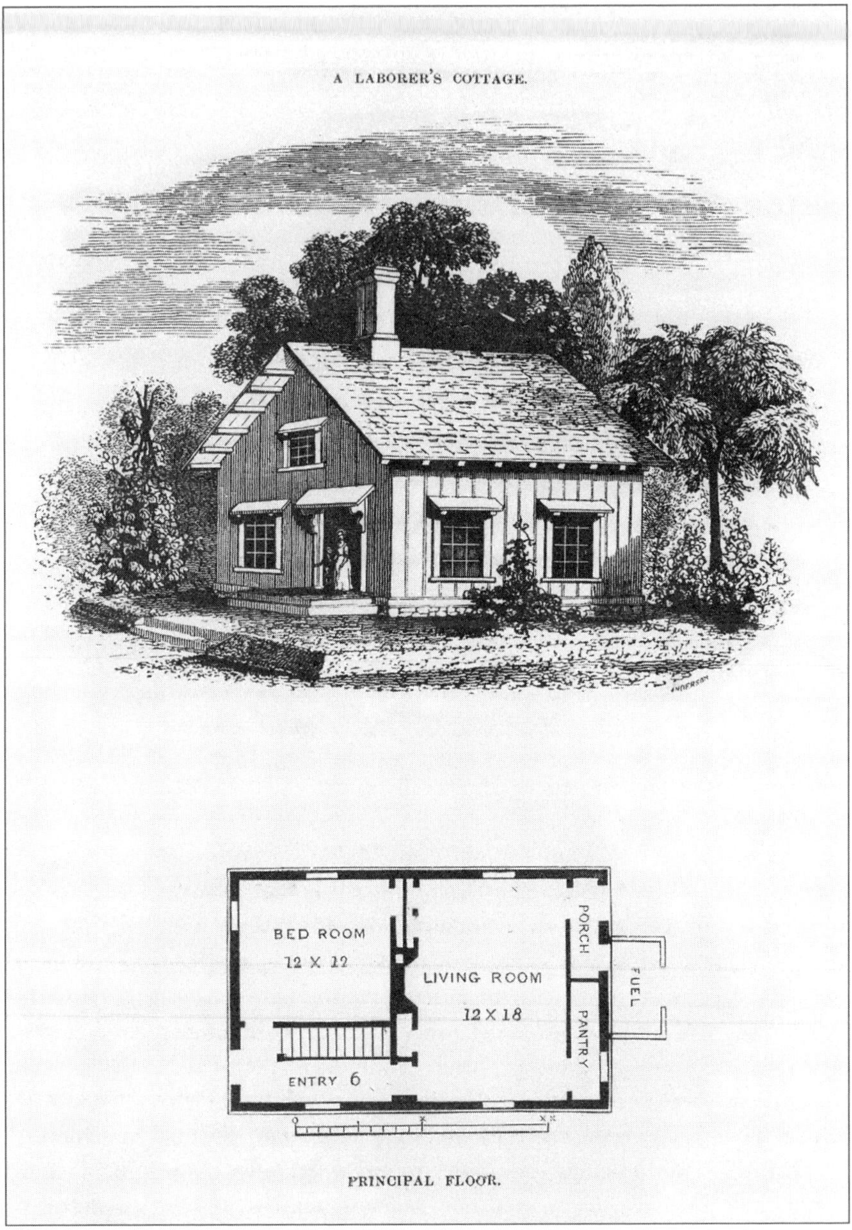

Fig. 4.1. View and Principal Floor Plan of Design I, *ACH*.

Fig. 4.2. Alexander Jackson Davis, American Cottage.

activities of dwelling were of primary concern for domestic design. In its fundamental and constant occupation, Downing considered dwelling as distinct from considerations of architectural style, where historical precedent or vernacular tradition sometimes dictated house design. He presented an alternative where this choice was based on individual expression and qualities of the land. He argued for the beauty of propriety for all houses—not only for large villas, but also for modest cottages and practical farmhouses. The effectiveness of Downing's work came from the method he employed to illustrate principles with physical attributes of dwelling.

All constructions are made up of decisions about parts and how they make a whole. For Downing, design decisions needed to provide for the "real" and "apparent" support of dwelling.[3] This means that domestic architecture required elements associated with dwelling to evoke emotional responses appealing to its occupants as well as the disinterested spectator. The power of Downing's work comes from identifying certain attributes of domestic architecture that are analogous to the basic and eternal types of dwelling.

In this, Downing followed accounts of the origins of architecture he knew from European theorists.[4] His architectural elements had a duty of purpose and a duty of expression in order to provide real and apparent support for dwelling. These elements (Downing used the word "feature") are prominent parts of the house.[5] Building elements were distinct things with underlying obligations; that is, each needed to say that this building is a *house*. Put another way, Downing's language of domestic architecture consisted not only of elements expressive of dwelling in real and apparent demonstrations, but its force came from their reference to original dwelling typologies.

In architectural theory, typology is a formal schema and not the form itself, or the very idea of architecture. Many scholars have started their examination of the subject with early nineteenth-century writer Quatremère de Quincy's definition of "type" as "less the image of a thing to copy or imitate completely, than the idea of an element which must itself serve as a rule for the model," and "the originating reason of a thing."[6] Typology investigates the symbolic representations of the origin and meaning of things. This is different from the building type, which is a classification system of building functions and their related form. Theaters, train stations, or office buildings are building types, for instance.[7] In order for a building to express its domesticity, Downing employed elements associated with domestic habitation as the fundamental characteristics of dwelling, and these are analogous to original dwelling types.

Usually studies of architectural origins for building begin with investigations of the primitive hut as the original dwelling type.[8] Joseph Rykwert has stated that "in the present rethinking of why we build and what we build for, the primitive hut will, I suggest, retain its validity as a reminder of the original and therefore essential meaning of all building for people: that is, of architecture. It remains the underlying statement, the irreducible, intentional core."[9] The primitive hut is not the only original dwelling type, however. While the hut with post and beam construction and a pitched roof to shed rainwater was a shelter type most open to human invention, there are other shelter types that rely on different habits of human activity. Ignored in architectural theory, the implication of this observation leads to a deeper understanding of original dwelling typologies and serves as the basis for my interpretation of Downing's accomplishment.

Quatremère de Quincy wrote what many consider to be the "first coherent and explicit formulation of an idea of type in architectural theory."[10] Quatremère's "type" was the vague idea, motif, or intention of the artist followed by a precise model. In other words, the model is a physical representation of an idea. Quatremère stated that it is "less the image of a thing to copy or imitate completely, than the idea of an element which must itself serve as a rule for the model."[11]

It is precisely this distinction between type and model that makes Quatremère's work critical to understanding the power of Downing's designs. Unlike domestic architecture, public buildings with a single purpose may have a strict ideal form clearly expressed in built shape. Downing gave the following example: "In Roman art, we see the ideal of the *state* as fully manifested as is in the Gothic the ideal of the church."[12] Downing observed that diverse people, domestic activity, and site conditions prohibited specific models. He offered no architectural recipes as model house designs—something he thought impossible to do well—although other writers had begun to publish examples and submit designs to competitions. (The popular magazine *Godey's Lady's Book*, for example, was publishing designs of model cottages by 1846.)[13] Rather than a single dwelling ideal, the variety of houses for domestic architecture required a correspondence between the reason for activities and the supporting and expressive architectural elements. For instance, houses designed for hot climates needed broad roof overhangs and protective window and door hoods to provide shade. These elements may have been executed in a style, but they were included more for the purpose they served.

According to Quatremère, "this theory . . . is based on the nature of things, on historical notions, on the most ancient opinions, on the most constant facts and on the most evident testimony of every architecture."[14] Distinguishing type in design is an exercise that separates the basic and essential from the accidental and arbitrary, which is part of specific models. For Downing, examining how and why something was originally made promoted fabrication grounded in the satisfaction of our common, inherited human nature. This, he argued, was superior to design based on divine inspiration or the blind following of the rules of proportion as used in classical architecture, something he thought impractical for most domestic design.[15] Downing observed, "In the country places which they create, the casual visitor may be struck with many beautiful effects; but when a trifling observation has shown him that this beauty is not the result of a harmony between the *real* and the *ideal*,—or in other words, between the surface of things intended to be seen and the things themselves, as they minister to our daily wants,—then all the pleasure vanishes, and the opposite feeling takes its place."[16]

Quatremère suggests that in order to understand the reasons behind science and philosophy, one must discover their original function or cause. This leads to an idealistic and eternal truth—an intrinsic essence of immaterial design—appealing to the very core of human experience. Thus, Quatremère identified three original building types linking architecture to the habits of man in his different activities as well as to environmental and social conditions. These are the cave, the tent, and the hut.

Many treatises begin the history of architecture with an account of the three original architectural types following the principle of fitness based, in part, on the fundamental truths evident from the study of nature.[17] Vitruvius began Book II on "The Origin of the Dwelling House" by observing that "they began in that first assembly to construct shelters. Some made them of green boughs, others dug caves on mountain sides, and some, in imitation of the nests of swallows and the way they built, made places of refuge out of mud and twigs."[18] Alberti's Book II on materials gives an account connecting imitation of nature to construction, and then to invention: "Some maintain that man first lived in caves, and that master and herd were sheltered under a common roof: they accept the account given by Pliny, that it was one Taxius, a Gelian, who was the first to imitate nature and build himself a house of mud. Diodorus states that the goddess Vesta, daughter of Saturn, was the first to invent the house. Eusebius Pamphilius, a respected scholar in matters of the antique, maintains, on the basis of ancient manuscripts, that the descendants of Protogenes devised the first dwelling place for man from screens platted of reed and papyrus."[19]

Quatremère's treatise on Egyptian architecture expanded consideration of multiple types based on human occupations, materials and cultures. His position may be summarized as follows:

> The cave, first found and then carved or made with stone, is the habitat of the hunter. It leads to the solid, massive and dark architecture of the Egyptians.
>
> The tent, assembled with frame and fabric, is the wandering shepherd's dwelling. It leads to the lightness of Chinese architecture.
>
> The hut or framed structure, built with permanent pieces, is the home of the farmer. It leads to the grace and harmony of Greek architecture.[20]

Quatremère joined architectural type with various activities: the hunter retires to a secure cave, the gatherer or shepherd who moves for herd grazing carries his house with him as a light structure of poles and fabric, and the farmer makes permanent stone or wood constructions increasing his convenience and comfort. Thirty years after Quatremère's formulation, Loudon restated the types:

> Another class of architectural writers, [Marc-Antoine] Laugier, John Wood, Francesco Milizia, and especially Quatremère de Quincy (whose opinions have been adopted by a number of English writers, without the slightest acknowledgment), maintain, that Architecture, in so far as it is an art of taste, is to be considered an art of imitation. According to this doctrine, the type of the Egyptian Architecture is a cavern; of the Chinese, a tent; of the Gothic, a grove of trees; and of the Grecian, a rectangular hut. An opinion of this sort, adopted by such a profound metaphysical author as Quatremère de Quincy, deserves to be examined with the utmost attention.[21]

Loudon has four types, adding the Gothic grove of young trees bound to form pointed arches. The Gothic was a vertical style Loudon distinguished from horizontal Greek architecture. He also noted differences in the Gothic column articulated with bound saplings and classical architecture that was made, at least at first, with hewn timbers. Including the Gothic is not surprising given that these two were Loudon's preferred architectural styles. The Gothic in particular was appealing because of its efficiency of parts, ornamental references to nature, and clarity of a message of progress.[22] Nevertheless, Gothic fabrications fall under Quatremère's category of a hut because of its permanent and load-bearing structural approach to construction.

The value of Quatremère's theory for Loudon was less in the number of categories, and more in his identifying geographic and social characteristics with architectural constructions. Historian Melanie Simo notes that "ultimately, it was . . . Quatremère de Quincy who offered Loudon the most important clue to something which every scientist, if not every artist, craves: a theory based on eternal principles."[23] The allure of eternal principles resides in the clarity and truth assumed in understanding the original and the essential. Loudon declared himself "more indebted to [Quatremère's *Essay*] than to all the other works on landscape gardening, or the fine arts, put together."[24] Principles outlined in this book were based on something more fundamental and inherent to human nature than rational rules of geometry and proportion. They were based, among other ideas, on the key difference between type and model where a specific model resembles a type without being an idealized imitation.

Downing certainly knew of Quatremère from Loudon. Simo notes that "Loudon strongly recommends that the young architect consult Quatremère de Quincy's *Essai sur l'imitation*."[25] Quatremère's discussion of eternal types brought Loudon's forty years of thought to a comprehensive summation.[26] Downing continued the formulation of relating design to human tendencies. Some of Downing's favorite authors had their own accounts, including Nathaniel Hawthorne and Ralph Waldo Emerson, who said in 1841 that:

> We see how each work of art sprang irresistibly from necessity, and, moreover, took its form from the broad hint of Nature. Beautiful in this wise is the obvious origin of all the known orders of architecture, namely, that they were the idealizing of the primitive abodes of each people. Thus the Doric temple still presents the semblance of the wooden cabin, in which the Dorians dwelt. The Chinese pagoda is plainly a Tartar tent. The Indian and Egyptian temples still betray the mounds and subterranean houses of their forefathers. The Gothic church plainly originated in a rude adaptation of forest trees, with their boughs on, to a festal or solemn edifice, as the bands around the cleft pillars still indicate the green withes that tied them.[27]

Downing began *The Architecture of Country Houses* with a chapter on "The Real Meaning of Architecture," in which he aimed to instruct the reader on the origin of dwellings as a means of expanding their notions of taste (see the quotation at the beginning of the chapter). Dwelling types and their fabrication were described in terms of both the owner's occupation and the climate in which he lived, as well as duration of occupation. This variable determines whether a dwelling is to be constructed as temporary or permanent. The wandering shepherd has a portable structure. The hunter builds a rude hut, as he was capable of supplying his needs in local forests. The farmer builds with cut timber or stone, or finds temporary shelter when working distant fields.

While Downing followed the idea of linking original types of habitation in the cave, tent, and hut to human activity and site situation for domestic architecture, he did not design different houses modeled on one specific original dwelling type with appropriate form, material, and detail. He offered no primitive hut. Rather, the ultimate conclusion of this book based on my interpretation of Downing's work is that its enduring appeal and continuing value comes from one fact: *Downing incorporated all three original architectural dwelling types through the use of specific elements in every house design.* Of the thirty-eight houses known to be Downing designs and published in his two books on architecture, there are at least 231 analogous elements corresponding to the three original architectural types: the found cave, the portable tent, and the permanent hut. Many designs have more than one element associated with each type. When Downing identified and consistently incorporated configurations of all three original architectural types in every design, he accommodated ideas of dwelling more comprehensively because they reflected a deeper understanding of human nature. The result is a sense of belonging and a satisfied sense of completeness between man and his work, and nature.

Downing's cave is found in an adjacent smaller room off a larger room with an articulated opening. A bay window or wall niche or the window's exterior hood trim conveys a sense of security and retirement because of their smaller size. The most frequent application of the portable tent typology is a veranda or porch, places of temporary occupation between building and land. The mediating character of a porch provides a unique place for contemplative leisure between inside and outside. Downing's hut is the permanent shelter for people and the devices or instruments kept at hand to enhance safety, comfort, and convenience. Architectural elements range from passive roof overhangs to labor-saving mechanical equipment for domestic operations. Downing designed and published cottages, farmhouses, and villas—some in no particular style, and suitable for a range of climates—with these elements consistently included.

There were prescribed steps in order to achieve the complete house.[28] First, a veranda could be added to the simple shed house, because it "not only protects the apartment against sudden draughts of air, but it also protects the privacy and dignity of the inmates."[29] The veranda or porch also indicated an aspect of daily life "besides ministering to the necessities."[30] Second, good proportions were to be observed through house masses that were not too narrow and not too high. The third directive was to extend the roof with large overhangs and brackets to protect the walls from the hot sun and violent storms. Articulated lintels, hoods, and dressings protected door and window openings, and grouping windows into projecting bays or oriel windows provided intimate nooks to be found within rooms. Finally, ornamental chimney tops were important because chimneys "should never spring out of the roof with no apparent preparation for it," and should have a base, shaft and cap in proportion to the whole.[31]

These elements superseded style as a chief determinate of appearance. Downing discussed the development of a national style, and proposed a "bracketed" style.[32] He acknowledged that the Grecian, Roman, and Gothic styles were the product of architecture developed through "a long series of years" and for various locations by climate, habit, and genius of the architects. America was "too distinct in its institutions," Downing believed, and "too vast in its territorial and social destinies, not to shape out for itself a great national type in character, manners and art."[33] But this was not done with the application of "the showiest *ornaments* of a certain style," but by bringing forward those inherent qualities that support dwelling in the land.[34] The complexity and variety of purpose required a complexity and variety of dwelling elements. This spoke to the character of domestic architecture. The general truths, once displayed, were how a house may be useful, beautiful, and meaningful, and "thereby satisfy us fully and completely—satisfy all the rational desires of the senses, the affections, and the intellect."[35]

Domestic architecture, Downing believed, must support domestic activity. While exact proportions, displayed order, and constructed geometry gave architecture strong thematic connections, these concepts were a poor basis for programming architecture if it was to reflect and respond to human needs and desires. The romantic attitude of perceptible appeal superseded rational systems Downing knew little about. And here his instincts and experience served him well. The contemporary historian Anthony Vidler criticizes architecture that "continue[s] this precise calibration of the minimum number of architectural events necessary at once to shelter function and to liberate thought."[36] Downing would agree, claiming that these very attributes should always be included with designs to enhance pleasurable architectural experience.

The following three sections take Downing's designs and identify the critical elements, not as a prescription reducing original architectural types to specific formulas for execution, but more as an argument for their expressive value. Combining elements into a composed form reads as a unit—similar to a group of words, to use a linguistic analogy—intended to have meaning. Downing's essential elements, when taken together, provide a satisfying design for dwelling.

THE SECURE CAVE

In French domestic architecture, *cave* is the name of a cellar room meant for wine storage. It translates as "hollow" or "ditch," and shares the Latin root for "cell" and "cellar."[37] There is also an action implied in the etymology of this word, interpreted as a "falling into" or "hiding in." Cellars are different from basements. Cellars are for storage; basements are for human activities. The basement is a constructed base for the house above and operates with rooms with windows supporting efficient household operations. Cellars have low ceilings and no windows, keeping cooler temperatures desirable for preserving fruits and vegetables. The idea of a cellar connotes feelings of security, comfort, and well-being because provisions stockpiled for the future are safely stored there. A cave, therefore, is a distinct place removed from the primary rooms for habitation, yet supporting them in ways that improve their performance.

The architectural type of the found cave in Downing's floor plans is interpreted as the withdrawn place. It is an intimate place to see and not be seen; a place with an outward prospect and reduced reciprocity. This place embodies privacy, security, and visual focus. One theoretician has observed that "the cave represents the first *spatial* element, in contrast to the vertical-horizontal relation which is an ordering principle."[38] The cave-type space is for inward contemplation and reflection.

Manifestations of cave types in Downing's domestic designs are found in two forms. The first is the carved-out cabinet-like recesses and niches set into thick walls. The other form includes alcoves, bays, or oriel windows that project out from the primary room.[39] These cave-type elements provide visual orientation within a room because they are not the room itself, but rather a distinct part of the room *found* within it.[40] Another key quality of the cave is the articulated opening between primary and secondary spaces where one passes through a boundary of sorts to gain entry to the cave. Crossing this threshold helps transform experience to a more intimate and personal scale, and thus one emerges in a transformed state. Often the cave element is a room appendage with more refined detailing increasing the richness of appearance. Part of its appeal is the intimacy and security achieved, because it is necessarily smaller than the adjacent dominant space. Smaller physical space promotes feelings of stillness, freeing the imagination.

Recessed cabinets are small because they have to fit into the wall construction. They are perfect for an individual's valuable possessions. Museums began as repositories of curiosities in cabinets.[41] Some house designs have thick masonry walls, creating deep window niches suitable for interior shutters and useful sills. One example is Washington Irving's house at Sunnyside (Fig. 4.3).

For alcoves, Design V in *Cottage Residences* has an area between projecting closets in the shape of a bay window for a window seat (Fig. 4.4, shown as *a*). Downing's chapter "Interior Finishing of Country-Houses" in *The Architecture of Country Houses* has eight interior elevation drawings showing examples of various styles for principal apartments where alcoves have lowered ceilings, four with built-in seating, and one with an area for a table and chairs (Fig. 4.5). In a vast majority of Downing's published designs, the cave type is found as a projecting bay or oriel window (Figs. 4.6 and 4.7). He referred to bay windows as "pretty retiring places for conference," where windows "projecting boldly, will give three distinct views to a person standing within it."[42]

Fig. 4.3. Washington Irving's Guest Bedroom at Sunnyside, Tarrytown, New York.

At the scale of floor plan composition, special rooms such as the boudoir, book closet, and pantry closet (originally for bread and today used for linen, dishes, and other dining provisions) perform the same purpose depending on their connection to the principle room.[43] The boudoir is a small, semi-private room adjacent to a principal apartment—a cabinet usually for the lady of the house.[44] In Downing's floor plan for Design VIII in *Cottage Residences*, the boudoir is in the campanile off the hall and is described as a morning room for receiving social calls or as a guest bedroom (see Fig. 3.14). Downing's Design XXVIII in *The Architecture of Country Houses* considered the boudoir to have an alternate accommodation as "the office or sanctum of the master of the house, into which strangers, coming on business with him, may be shown" (Fig. 4.8).[45] The alternate floor plan provided for Design V in *Cottage Residences* modified the principal floor library by turning it into a bedroom with closet and "a pretty little boudoir" with access off the bedroom or drawing room (Fig. 4.9). One definition of the French boudoir is a "place to sulk in"—a quiet room to sit with mirrored walls, giving it an air of infinity and

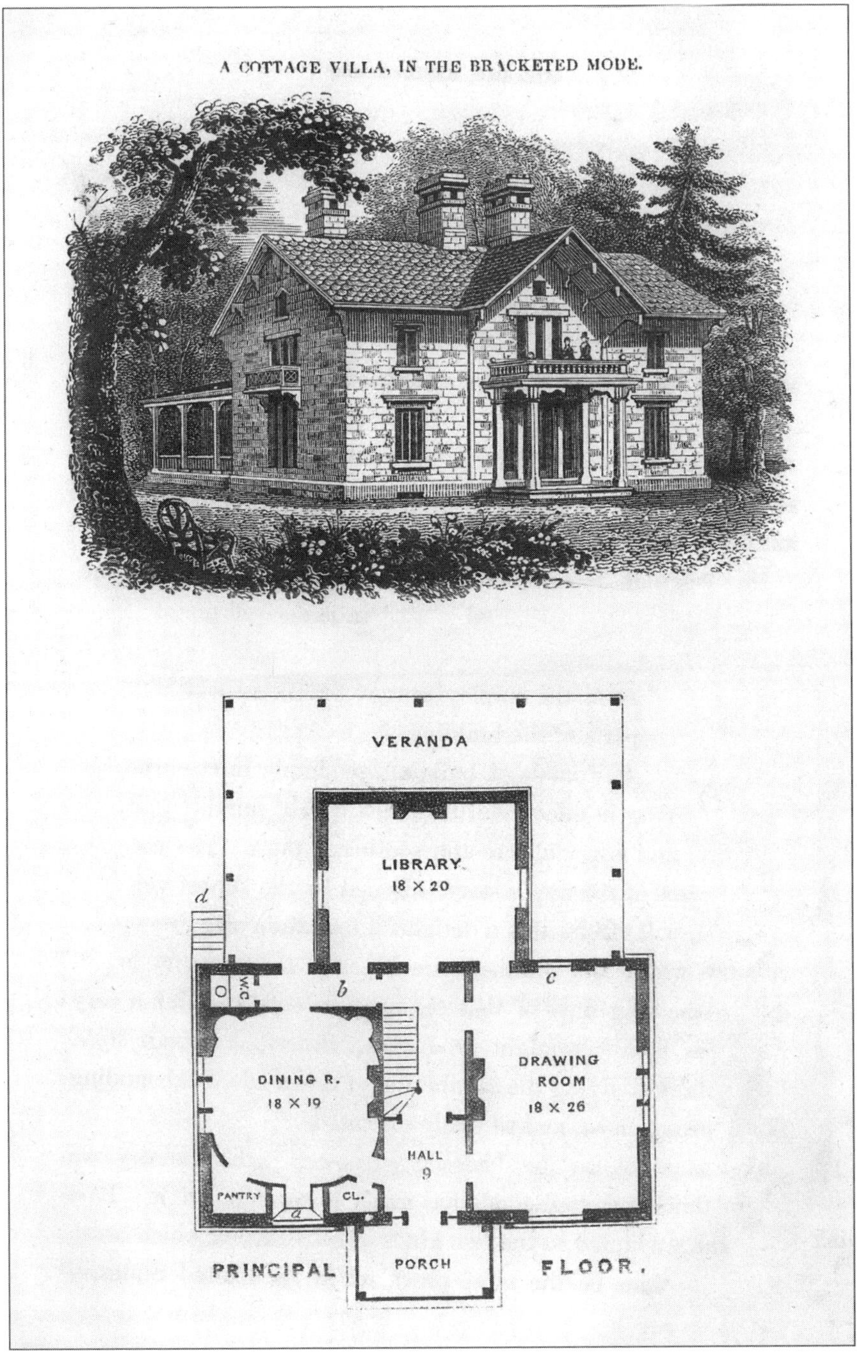

Fig. 4.4. View and Principal Floor Plan of Design V, *CR*.

Fig. 4.5. Dining Room—Italian Style.

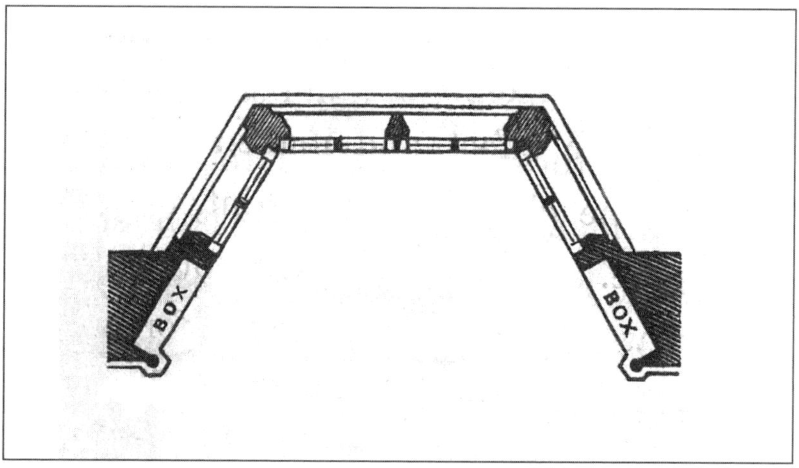

Fig. 4.6. Cottage Bay Window Plan.

Fig. 4.7. Oriel Window Section.

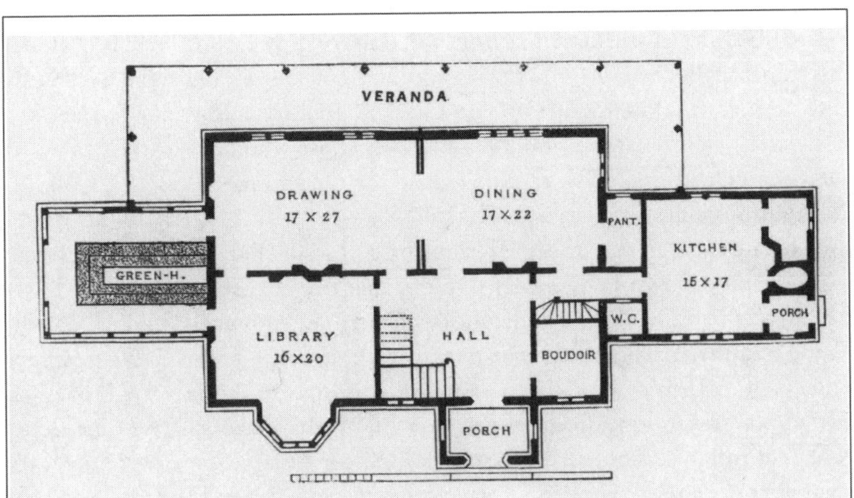

Fig. 4.8. Principal Floor Plan of Design XXVIII, *ACH.*

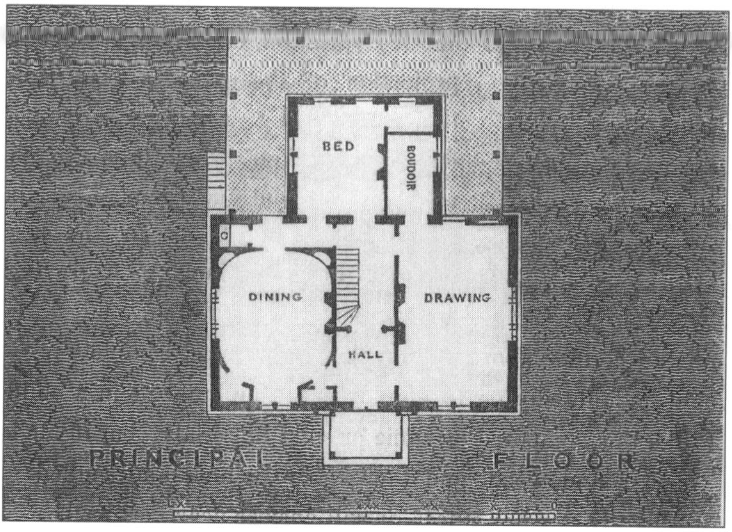

Fig. 4.9. View as Constructed in Wood and Alternate Principal Floor Plan of Design V, *CR*.

of endless reflection. The reflection and transparency of bay or oriel window glass provides an effect similar to boudoir mirrors.

THE DISCOVERY of intimate places is a delight of habitation. French philosopher Gaston Bachelard finds that nooks and corners are desirable because it is there that "we like to curl up comfortably. To curl up belongs to the phenomenology of the verb to inhabit, and only those who have learned to do so can inhabit with intensity."[46] This is true for the intimate domestic interior, and it also applies to a larger social scale.

For a community, groups of rural or suburban houses are safe retreats from the city. Downing certainly thought that the dual existence of city businessman with a townhouse and country gentleman with a villa applied chiefly to the wealthy. He observed that retreat to suburban homes was increasingly possible for the middle classes who migrated from farm to factory. Proximity and public transportation made this possible. Perhaps aware that other architects had published numerous house designs for urban locations, Downing's designs were not for the city.[47] He recognized social trends of retreat. Sociologists have observed that "in the eighteenth century, the family began to hold society at a distance, to push it back beyond a steadily extending zone of private life."[48] For Downing, private life was centered in a home on private land, which made urban ventures tolerable. Or, as architectural historian Robin Evans puts it, private life was about "finding liberty always in the escape from the tyranny of 'society.'"[49]

In the landscape designs Downing published in *Cottage Residences*, intimacy was achieved with meandering walks leading to secluded places lined with dense shrubbery. Along the walk, a shady retreat or bower might be found.[50] From this place of seclusion, good prospects were revealed and emphasized, with framed gaps or breaks in verdant barriers. Cave-type places are sites for architecture to provide a place for the body, and for the body to find a place in the landscape.

THE MEDIATING TENT

The architectural typology of the portable and fabricated tent is interpreted as the place between inside and outside where occupation is transitory. It is a mediating place between the house where one settles and the landscape where one wanders. For Downing, it is usually identified as some kind of ground-level porch or veranda, or a balcony off a front-facing room on the floor above. In total, Downing used twelve different terms for these places between house and grounds, each with related specifications of floor, enclosure, and roof conditions, and construction materials. These terms are listed below, with descriptions and notes about Downing's published designs in his two books on architecture.[51]

Arcade. A covered, perhaps vaulted walk between two buildings with side walls of continuous arches (Fig. 4.10, and see Fig. 3.14). Similar to a colonnade enclosed with a range of evenly spaced columns.

Balcony. An uncovered projection with a railing on the chamber floor usually on the front of the house facing the street (Fig. 4.11). Downing's villa Design XIX in *The Architecture of Country Houses* has a large covered room called a balcony, but it is more like a covered sleeping porch where Downing said, "the ladies of the family will find it agreeable to pass their summer mornings in *demi-toilette*" (Fig. 4.12).[52] In one case, Downing used "balcony" on his sketch for Design XIV (*ACH*), and Davis changed it to "gallery" on his drawing prepared for engraving.

Entrance. Also called an entry, an exterior space for preparing to enter (see Fig. 1.28 for the office entrance and Fig. 1.30 for the servant's entrance) Not to be confused with an interior vestibule, which is a room wider than a corridor and leads to the hall (see Fig. 1.17).

Gallery. A covered wrap around walkway with railing used for walking (see Fig. 3.15). For Downing, it is an exterior corridor used for his Swiss style designs. None of his house designs are large enough to have an interior room similar to the English picture and sculpture gallery, especially useful for walking during inclement weather. French houses in the lower Mississippi valley had galleries, which were covered porches that encircled and shaded their buildings.

Loggia. A covered room on the chamber level open to the view on one side with rooms on the other sides. It usually has an arcade above the railing (Fig. 4.13). Richard Upjohn's "Villa in the Italian Style," Design XXVII in *The Architecture of Country Houses* shows a loggia, but Downing did not include the second floor plan and so this room is unnamed.[53]

Pavilion. A tent-like structure outdoors. If attached to the house, Downing called it a "noble veranda" or covered room with a distinct shape and railing enclosing a sitting room for conversation (Fig. 4.14).

Piazza. An uncovered open square surrounded by an arcade. Downing used the word "piazza" once on his sketch for Design IV in *The Architecture of Country Houses* (Fig. 4.15) and Davis changed it to "umbrage" on his drawing prepared for engraving (Fig. 4.16).

Porch. A covered area that is part of the ambulatory entrance, partially enclosed with a railing and flanking benches (Fig. 4.17, and see Figs. 1.22 and 3.16). "Portico" is used for a carriage porch. Downing sometimes uses the terms "projecting porch" and "carriage porch" for a portico entrance.

Stoop. A small entry platform and no enclosure (See Figs. 1.11 and 4.1).

Terrace. In gardening, a raised bed with sloping sides and level, gravel upper surface. In architecture, an uncovered gravel area enclosed with a low railing adjacent to the house often serving as an extended base (see Fig. 3.10). Or, overlooking an "architectural flower-garden," an exterior room with a hard floor surface and railing pedestals with urns (see Fig. 3.14).

Umbrage. A covered room meant to provide shade and to have a mysterious effect (see Fig. 1.11).

Veranda(h).[54] A covered room with an almost flat roof (Fig. 4.18). In one case, Downing used "verandah" on his sketch for Design II in *Cottage*

Fig. 4.10. Arcade Elevation.

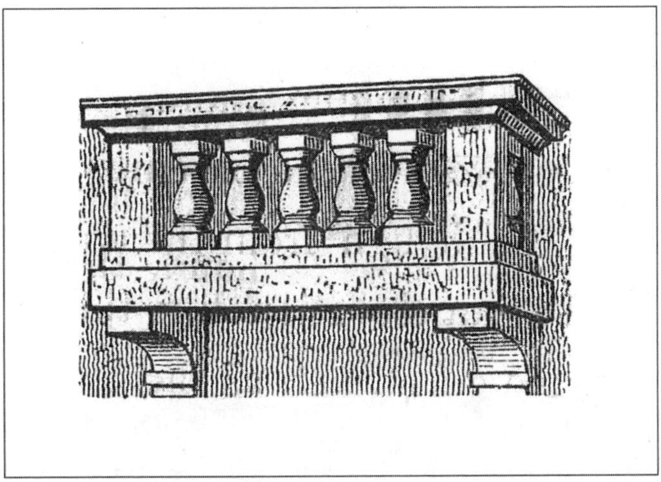

Fig. 4.11. Italian Balcony.

Residences (Fig. 4.19) and Davis changed it to "umbrage" on his drawing prepared for engraving (see Fig. 1.11). Sometimes it is partially enclosed with a railing (see Figs. 1.17, 1.22, and 1.32) or with trellis panels attached to posts (see Fig. 3.10). An arbor-veranda is sometimes made as a trellis roof for vines.

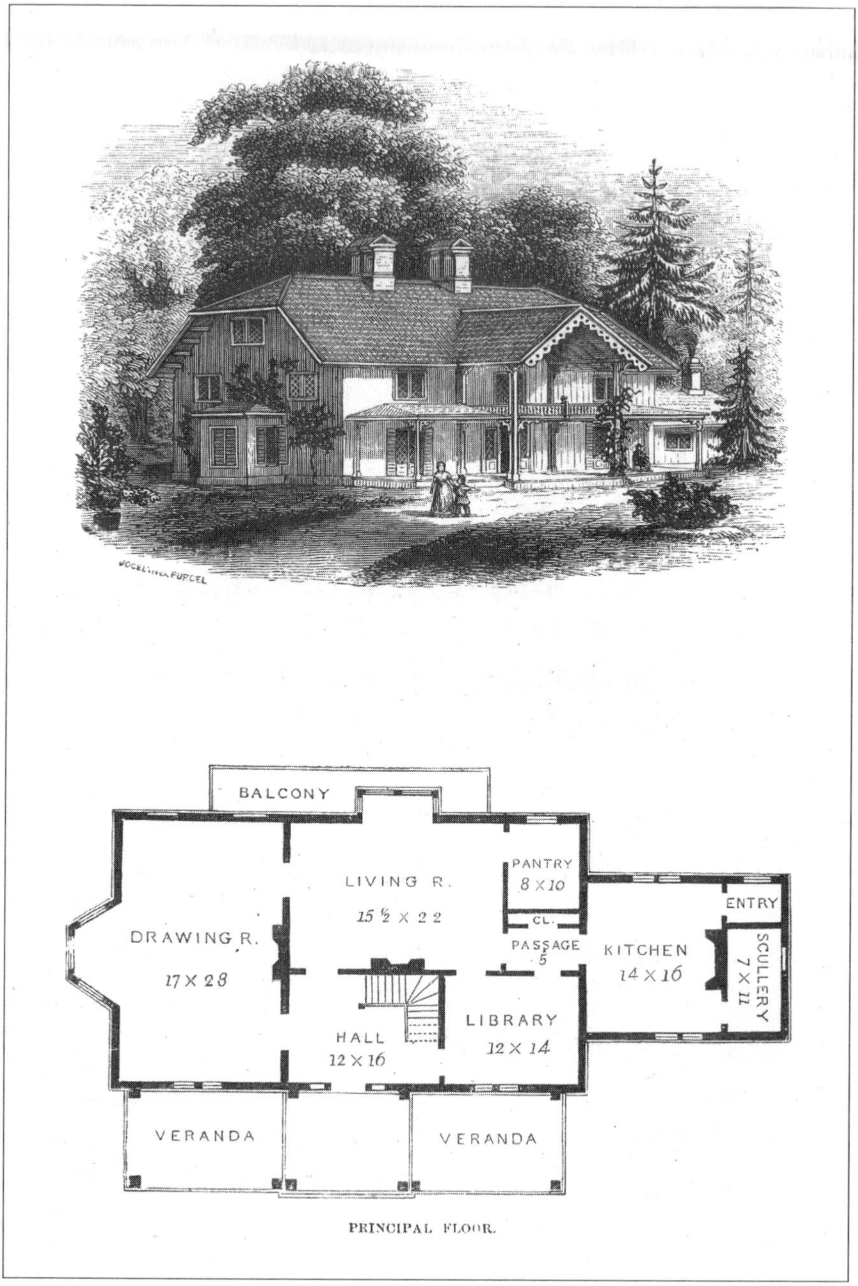

Fig. 4.12. View and Principal Floor Plan of Design XIX, *ACH*.

Fig. 4.13. View of Design XXVII, *ACH*.

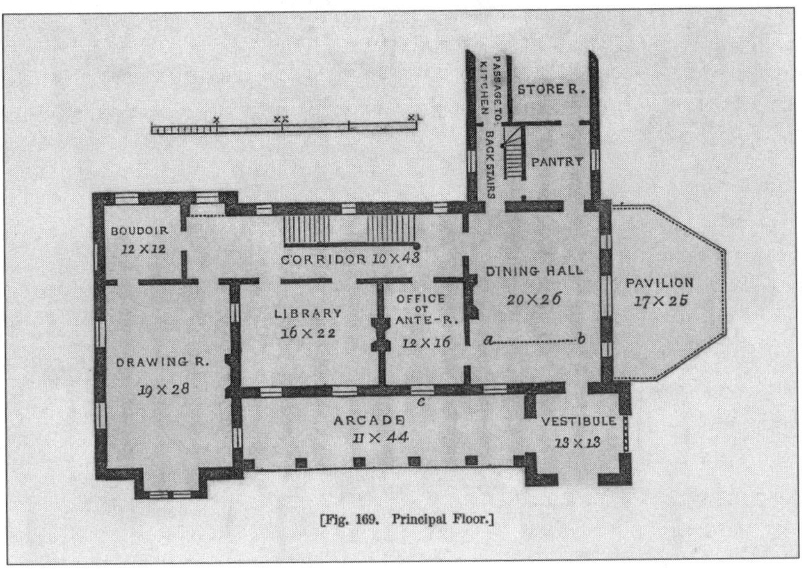

Fig. 4.14. Principal Floor Plan of Design XXXII, *ACH*.

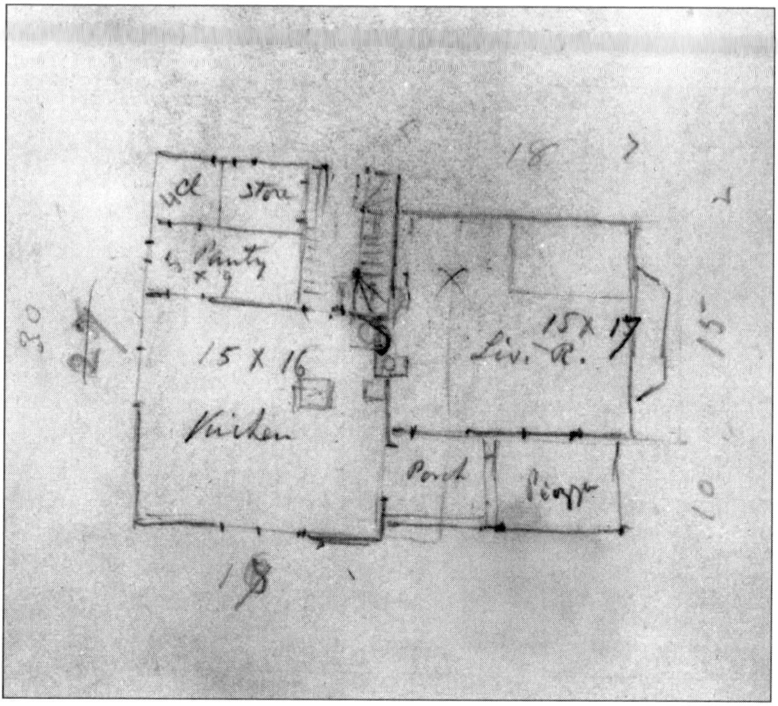

Fig. 4.15. Downing sketch of Design IV, *ACH*.

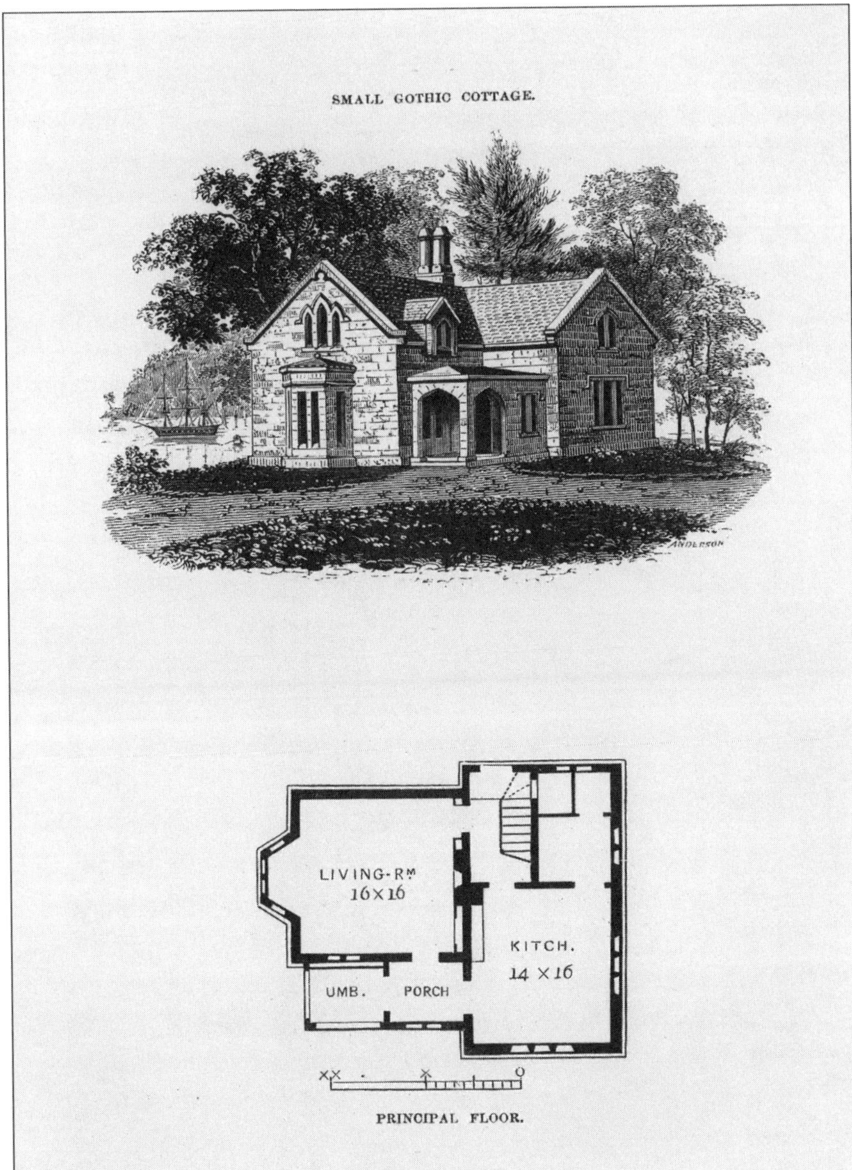

Fig. 4.16. View and Principal Floor Plan of Design IV, *ACH*.

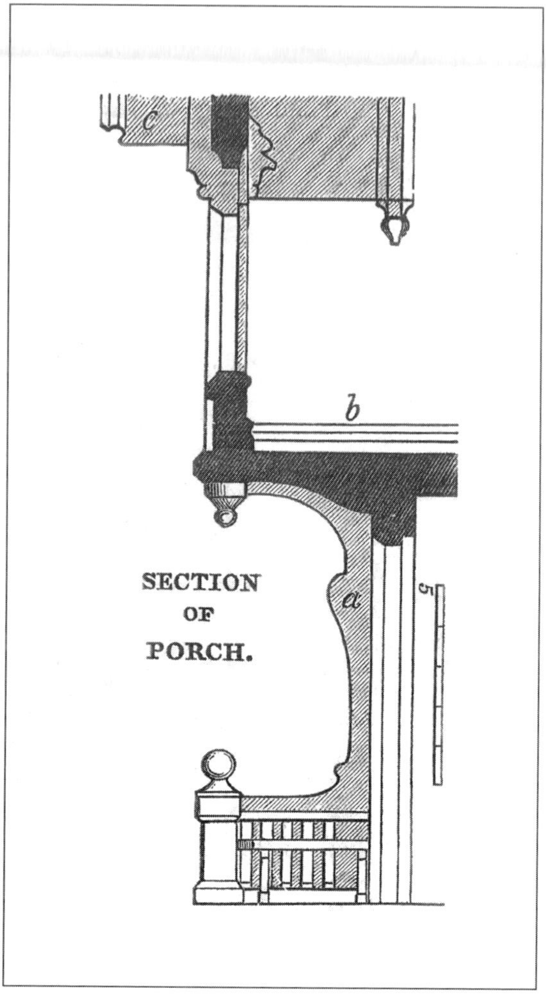

Fig. 4.17. Section of Porch.

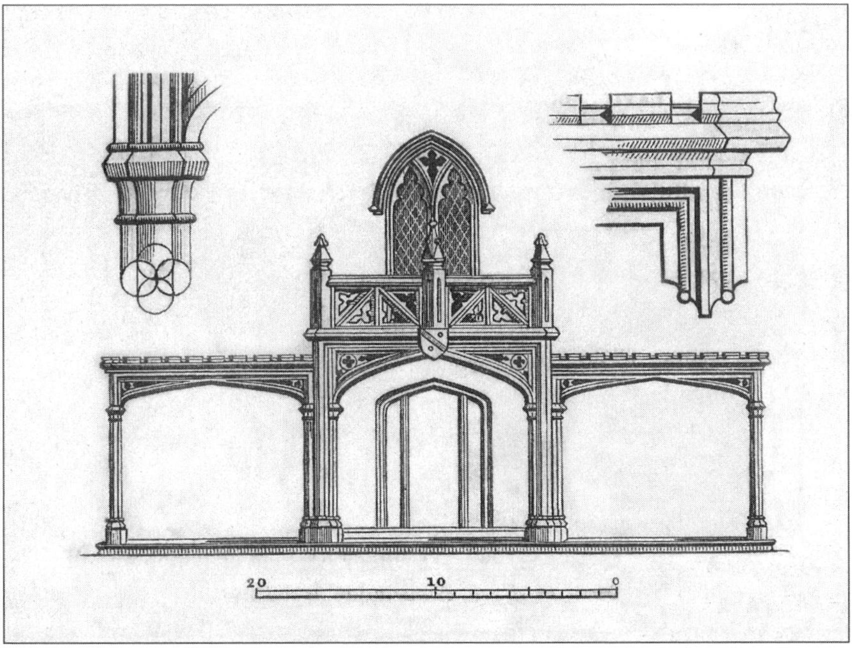

Fig. 4.18. Porch and Veranda Elevation and Details.

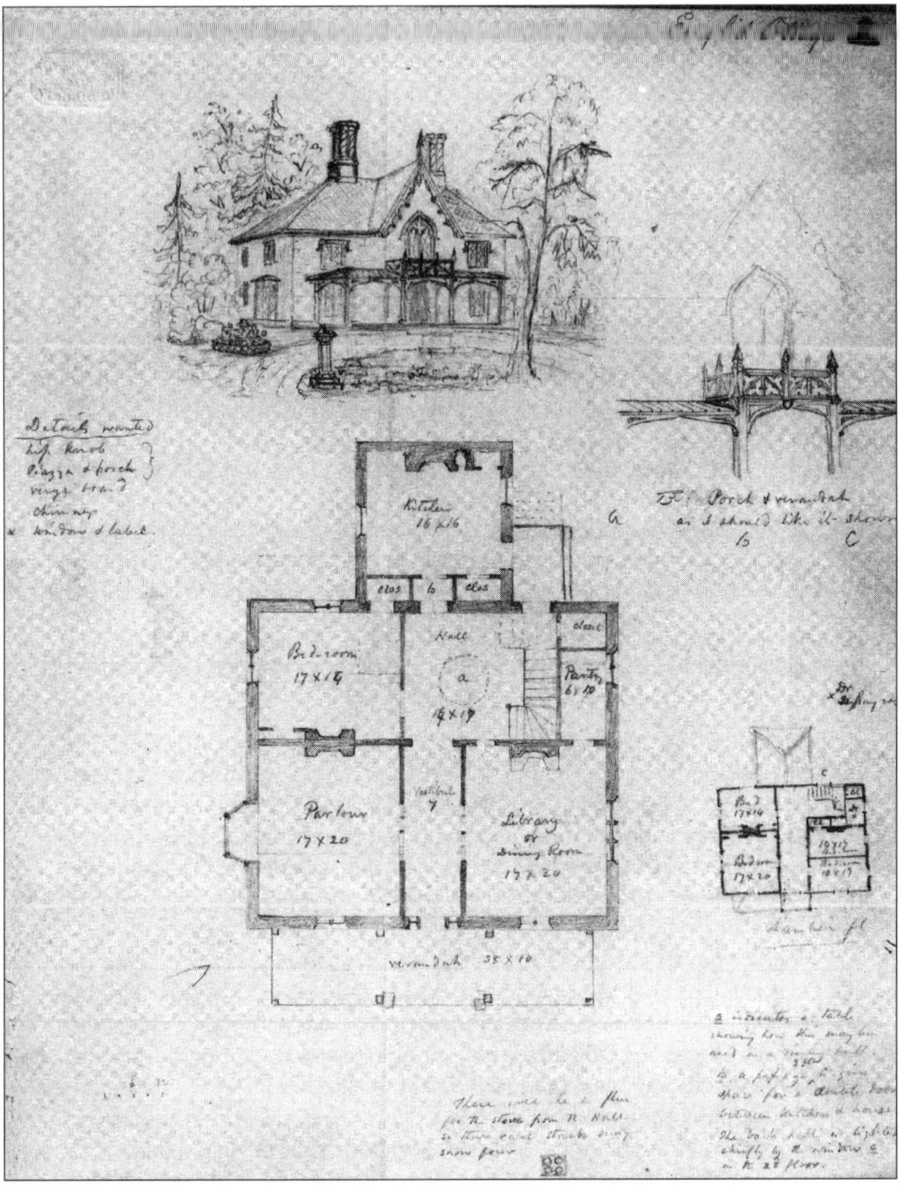

Fig. 4.19. Downing sketch of Design II, *CR*.

HISTORIAN MYRNA KAYE, in a recent book on the history of American interiors and especially the peripatetic porch, gives some background on these words and concludes that for the most part they should be regarded as a sitting room outdoors.[55] Downing's use of words such as loggia, piazza, umbrage, and verandah reflects some pretension given to elevated foreign culture.

The terrace was seldom used, but did provide the perfect design for what Downing described as the "harmonious union between the architecture and the landscape, or, in other words, between the house and the grounds."[56] This was especially important for Design VIII, a Villa in the Italian Style in *Cottage Residences*, which has a geometric, formal garden, a style Downing calls "architectural" (see Figs. 2.18 and 3.14). Together, Downing claimed that terrace and garden provided an extension from the house, a highly artificial object, to the forms of natural objects in the landscape, mediating between the two.

As a landscape designer, Downing knew the advantages of outdoor sitting rooms for contemplating favorable prospects. The tent type also improved the appearance of the house—an enhanced aspect—where the dignity of contemplation is displayed because a place is provided. A display of leisure reflected life with some rele;'ase from hardship and drudgery. "The moment the dwelling rises so far in dignity above the merely useful as to employ any considerable feature not entirely intended for use," Downing declared, "then the veranda should find its place." It hints of refinement and the presence of a gentleman.

He continued:

> To decorate a cottage highly, which has no veranda-like feature, is, in this climate, as unphilosophical and false in taste, as it would be to paint a log-hut, or gild the rafters of a barn: unphilosophical, because all that relative beauty suggested by features which indicate a more refined enjoyment than what grows out of the necessities of life should first have its manifestation, since it is the most significant and noble beauty of which the subject is capable; and false in taste, because it is bestowing embellishment on the inferior and minor details, and neglecting the more important and more characteristic features of a dwelling.[57]

The tent type is also a place of social decision. It belongs neither to the private domain of the house and grounds, not is it the public street. It mediates between the two, revealing and reconciling each other. It causes an unsettling that is liberating and risky, and hosts closer emotional connections to the forces of nature where one senses the rain without getting wet, or feels the breeze in the shade. This area mediates the effects of nature where dimmed daylight provides cooler air for the adjoining rooms, a passive air-cooling procedure often worth the sacrifice of direct sunlight. Tent-type places also mediate behavior. To step up onto a porch is not the same as knocking on the front door. Downing called this feeling "a note of preparation," because a decision about entry is required. One must question if it is appropriate to enter this transitory place simply because it is possible. Entry implies legitimacy and sufficient acquaintance with the proprietor. The terms "out-of-doors" and "indoors" refer to opposite sides of a threshold boundary, broadened into a place by a veranda or other mediating element. When omitted, Downing compared the effect to "a well printed book without a title page."[58]

All of Downing's published designs have at least one of these tent-type mediating places. Modest cottages sometimes have only a stoop. Downing defended this reserve, saying that "the exterior of this cottage would be raised in character as well as comfort, by a veranda. This could easily be added; but we have preferred in this example to make the interior accommodation the first object."[59] The veranda "shelters the entrance-door, and affords an agreeable place both for walking in damp or unpleasant weather, and to enjoy a cool shaded seat in the hotter portion of the season."[60] This ambiguity of function enhances its poetic capability where various interpretations are possible.

One way the tent type expresses its subordinate purpose is through form. It is not as wide or as high as the house. Downing said that "as the spirit of Gothic architecture lies in vertical lines, a long unbroken horizontal line of veranda would destroy or mar the architectural character of the cottage" (see Fig. 1.11).[61] The veranda roof is made as flat as possible to serve this purpose as well. The resulting horizontality, a horizon in fact, distinguishes this kind of element from those of the cave or hut. It is associated with the unending plain without mountainous barriers or impassable water, and suggests a feeling of freedom. It is bound below with edges cut into the land, and appears boundless above with a light, low and thin roof.

The use of materials that provide minimal protection between full exposure to the forces of nature and the full shelter within the house is another distinctive characteristic of these kinds of places. An alerted, heightened sensibility, or even a teasing or testing of human ingenuity against natural forces, is part of the appeal. This feeling is impossible to achieve with buildings raised on columns above ground level, leaving an ambiguous open area below. The heaviness of such spaces cannot convey a tent effect because they are not made thinly. Tent-type thinness is achieved as Downing specified, with "the roof made of nicely jointed stuff, nailed upon the joist rafters, which are beaded and left exposed, so that no other ceiling is required."[62]

The exposed structural frame on the underside of porch roofs was sometimes imitated on the interior, under eaves and inside dormers. The sloped ceiling in Washington Irving's bedroom at Sunnyside is finished in the French tent fashion (see Fig. 4.3). Irving described the room as "left with the natural pitch of the roof . . . and beneath it the slope of the roof might be papered with striped paper, so as to resemble the curtain of a tent—I have seen an irregular attick room managed in that way in France with a very pretty effect. The very irregularity became a source of ornament."[63]

It is interesting to observe that the number of tent-type elements in Downing's designs increased as the house size increased, and when they were client commissions. The villas in *The Architecture of Country Houses* all have porches, verandas, and balconies. The design Villa in the Romanesque Style also has a pavilion and arcade; some scholars think that Downing considered this to be his finest design (see Figs. 4.14 and 4.20). His larger commissions designed with Vaux have the balconies and verandah/porch/verandah arrangements, and some also include arcades, pavilions, and terraces.[64]

Downing sometimes includes rustic buildings in his landscape designs. They are cave types in their location when found along paths, and they are also tent types in their construction with undressed materials of bark-covered branches for frames and platted screen walls. Downing identified them as a rustic summerhouse (Fig. 4.21, shown as *c*) or rustic arbor that "serves as a resting-place, and affords a pleasant view" (see Fig. 3.17, shown as *k*).[65] They were places of transitory occupation closely related to the land.

THE HUT OF INSTRUMENTS

In Downing's architecture the hut is not a rough, crude shelter, but an *idea* of sheltering. Hut-type shelters not only protect people from harsh weather, but also protect their accoutrements and mechanical devices. Just as part of a policeman's uniform includes equipment needed for efficient job performance—such as handcuffs or a radio or a flashlight—building accoutrements are useful because they increase human comfort, safety, convenience, and pleasure. Sinks and drains, pipes and stoves, and water closets and rising cupboards are all instruments of dwelling that might be sheltered in the hut type.

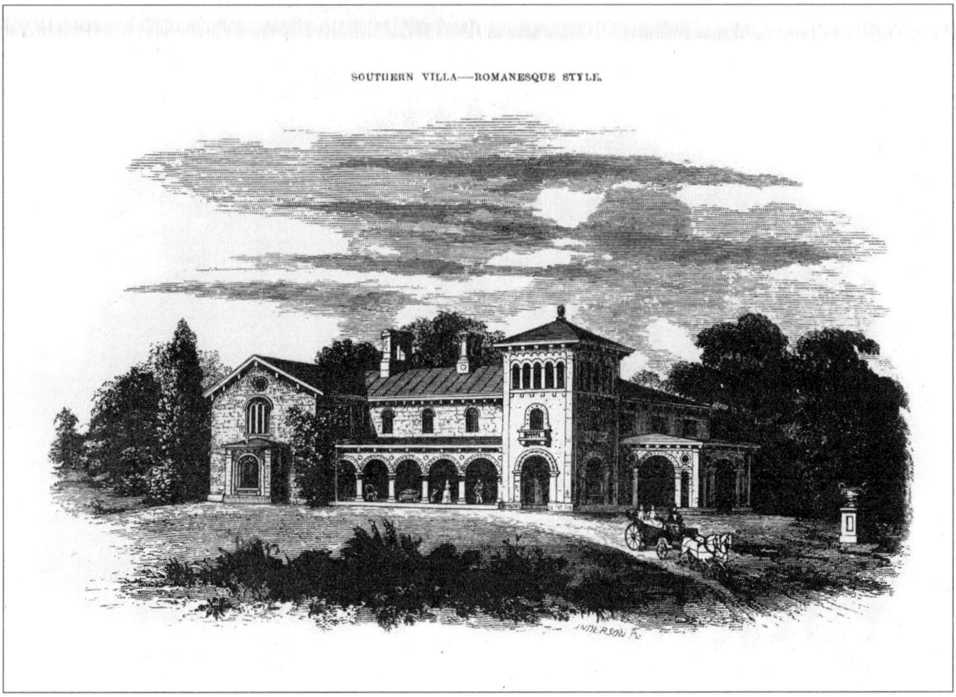

Fig. 4.20. View and Principal Floor Plan of Design XXXII, *ACH.*

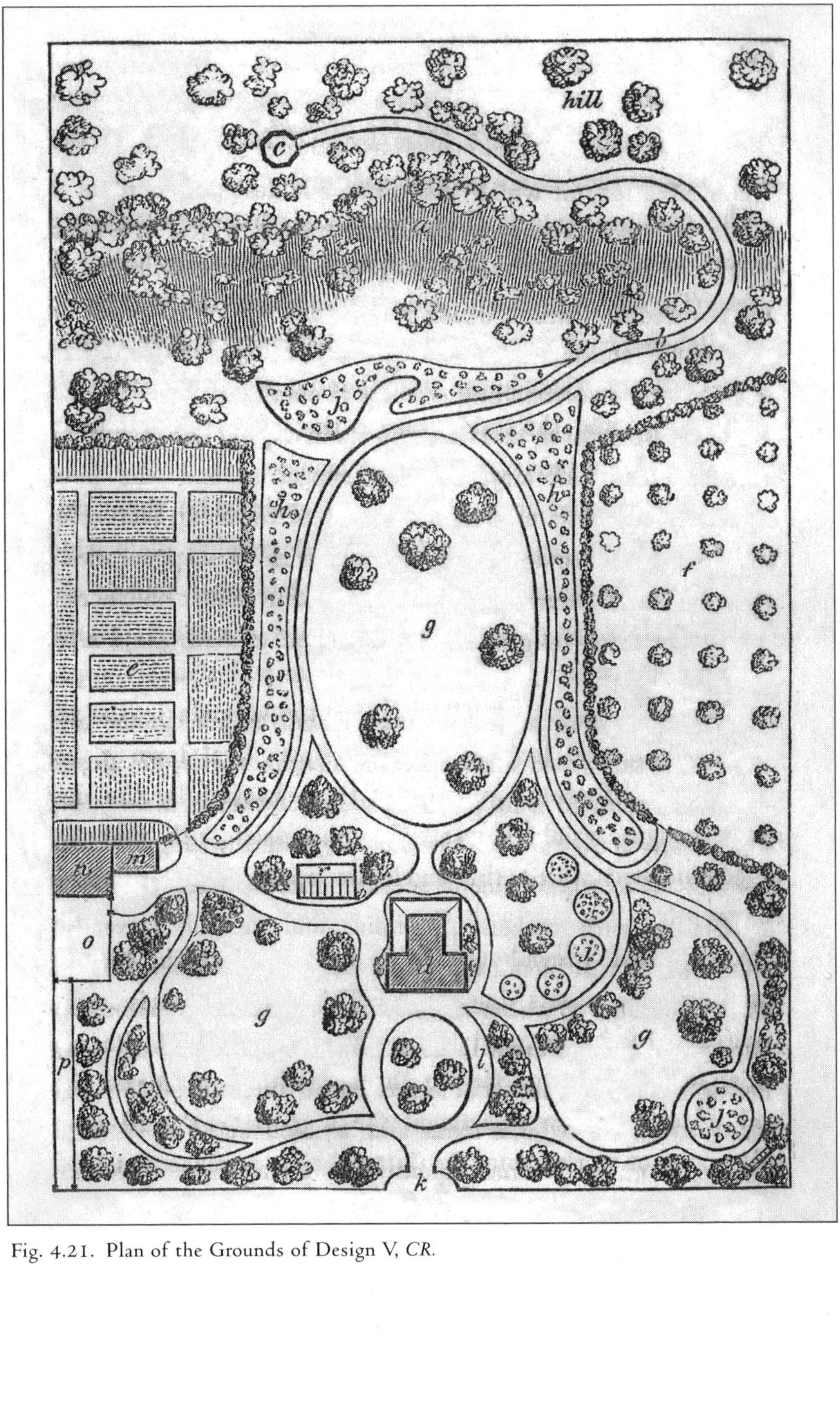

Fig. 4.21. Plan of the Grounds of Design V, *CR*.

The *cabane* or hut was of particular interest to Quatremère as the most suitable constructive type between the heaviness of the cave and the lightness of the tent. It was the type most open to harmonious rules of proportion. Quatremère defines "hut" in two ways: first, as a meager, wooden shelter (which he noted did not belong in an architectural dictionary), and second, "an abstract and theoretical respect." This approach "presents a trial or an adumbration of construction in the origin of every society; hence it is possible to discern the seed whose succession of ideas and efforts fostered later development."[66] Quatremère's hut was the sole building type that relied on nature's three kinds of building material—wood, stone, and earthy clay formed into bricks—all with a load-bearing rapport between parts. The hut was also especially able in its fictive or metaphorical ability to transpose corporeal proportions and expressive characteristics into architecture.

In historian Ann Cline's investigations of the architectural limits of habitation, the hut is most easily homely as it is devised for homo-sapiens. As she notes, "the hut was not beautiful, nor aggressive; not even clever. All the same, the hut was a well-crafted thing, difficult to dismiss. In a word, the hut was *homely*, and precisely this plain unpretentiousness was what people either hated or loved. Because it moved them in ways that architecture seldom did."[67]

Meant for human occupation, the hut as shelter includes the exterior enclosure with its attributes; on the interior, the hut shelters things that support occupation. Downing thought that the most important expressive elements of a house that showed its true character as domestic architecture were the entrance porch and the chimney top "breaking against the sky boldly" (Fig. 4.22).[68] Because Downing located fireplaces on interior walls to maximize the thermal benefit of radiant heat, they were invisible until they emerged from the roof, making the chimney top the expressive form of the hearth. Also important were roof overhangs necessary to protect exterior walls from exposure to harmful weather. This was especially true for wood construction, something he recognized as likely because of the economy and availability of the material. The accompanying roof brackets (Fig. 4.23), ornamental verge boards (Fig. 4.24), and built-in gutters that hold and channel rain (Fig. 4.25) were all elements which combined to make apparent what Ruskin says of the roof, describing it as the very soul of the cottage where "beneath my roof" is very different from "within my walls."[69] These elements were expressive and integral devices to shelter. They respond to notions of dwelling by helping the house resist the destructive forces of nature.

On the interior, instruments also supported dwelling. Downing introduced devices he thought were new to his audience very systematically in

Fig. 4.22. Stack of Chimneys.

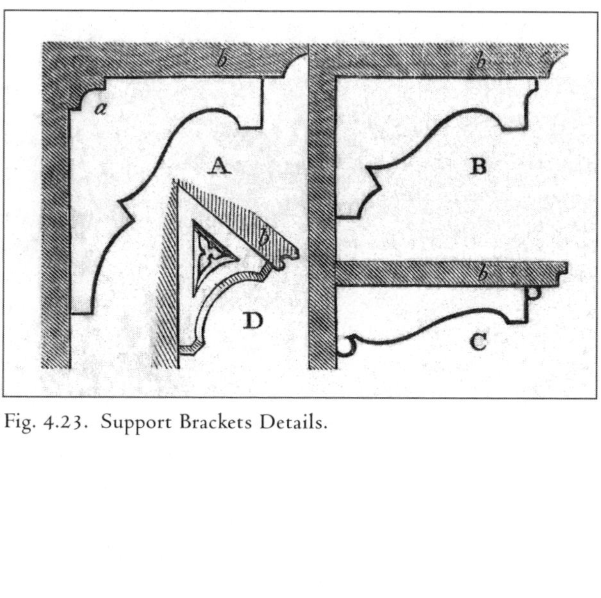

Fig. 4.23. Support Brackets Details.

Fig. 4.24. Verge-board Elevation Detail.

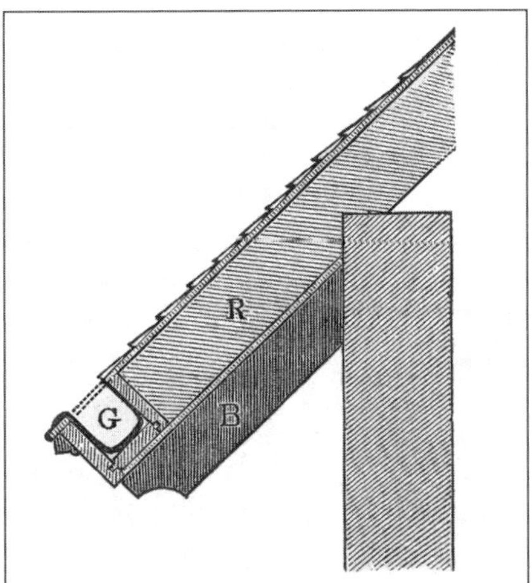

Fig. 4.25. Gutter in Projecting Eaves Section.

Cottage Residences, usually providing information about one device per house design. These items included a bricked drain from the kitchen sink to a reservoir, improved if possible with a leaden pipe and pump (see Fig. 3.12); a dry closet and a stove to heat the hall for winter dining (see Fig. 1.11, shown as *a*); a rising cupboard or dumbwaiter which could be added to the pantry connecting to the kitchen below (Fig. 4.26, and see Fig. 1.12); a slide to convey a cartload of root vegetables to the cellar; a water closet (Fig. 4.27, and see Fig. 4.4); stripped canvas window-shades or canopy awnings (see Fig. 3.10); a water closet with a concealed discharge pipe and a bathroom with hot water piped from a boiler in the kitchen located in the basement (Fig. 4.28); a French-designed wind-powered water-ram drawing water from a cistern to a garden fountain or as an alternative, a hydraulic ram (Fig. 4.29) and a hot air furnace (Fig. 4.30).

The list above reflects experience Downing gained over time. One regret he had with his own house design was that there was no dumbwaiter between the basement kitchen and the dining room on the floor above; he included one when he designed his brother's house three years later. Downing praised the advantages of indoor toilet closets—at first merely a room located on an exterior wall where refuse could be taken from an access door directly to the fertilizer pile where it would turn, in Downing's words, into "valuable account." Three designs later, he noted that there were New York plumbers who had equipment for a wet system where a lever on a pull-cord opened an elevated cistern valve to flush water by gravity to a basin with a smell trap, which connected via leaden pipes to a covered drain or liquid manure cistern for later use in the garden.[70]

Downing was less systematic in *The Architecture of Country Houses* in introducing devices likely to be unfamiliar to his audience. Additional equipment for the cottages and farmhouses included two with a piped kitchen sink, three with water closets, and one with a wind-powered, water-raising device. The villas, on the other hand, had many devices, including one with a Chilson furnace; seven with bathrooms with water closets, usually on the chamber level; one with a hot-air heated greenhouse and another with water stored in a garret cistern; and two with a roof ventilator located over a large stair hall. Downing described Emerson's "ejecting ventilator" and showed several decorative roof cupolas.[71]

Projects designed with Vaux had even more instruments. All houses have indoor plumbing with water closets on the principle floors and bathrooms on the chamber floors. Also, three have lifts, one has a furnace and skylight, and another has speaking tubes and gas piping, anticipating future munici-

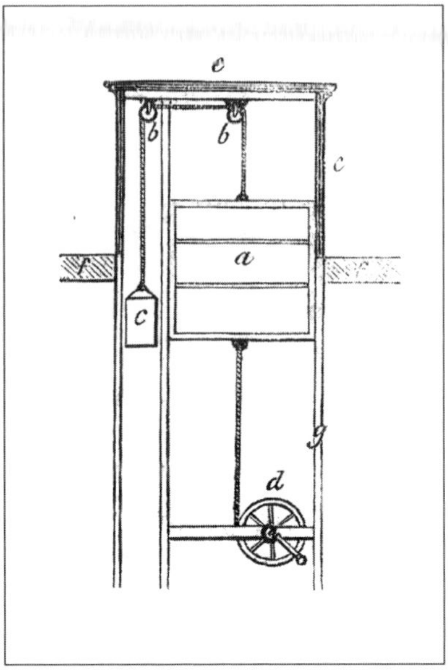

Fig. 4.26. Rising Cupboard Section.

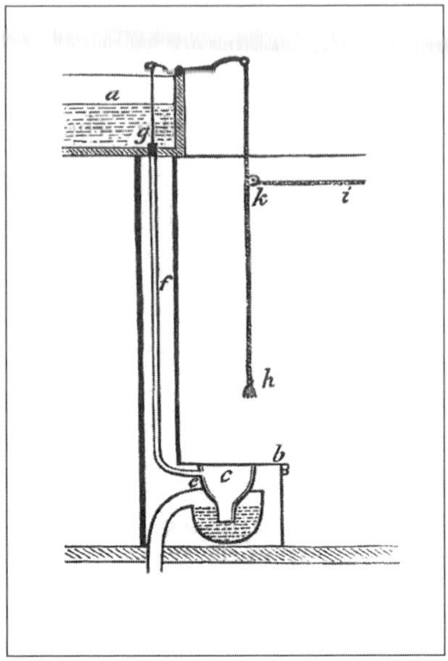

Fig. 4.27. Water Closet Section.

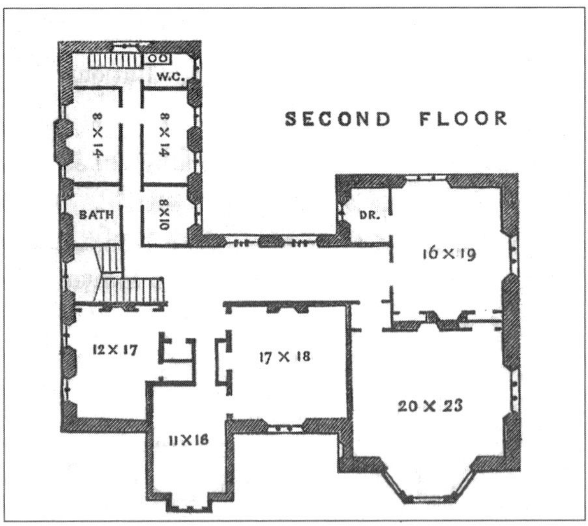

Fig. 4.28. Design VII, Second Floor Plan, *CR*.

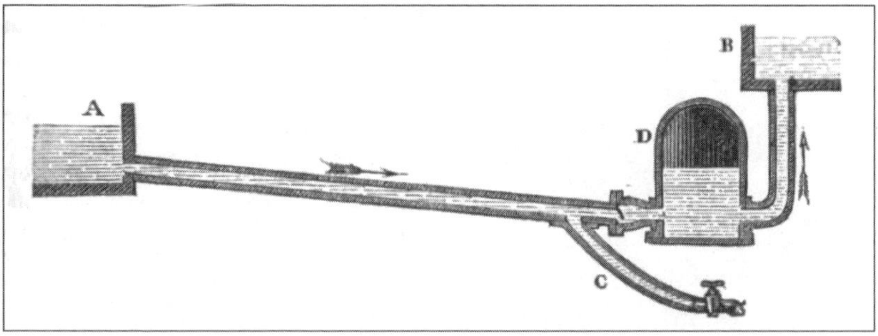

Fig. 4.29. Hydraulic Ram.

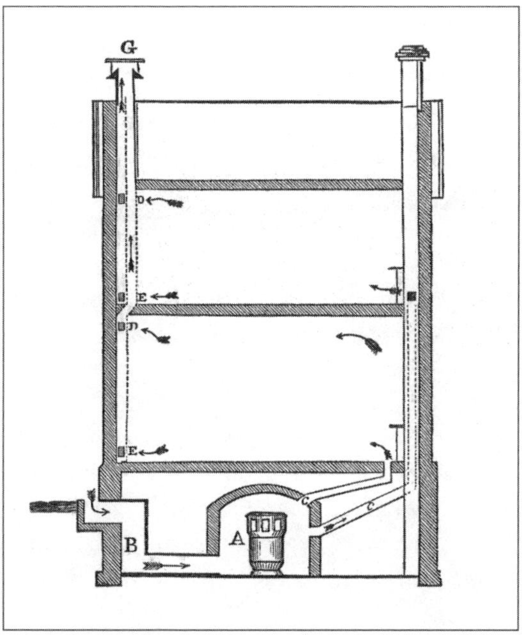

Fig. 4.30. Hot Air Furnace Heating House Section Diagram.

pal service.[72] Because Downing's larger projects designed or intended for specific clients often had more of these instruments, they had higher costs per square foot: the average villa in *The Architecture of Country Houses* is $1.34 per square foot, while the average project designed with Vaux cost more than double, at $2.76 per square foot.

The Architecture of Country Houses ends with three chapters unique for design books at that time. The section called "Interior Finishing of Country-Houses" included discussions of wall finishing and trim, floors, and window shades and curtains for all house sizes. The next section was about ready-made furniture. The third section covered the latest inventions for warming and ventilating. Downing argued that indoor air quality affected health and included diagrams showing his understanding of necessary air circulation (Figs. 4.31 and 4.32). Chilson furnaces, available from New York City, supplied early central heating systems and were described in detail. Downing also included drawings of cast-iron hinged louvers and double-wall construction to aid circulation (Fig. 4.33). Knowing the costs and layout consequences of providing wood-burning masonry fireplaces in every habitable room, he suggested that room registers connect to a centrally located furnace as an economic and operational improvement. Even with the advantages of mechanical heating, he hoped that at least one fireplace would be built in the main room for "the genial expression of *soul* in its ruddy blaze, and the wealth of home associations that surround its time-honored hearth."[73] Downing particularly appreciated equipment for heating, moving, storing, and distributing steam heat and water when these systems were extended to greenhouses and conservatories.

In terms of air flow, Downing discussed the advantages of Emerson prefabricated roof ventilators for cooling the house by increasing air circulation; equipment recently available from New York City (Fig. 4.34). Downing knew that poorly built fireplaces made unpleasant smoky interiors, and recommended numerous publications on how to build better fireplaces and chimneys.[74]

And, then as now, along with instruments come instructions. To this end, Downing needed to convince owners about the practical advantages of these labor-saving devices and approaches to construction. Comfortable and convenient habitation depended on devices to reduce the difficulties of moving warmed or cooled air, providing running water, and disposing of waste.[75] They also compensated for one difficulty with servants. As Downing noted, "in a country like ours, where the population is comparatively sparse, civil rights equal, and wages high, good servants or domestics are comparatively rare,

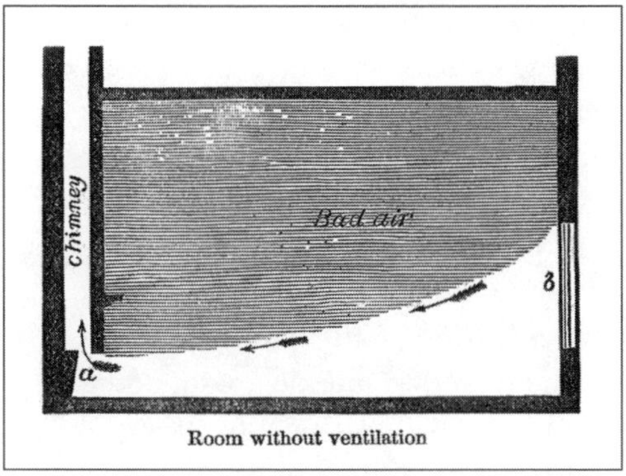

Fig. 4.31. Bad Room Ventilation Diagram.

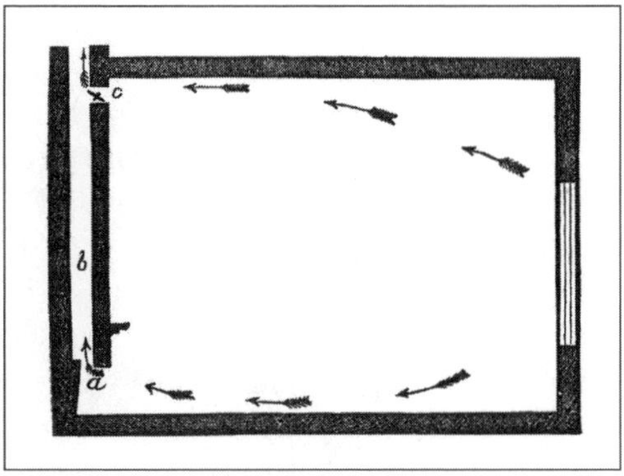

Fig. 4.32. Good Room Ventilation Diagram.

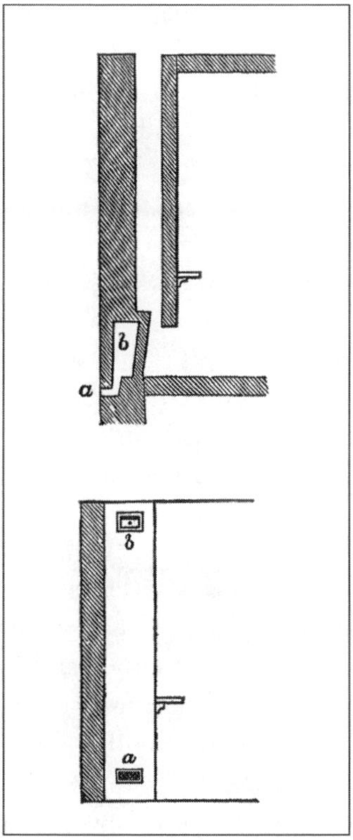

Fig. 4.33. Chimney Construction Details.

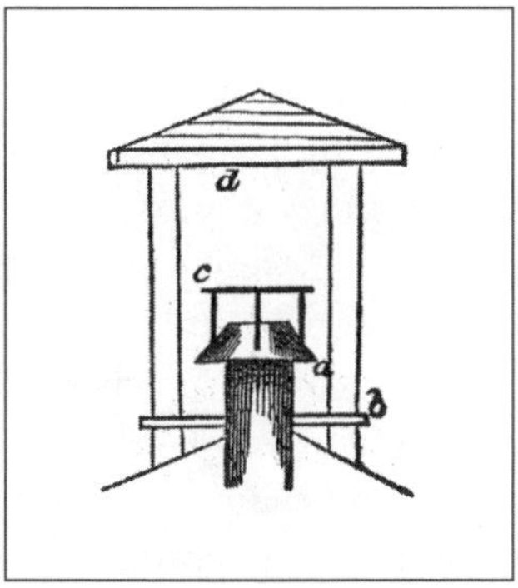

Fig. 4.34. Roof Ventilator.

and not likely to retain their places a long time. The maximum of comfort, therefore, is found to consist in employing the smallest number of servants actually necessary. This may be greatly facilitated by having all the apartments conveniently arranged with reference to their various uses, and still further by introducing certain kinds of domestic labor-saving apparatus to lessen the amount of service required, or to render its performance easy."[76]

Downing believed that "each department of the house being complete in itself, and intruding itself but little on the attention of the family or guests when not required to be visible, which is the *ideal* of domestic accommodation."[77] This statement points to a key requirement of instruments. As architectural scholar David Leatherbarrow puts it, "the first duty of equipment is to provide a response to the expectations of the body, not the disinterested gaze."[78] The lift or dumbwaiter that communicated between the kitchen and dining room was to be located out of sight in an adjacent pantry. If the kitchen was on the principal level, a double set of doors was needed to prevent disagreeable smells and noises from entering the rest of the house (see Fig. 1.11, shown as *b*). A skylight illuminated the attic hall and the hall below through a floor opening protected with a handrail (see Fig. 1.22). (Downing did not think of the skylight itself as an expressive element, but noted that natural light was a benefit to center stairs and halls before artificial lighting was available.) Gas fittings, water piping, and speaking tubes were concealed in the wall framing. Only the bathing room has evolved from a water closet to a larger room with a tub, to a room with windows and furniture. Downing was one of the first to call this room the bathroom.[79] Unlike the exterior accoutrements of roof overhangs and chimney tops that had duties of expression, Downing considered these interior instruments to be silent servants, useful and invisible to varying degrees.

Cultivating the land was backbreaking work made easier with animal assistance and equipment. Settlers cleared forests for roads and leveled fields for planting. Maintaining productive and pleasure grounds also benefitted from technical improvements. Downing somewhat generously—and inaccurately—credited his client and friend Robert Donaldson for the invention of a horse-led gravel road scraper, used to clean and smooth paths (Fig. 4.35). He also claimed that his friend Henry Winthrop Sargent brought the mechanical lawn mower to America in the 1850s, although mowers were actually not manufactured here until the 1860s.[80] Downing appreciated this particular invention because he knew that using a sharp scythe was a dangerous and time-consuming chore; he recommended a few sheep instead to keep the lawn tidy.

Fig. 4.35. Implement in use at Blithewood for smoothing gravel roads.

Improvement to the hut type was a matter of accumulating more and better instruments. In the mid-nineteenth century, every household (with the exception of some in Philadelphia where limited municipal water service was provided), had to have its own water well and method for waste disposal. Today, few fail to appreciate the convenience of indoor plumbing, the safety of electrical lighting, and the comfort of mechanical heating and air conditioning. However, substituting energy-consuming mechanical devices for passive elements such as shady overhangs has economic and emotional consequences. Taken to an extreme, as contemporary critic Albert Borgmann has observed, "our contact with reality has been attenuated to the pushing of buttons and the turning of handles. The results are guaranteed by machinery that is not of our design and often beyond our understanding. Hence the feelings of liberation and enrichment quickly fade."[81]

IT IS NÄIVE to assume that Downing's principles for beautiful and truthful homes were absolutely democratic, especially if you were the one doing the work. The point then and today is that houses dedicated to efficiency alone fail to support a sense of dwelling that has little to do with size or cost. John Crowley, in his recent study of domestic life, observes that women associate female domesticity with work and men associate male domesticity with leisured privacy.[82] Gender issues aside, it is neither work nor leisure that strictly makes up the vital activities of home occupation. It is both.

From bathroom fetishes to every facet of the virtual electronic information age, instruments have come to dominate domestic life. As Borgmann states, "we have progressively divided and decomposed the fabric of our lives. This is particularly evident when we consider how technology has step by step stripped the household of substance and dignity."[83] Our dependence has reached a point where their use is unquestioned, and assumed as integral and necessary to daily life. While we cannot imagine living without some of them, we can insist that their costs and full environmental consequences remain apparent.

A hut of instruments permits human activities to extend far beyond our natural human reach. Building on flood plains or reclaimed land, on unstable soils in earthquake-prone areas, and in excessively hot or cold climates requires extreme commitments to constructing and maintaining technologically advanced engineered infrastructure. While this achieves a standard of comfortable living in more parts of the world, it risks minimizing the qualities that make various places ecologically unique and valuable to natural systems that suffer from human presence. The ability to alter natural forces to the extent necessary for human occupation also reduces human awareness of our own limited physical character as well as an appreciation of the complexities of nature that has nothing to do with human presence or appreciation.

These three interpretations of architecture's original dwelling types became for Downing the consistent and essential requirements for domestic fabrication. In Edmund Burke's exploration of the cause of beauty he submits, "For *deformity* is opposed, not to beauty, but to the *compleat, common form*."[84] The formal elements of cave, tent, and hut as bay window, veranda, and interior and exterior instruments make up a complete state—a desirable attribute of any production—and the commonality of its expression suggest a valid appreciation likely shared among people.

Downing's definition for dwelling as a place that supported contemplation and the routines of operation required expression to convey ideas of sentiment beyond economy and industry in a meaningful and significant way. Through the consistent and combined use of cave, tent, and hut typologies, he had the means to show how architecture and landscape designs appeal to human sensibilities. The final discussion of his principle of expression now becomes critical, because its application shows the completeness of Downing's domestic architecture.

5

APPLYING A LANGUAGE OF SENSIBILITIES

> He who studies how to combine beauty of form, the expression of domestic feeling, and unity of style or composition in his designs, will always both delight and satisfy us in the houses which he produces.
>
> —Downing, *The Architecture of Country Houses*[1]

ONE OF Downing's great contributions to the profession is the emphasis he placed on using precise terms of architecture and landscape to express certain sentiments about dwelling. The importance he placed on expression in design required a high level of communicative precision to execute effectively. Quatremère insisted that "it is extremely important, and I will not stop repeating this point, that if the language of architecture is to have value, if its signs are to be understood and are to have the effect of which they are capable, . . . if these signs are to say something, they must not be used to say nothing."[2] It is clear that Downing knew something of European theories of original dwelling typologies. It is also clear that he designed and published domestic projects that were usually not commissions for specific clients. He did not publish his portfolio as a pattern book or offer a builder's guide.[3] Instead, his work directed American taste in the rural arts with architectural principles as his guide, and he did so by introducing a vocabulary of domestic elements. He taught Americans to expect their home improvements to say something about their country, their constructions, and themselves.

Keeping in mind his three principles of design—fitness or usefulness as the beauty of utility, expression of purpose as the beauty of propriety, and expression of style as the beauty of form and sentiment—we can see that

Johann Gottfried Herder (1744–1803)

German philosopher and literary critic Herder studied under Immanuel Kant at the University of Königsberg from 1762. His work attacked eighteenth-century assumptions of the Enlightenment and helped lay the groundwork for German Romanticism. Herder and compatriot Wolfgang Goethe's early work crossed the line from classical or enlightened to the romantic, later influencing utopian writers Thomas Carlyle and John Ruskin in England, and then the American Transcendentalists. The English translation of his Treatise upon the Origin of Language *appeared in 1827. Herder's writing questioned the relationship between language and thought as it reflects a culture and its history. Romantic themes included a love of the picturesque, exotics, and a delight in the mysteries of nature idealized.*

for Downing, the art of design comes from expressing purpose and feeling. A communicative language needs to correspond between idea and act. Downing's vocabulary is comprised of elements that bring specific form and material to the found cave type in the form of a bay window, the mediating tent type in a veranda, and the sheltering hut type in instruments such as a chimney top. But language is also composed of grammar, a structure for how elements—words or building parts—are arranged and meaningfully employed. If a visual language is to evoke emotional response and arouse sentiment, then nouns as attributes of dwelling experience benefit from association with verbs to make intention real.

The elements Downing consistently employed in his designs are specific to domestic architecture and landscape design. In general, all buildings have floors, roofs, and walls, as well as doors and windows. Comfortable shelter for people in most parts of the country in the mid-nineteenth century required heat supplied by fireplaces. A domestic vocabulary needs elements that are, as Downing put it, "chiefly confined to our own dwellings."[4] This vocabulary must denote "more forcibly those elegant enjoyments which belong to the habitation of man in a cultivated and refined state of society."[5] Downing's list of dwelling elements are represented on floor plans, shown on perspective views, and described in the text of his books. But how do these things speak to say that this building and these grounds are for domestic habitation? What is this relationship between the object as a noun and the action or verb activating the expression Downing considered part of design?

In Isaiah Berlin's lectures on the roots of Romanticism, he noted that Johann Gottfried Herder identified three "doctrines" that contributed very powerfully to the Romantic movement. They are expressionism, the notion of belonging, and the notion that true ideals are desired but are often incompatible and cannot be reconciled with each other. Taking Herder's doctrines in reverse order, a true ideal can never be obtained, but working toward it gives life purpose. Belonging, as discussed earlier, is part of truthful architecture that yields to landscape and enters its whole universe in order to fit together. Expanding on the idea of expressionism, "Herder believed that one of the fundamental functions of human beings was to express, to speak."[6] For Downing, to express the attributes of dwelling visually is to voice meaningful and common concerns about privacy, comfort, security, permanence, and contemplation. Dwelling experience began with visual appearances and practical functions, and then extended to include the realm of emotional response. The predication of domestic elements allows one the means to occupy a building and feel "at home."

Downing specifically wanted houses to say something about dwelling that is *possible* to express through meaningful elements. Bay windows, niches, and alcoves convey a sense of privacy and intimacy; verandas enable our ability to picture nature as landscape and to display a civilized state of leisure; and chimneys tops are associated "with all our ideas of warmth, the cheerful fireside, and the social winter circle."[7] These elements become actions when they conveyed, pictured, displayed, associated, and sheltered domestic life.

In order for architecture and landscape's inanimate elements to communicate, they need to take on lifelike qualities. Downing's language, like all architectural language, relies on images and not words. Architecture and landscapes are made; they are artifacts. If they are to appeal to human sentiment, then the metaphoric transfer from seeing a terra-cotta chimney top to feeling warmth and family communion requires a language that bypasses verbal forms of communication. Downing's association of "this" with "that" is clarified in the warning that these essential elements cannot be omitted in domestic design if it is to express human purpose. In other words, they must be combined in ways to affirm sensory and reasoning definitions of dwelling.

Downing's world was a time of landscape painters and romantic writers. Their work combined selected realities with fictive imagination to create the story narrative. The significance of each part of the painted composition—foreground, middle ground, and background—contributed to an overall statement. For instance, the content of the painting by Frederic Edwin Church, "New England Scenery" (1851), is less the precise details of the covered wagon, and more the idea of progress signified (Fig. 5.1). For Emerson, there was a difference between the materialist who relied on sense data alone and acted as a result of experience, and the idealist who considered sense data insufficient and therefore relied more on reasoning.[8] Architecture and landscapes are made

Fig. 5.1. *New England Scenery,* Frederic Edwin Church, 1851.

out of materials. Sensory experience requires us to touch it, see it, and interact with it using all our senses. However, perceiving the world is not enough. We want more from our engagement. Thinking helps understand life experience. Understanding experience addresses our question of how inanimate objects can express something. Architecture speaks through an emotional vocabulary because we *think* we hear what it says. Therefore, inanimate objects become expressive in created conditions of personification, setting forth its character in ways that are comprehensible. These created conditions, when arranged allegorically, amplify the effect. Finally, qualities of animation affirm experiences Downing related to dwelling. These methods of personification, allegory, and animation are ways of thinking about design, then and now, that show how architectural expression leads to satisfying experience.

METHODS OF PERSONIFICATION, ALLEGORY, AND ANIMATION

Personification is a literary trope, defined as "the giving to an inanimate being the figure or the sentiments and language of a rational being." The dictionary's earliest example is "*Confusion* heard his voice."[9] A better example might be the personification of church and country, even boats, as female. Romantic poets and European and American landscape painters of the eighteenth century used this artistic device liberally to present images intended to evoke emotion.

Once painters treated their landscapes as compositions of selected real and fictive elements, their art freed itself from responsibilities related to the portrayal of literal subjects. Thus art became more a matter of expression and artistic sentiment than record-keeping (Fig. 5.2). This allowed landscape paintings to be understood more as compositions arranged for effect and message, and less as photographic records of nature, historic place and fact. Architectural scholar Rudolf Wittkower points out that thinking about nature and man's interpretation in art had ancient roots in arguments about mimesis. Wittkower observed that "the closer the imitation the more perfect the work of art—implies that art can never surpass nature." Wittkower continued with a key departure in thinking about the purpose of art; that is, "nature is regarded as accidental and imperfect, and for this reason the artist has to choose the most perfect parts from nature and to combine them in his work. Thus the work of art surpasses nature."[10]

Arguments about mimesis and the connection between art and nature had another interpretation in Quatremère's work. He considered the fine arts of painting or poetry differently from the building arts. The fine arts attempted to *imitate* nature, and the quality of the result was therefore judged for its close resemblance. The intent of the building arts, on the other hand, was to *extend* nature through artifice. As I have attempted to show throughout this book, Downing's intent was to provide instruction about the relationships between the land and the proprietor's character and its tasteful improvement. His position suggested that nature has qualities understood as types of landscapes, and further, that people with different characters and buildings in different styles may fit together harmoniously. One way in which Herder's second doctrine about the notion of belonging applies is through a truthful yielding of one to another, thereby extending nature through human presence.

Using the literary trope of personification for the building arts requires Downing's domestic elements to have expressive voice. Unlike civic architecture with applied ornament of iconographic painterly or sculptural referents, Downing's typological vocabulary has more direct and less abstract reference to ideal acts of dwelling. If a chimney top says anything, it is in association with warmth and the society of the hearth. Or if finding a bower

Fig. 5.2. *Montagne Sainte-Victoire,* Paul Cézanne, c. 1887.

in the woods prompts sentimental reactions, it is because it is recognized as an invitation to certain kinds of occupation. Spectators see and read domestic elements, recognizing them from their own remembered experiences and coming to a common understanding of their current meaning. In this sense, personification is literally applied because it affirms association without much resistance. Conflict arises when domestic architecture is seen as being unable to rely solely on the inclusion of a list of things in order to express its distinct purpose. Understanding the full strength of Downing's designs requires something more than reading a collection of elements assigned with memories of human actions that predict certain human emotional response. The sequence of experience is also important.

One example of how a designed sequence heightens experience is described in Quatremère's essay "On the Use of Allegory in Architecture," which Loudon published in 1837. Quatremère gave an account of Marcellus of Rome's decision to build two temples to the deities of virtue and honor after it was determined that the two deities could not share the same temple. Therefore it was decided a visitor should go through the Temple of Virtue in order to get to the Temple of Honor because "by virtue alone honour can be attained."[11] In this example, the three inner senses—understanding, memory, and desire—are informed through allegorical reference in an arranged and sequential experience.

In a similar way, Downing's house designs appeal to fundamental human sentiments because personified elements are arranged in ways that add to their expressive capacity. For instance, the entrance sequence begins with a stoop or porch for small cottages, and a veranda for larger villas. These tent-type mediating places lead to an entry, vestibule, or hall, which connects the principal adjoining apartments. In just over half of Downing's published designs, halls contain stairs that lead to the private chamber floor above. Designs for three houses in the Norman, Italian, and Rhine style have separate stair towers (Figs. 5.3 and 5.4).[12] In the other designs the stair is concealed from view, separating the more public apartments on the principal level from the private rooms above and service offices below. Revealing the stair displayed an openness and informality, while concealing it protected a sense of privacy. In either case, the location of the stair silently communicated how household operations were to be understood and the level of formal conduct expected.

Internal movement, expressed or concealed, had other facilities shown on Downing's floor plans. Unlike room-size halls, narrow passages connected the principal apartments to kitchen offices in a concealed way, desirable because these passages were meant for servants (see Figs. 4.12 and 5.3). In another case, a passage is used for access to the water closet—something new in 1842, when the rules for behavior in this regard were uncertain (see Fig. 4.4, shown as *b*). Passages for servants or for access to "invisible" activities are different from corridors intended for family use. For instance, Design XXXII in *The Architecture of Country Houses* was intended for a location in warmer climates, as suggested by the title a Villa in the Romanesque Style, for the Middle or Southern States (see Fig. 4.14). The family would use the arcade to enter the principal rooms and the vestibule would be reserved to receive visitors. The family would use the corridor and stair, and the servants would use the passage and back stair. Separating internal circulation promoted certain patterns of behavior; that is, quiet reflection and uninterrupted enjoyment for the family, and more efficient operation for the staff.

Designs for exterior movement are evident in Downing's layout of the grounds in *Cottage Residences* and become increasingly sophisticated. The simplest, Design I, described as located in a suburb of a town or village, had the entrance centered on the house and close to the road (see Figs. 3.12 and 3.13). The next designs have more extensive gravel carriageways and

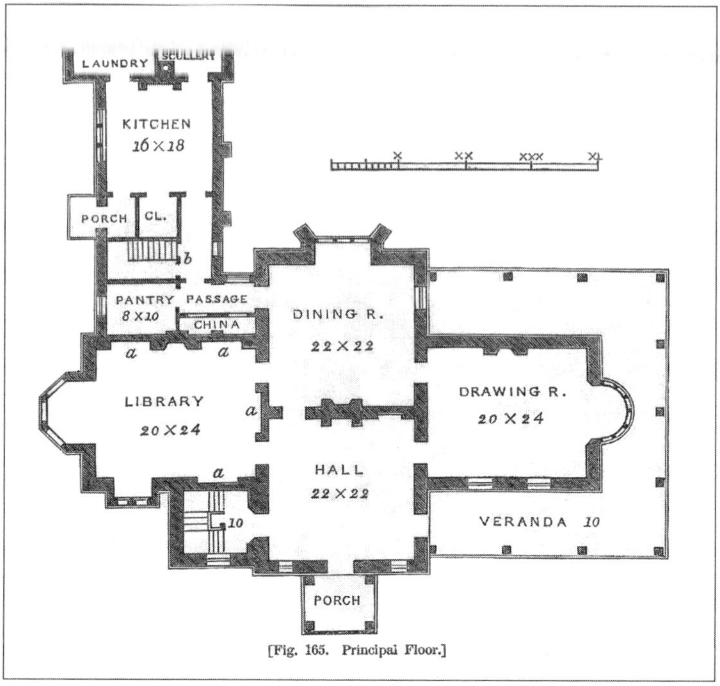

Fig. 5.3. Principal Floor Plan of Design XXXI, *ACH.*

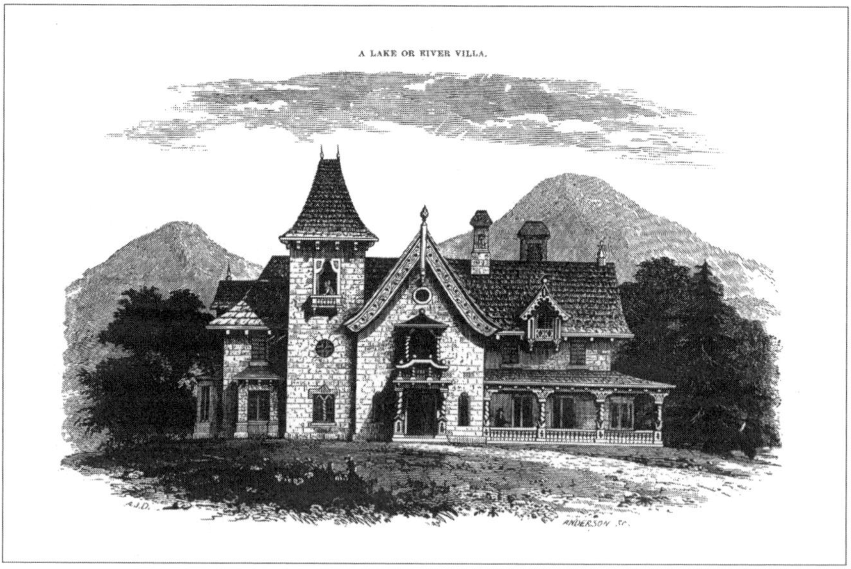

Fig. 5.4. View of Design XXXI, *ACH.*

footpaths. Downing recommended keeping the wider roads short for lower installation costs and less maintenance. Almost all site plan designs show gradually curving entry roads, allowing the house to first be concealed and then to burst into view. Roads continue directly to the kitchen yards and end at the stables. Separate pleasure paths follow land shapes and curve towards elevated spots enjoying beautiful or extensive prospects. Verdant barriers shield productive grounds from view. The extent of the grounds was usually concealed with thick plantings or espaliered fruit trees along fences. Thinned forests, mossy dells, and sunny glades serve as backdrops to turf lawns, often located in front of verandas that were oriented to the view. Sequences of approach set up the contrasting experience coming from "the highly artificial and populous city" to a place of cultivation and "full of wildness, only sufficiently subdued by art to heighten its natural beauty." Movement through Downing's landscapes was meant as sequential experiences of due concealment and truthful revelation, giving the pleasure expected of such grounds. According to Downing, "the *natural expression* . . . must be thoroughly studied before making any improvements; as otherwise the latter will, instead of heightening and developing its original charm, only weaken and render it incongruous and unsatisfactory."[13]

Using personified elements and allegorical movement sequences is further enriched, becoming more expressive with the use of still one more device. Inanimate objects are said to be vivid and full of life through a method of animation defined as "the act of *infusing* life."[14] This action extends what is possible beyond the useful and appropriate, reinforcing the match among occupant, house, and land. Where meaningful associations are *given* to architectural elements in personification and to experience through choreographic sequences, we can now consider a way in which design *infuses* elements with lifelike properties.

Vitality is infused using three definitive and signature qualities of life: growth, regeneration, and movement. These facets of animation are the necessary conditions defining life. In general, a thing is alive if it grows, regenerates, and (in most but not all cases), moves. Examining Downing's design for these three actions shows ways that his designs animated dwelling.

Growth assumes a dynamic state capable of change. Architectural growth is interpreted in the way that floor plan designs expand. As discussed in chapter 3, this is possible in two ways. Design through subdivision grows with the addition of more elements, dependent on one another and arranged with a clear hierarchy. Design through assembly grows through the accumulation of individual elements, ordered strategically. Dynamic floor plan

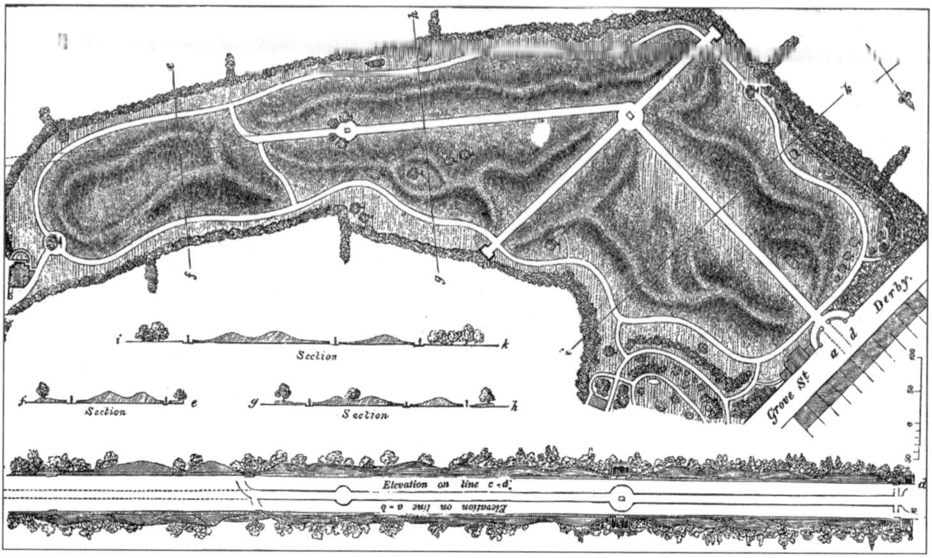

Fig. 5.5. Plan of Derby Arboretum, J. C. Loudon, 1838.

design is capable of growth when its design can respond to changing circumstances—when it can evolve and remain useful.

Pleasure grounds grow by adding paths for access to uncultivated forests, for instance. Loudon's Derby Arboretum in England and Downing's Washington Mall had distinct boundaries, and their interior space was subdivided into smaller, more private places enclosed and shaped with mounded berms, vegetated shrub belts, and clumps of trees (Fig. 5.5 and see Fig. 1.36).[15] In this way, many people were able to enjoy a greater degree of privacy in a public place. Picturesque public parks and rural cemeteries were designed with this graduated experience in mind.

The second animating quality is regeneration, a word that comes from the Latin *rēgēnerāre*, "to cause to be born again or reproduce; to carry back, to bear back, to throw back."[16] The effect of the repetitive experience is an interpretation of regeneration applicable to animated architecture. Repetitive experience is possible in places composed of a serial pattern of single, familiar elements repeated regularly. Walking along an arcade or colonnade, or one of Downing's long or wrap-around verandas, for example, offers such an experience (Fig. 5.6 and see Fig. 4.8). One way to turn wilderness into landscape is to edge the forest with a series of regularly spaced trees.

Any design with repetitive elements provides a location for experiences that unfold in a multiple and layered event. In Greek drama, repetition is

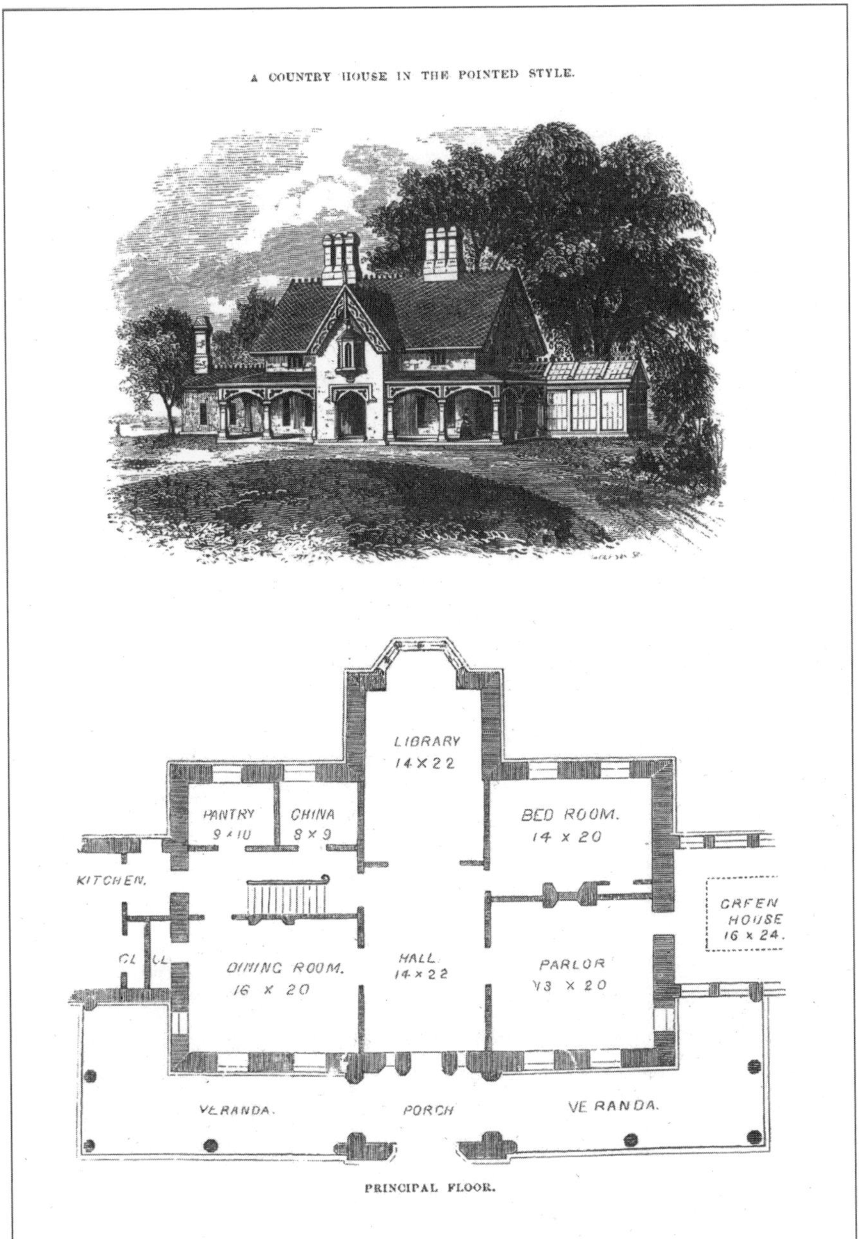

Fig. 5.6. View and Principle Floor Plan on Design XXV, *ACH*.

the simplest method of establishing order. In the landscape, walking through a grove or along an alleé with regularly spaced trees of the same species provides a heightened feeling because it requires an attention distinct from other kinds of landscape experience. It is similar to moving through an exterior arcade or interior gallery with regularly spaced openings in the enclosure. In these places, entries and exits are secondary to the internal movement. The rhythmic pace along regularly spaced niches and openings promote an awareness that expands simultaneously in opposite directions (Fig. 5.7 and see Fig. 3.9). Awareness diminishes in one sense because there are no decisions negotiating direction, and it elevates because one attends to other sights and sounds. Repetition displays an orderly logic that is perceptible and movement that alters concentration.

In architectural experience, there is an obvious unity in experience of places made with repetitive elements due in part to the portrayal of plan in elevation. The equal, exact placement of each post or column anticipates plan form, resulting in an intuited understanding of the whole architectural intention. The dynamic experience is rhythmical in its mark and gap, and, once begun, it is circular in its suppression of beginning and end. It provides a sense of unity and order through the repetition of single elements.

Downing described the arcade and vestibule of Design XXXII as "a broad and airy promenade, nearly 60 feet long, sheltered from sun and rain" (see Fig. 4.14).[17] When Downing identified the arcade as a promenade, he referred to both the feel and the purpose of this place. Experience here is not only visual, but also built up into a whole understanding from noticing subconsciously. This kind of rhythmic movement past various elements—windows, doors, panels, niches, cabinets, and fireplaces repeated in consistent patterns—allows anticipation and memory to build up into a full, vivid, and regenerative experience. One's place is found through movement. Theorist Michel Foucault assigned verbs the purpose of movement between signs as necessary for language to give expression a foundation of truth.[18]

Movement, the third signature action of life, is, according to landscape historian Christopher Hussey, the first requirement of the picturesque. Static, symmetrical buildings perched on open lawns were changed to a romantic vision of design, with contrasting and irregular architectural form set in a landscape with a sense of mystery.[19] Downing's tent-type mediating elements provide places to observe movement in a unique way because the observer is at rest. But watching movement is not the same as being in motion.

The French term *marche*, part of the École des Beaux Arts education pedagogy, suggested that thinking of a heightened sense of approach was as

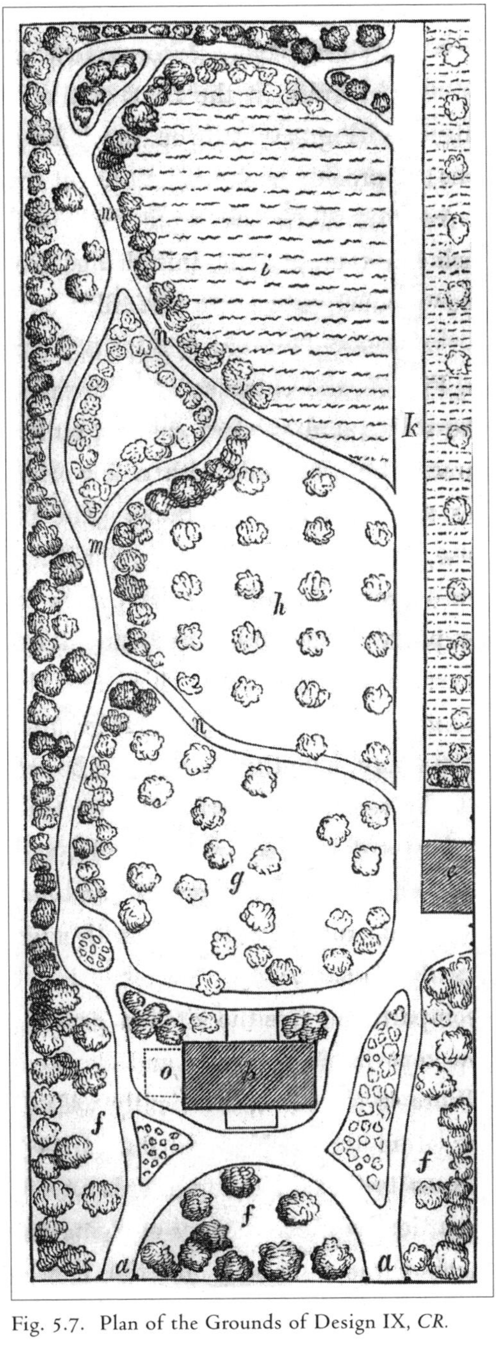

Fig. 5.7. Plan of the Grounds of Design IX, *CR*.

important as the design of the room. In this way, the baroque floor plan of nineteenth-century France shifted the emphasis from distribution to composition. Circulation design became the means to order the floor plans. Now it was the hall or "the marche (that) makes one aware of the impact of the enfilade (rooms with aligned openings) and the shift in character from one space to the next."[20] Circulation organized to reveal or to conceal space and scene was for Downing a means to design experience appealing to those of imagination and sentiment.

Downing used composition in floor plan and site plan to demarcate areas with distinct places for different uses and users to connect in different ways. In his larger houses, passages for servants and corridors for families connected rooms differently. The entry hall served another purpose beyond circulation; this place merged purposeful movement with free movement. Halls, like paths of all kinds, allow for convenient circulation; however, this is another kind of movement experience worth considering.

Design XXXI in *The Architecture of Country Houses* has a hall designed for free movement (see Fig. 5.3).[21] It was meant to be a room and to allow unrestricted movement of people and air. A hall's openness provided a coolness and airiness to the surrounding rooms in summer, and Downing's text described how the rooms could be closed up to conserve heat in the winter. Halls have a less programmed purpose, and this allows people to move more freely. Its openness is more felt as movement than seen as a place, in contrast to the principle that rooms had specific duties and were positioned for practical reasons, or to take advantage of a view.

In Loudon's early treatise on country residences published in 1806, he described three categories of improvement related to landscape design.[22] The first was the necessary or permanent change that included rocks, trees, water, and buildings—things difficult to move once exposed, planted, or constructed. The second category was the occasional or appropriate in design that included roads, walks, and fences, which are constructed things that can be moved with some effort as circumstances change. The third was the fleeting or accidental, made up of moving objects and changing weather that are nearly impossible to control. These included the presence of wild animals, fish, birds, and boats on ponds as well as the setting sun, clouds, fog, and other atmospheric conditions. Landscape design that made the third category of mobile elements more prominent was desirable because it resulted in an animated experience that was more inhabited and more vivid in its presentation of lifelike qualities.

Literal devices of personification, allegory, and certain places of animation arise from a correspondence between design and experience, and exemplify Downing's third architectural principle of the expression of style as the beauty of form and sentiment. The expression of life is possible with Downing's elements combined and arranged in specific ways that allow growth, repetitive perception, and free movement. This intent reflects the truthfulness in design that Downing thought possible in architectural expression.

In horticultural terminology, "vital actions" refer to the germination, growth, and other actions of leaves, flowers, and fruit.[23] Cultivation of these vital actions altered certain parts of plants by reinforcing and enhancing their inherent properties. In order for Downing to elevate taste in the rural arts, improvement as cultivation meant design for the real and apparent support of dwelling. In order to satisfy Downing's definition of domestic architecture, design needed to possess vivid, expressive elements. Fidelity to the expression of domestic life was not to be downgraded. The bay window, the veranda, and the chimney top must be real, and they must be significant. A mere suggestion cannot give weight to association in a meaningful way. When omitted, the result fails to express anything of home beyond a mean shelter. Expressive elements activate architecture that embodies lifelike properties. To Downing, architecture and landscape had a duty to people beyond what was seen; it must also be felt. And this emotional support came not just from ideas, but from experience.

CONCLUSION

> Hence, as society advances (and) the primary wants of human nature are satisfied, we naturally find that literature and the arts flourish. Along with great orators and inspired poets, come fine architecture, and tasteful grounds and gardens.[1]
>
> —Downing, "On the Moral Influence of Good Houses"[1]

WHERE DOES Downing fit among the company of important early American architects and landscape architects? Surely Benjamin Latrobe and Thomas Jefferson in the eighteenth-century, followed by Richard Morris Hunt and Henry Hobson Richardson in the nineteenth, were more influential in directing civic architecture. The important and extensive work of Fredrick Law Olmsted and Calvert Vaux on Central Park began shortly after Downing's death. The limited number of Downing designs—and built projects in particular—cannot support the claim that he was a great or prolific architect, although had the Washington Mall been completed with his specifications, he would be better known today. Rather, Downing's contribution and subsequent influence follows a literary path. Downing published his observations and ideas with clear descriptions and engaging illustrations. Vincent Scully, among other architectural historians, has commented on his theoretical bequest to architects from Richardson to Frank Lloyd Wright, which set expectations for the domestic ideal as living in suburban single family houses set in lawns on gently curving, tree-lined streets.

Understanding the history of design in this country is important, but why Downing and his work? What matters to us today? Downing knew that in order for the house and grounds to fit and to belong together, form and placement needed to correspond. For design, this begins with attention to topography, climate, and site orientation; to the presence of mature trees, rocky outcroppings, and other found conditions; and leads to matching house style choice to the characteristics of the land. What is built—small or large—comments on the proprietor's character and reflects his interests and manner of life. And Downing understood his mid-nineteenth century audience and how to reach them, through advances in printing technologies and the power of the image. His publications addressed a democratic audience idealistic in its reach for freedom from class and wealth distinctions, and instructed those interested in self-improvement.

This legacy begins to explain the appeal of his house designs. Deeper inquiry shows that Downing's houses speak to us because we sense a relationship between the three original dwelling types and fundamental human tendencies. Made apparent through specific elements expressing domestic physical activities and emotive associations, these designs are complete because they support the complete experience. Architecture and landscape design satisfy the human desire to dwell in all its manifestations.

Two final examples illustrate this accomplishment. Downing described a Southern Cottage Villa with a subdivided floor plan as "simple, rational, convenient and economical" (Fig. C.1).[2] Downing's composition included the three original types in the dining room bay window, the wrap-around veranda, and a roof ventilator (described in the text) connected with air ducts from cellar to garret. The house elevation conveys a sense of growth, with the location for the kitchen wing based "on the side offering the greatest facilities for their uses, and, at the same time, keeping them most in the background."[3] The veranda serves as a shady walk, protects the walls from sun and rain, and provides a contrasting effect of light and shadow with evenly spaced bracketed posts. Inside, the free movement of air from the front hall and open stair to the back porch, and vertically through floor levels, is desirable for a house design proposed for warmer climates. The design is complete in composition and expression.

Another design with an assembled floor plan is a good example of how Downing combined elements in animated expression (Fig. C.2 and see Fig. 4.4). Downing suggested that the Cottage Villa in the Bracketed Mode could evolve into the new, dominant American architecture style because it abounded in the picturesque, was made with wood, and was more easily executed than many other styles. Here, the cave type is found in the dining room window seat, created with projecting closets; the porch, balcony, and wrap-around veranda represent the tent type; and the interior water closet

A SOUTHERN COTTAGE VILLA.

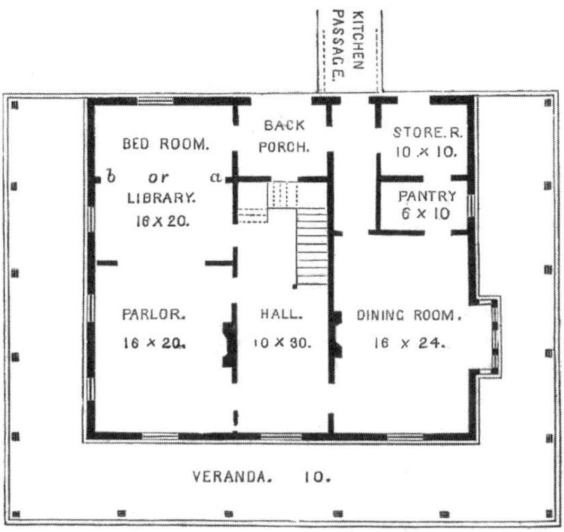

PRINCIPAL FLOOR.

Fig. C.1. View and Principal Floor Plan of Design XXVI, *ACH.*

Fig. C.2. View as Constructed in Wood of Design V, *CR*.

is the hut type. The house could grow by extending the porch to the sides. The veranda post and railing pattern suits the orderly observation of the surrounding pleasure grounds. There is free movement from entry hall to stair hall and back passage and up to the chamber floor, terminating in a large balcony over the porch. Downing described the apartments of the upper story as cool and airy because the broad, veranda-like roof overhang would "shelter the windows from the summer sun during all the sultry portions of the day; while in winter, the sun being low in position, this effect will not be felt when it is not desirable."[4] And, at the same time, the entire house would be warm and dry because of protected walls and techniques of construction. This displays a harmonious condition between architecture and environment where the same design can work in a climate with varying seasons and temperature. In this way, a house and landscape belong together.

The same completeness is discerned in the landscape plan (see Fig. 4.21). Downing arranged productive gardens (shown as *e* and *f*) separated from ornamental grounds (*g* and *j*) by borders (*h*). A nearby greenhouse (*r*) was positioned diagonally from the house (*d*) to be close and at the same time less noticeable; judicious position and plantings concealed views of outbuildings (*m*, *n* and *o*); and a distant rustic summerhouse (*c*) was placed to embellish a hill Downing described as picturesque. All are assembled into a unified composition with distinct forms that fit together to express their purpose, thereby appealing to sentiments of dwelling.

Houses today may be just as well designed in their completeness from the smallest flat to an estate so large that it requires a staff to run it. For the cave type, a small alcove off a large room or a bay window large enough for sitting provides a place for intimate retreat and for transformed emergence. The tent type has many possible elements that mediate between interior and exterior, providing places for the contemplation of nature and display of leisurely repose. For the hut type, considerable sophisticated technology has been invented since Downing's time. Buildings with photovoltaic fuel cells for sun-generated energy and cisterns for rainwater collection reduce dependence on municipal utilities, and provide a more symbiotic relationship between environment and human consumption. Sustainable practices for energy-efficient building construction and operation, computers for systems and information management, labor-saving equipment for cleaning, and monitoring devices for increased safety and comfort are being incorporated as quickly as they are invented and made affordable.

Downing's contribution to American architecture began with his departure from late eighteenth and early nineteenth-century European aesthetic theories. His writings reflect his keen appreciation for the struggles of his fellow countrymen seeking identity and definition in the rural arts. Now considered the father of American landscape architecture, Downing's influence was extended primarily through his publications.[5] His writing on the improved landscape, homes of convenience, beauty and imagination, and industrious Americans directed public taste during his time and beyond. The variety of Downing's floor plan designs illustrate areas of appropriate architectural concerns from truthfulness of expression for materials and ornamental details, to issues of aspect and prospect that make apparent how artifact and nature can belong to each other.

"Real and apparent support" is a phrase Downing used when emphasizing the importance of practical elements. For him, every element is intended to simultaneously give *real* support and to express *apparent* support for dwelling. His intention was not new, nor was his insistence on expressing the elements of architecture. But what was important then and is now are the ways in which he *consistently* used these element types to affirm the vital actions of human dwelling.

The term "complete" admits no comparison. Downing's modest and cheerful cottage, practical farmhouse, and dignified and luxurious villa are not diminutive or expanded replicas of each other. They are meant to be complete in themselves. There was no single ideal house—only designs with ideal accommodations that appealed to the inherent character of man whether he had common sense, sentiment and feeling, or imagination, and whether he was a cottager, farmer, or country gentleman. We learn from Downing that all homes need small elements designed for individual occupation that satisfy a need to retreat, to feel secure, and to be embraced by architectural form. Homes need transitory areas that are neither inside nor out, where architecture shelters what is otherwise exposed and where protected observation of the landscape is possible. Finally, homes also need to support the routines of operation with devices to move and heat water and air, improving health and easing the mechanics of living.

The charge of domestic design is to transfer significant expressive elements through emotional associations. Downing's insistence on the meaningful expression of man's dwelling becomes possible to a greater extent when affirmed in animate fashion through constructions permitting growth, regeneration, and movement. To put it in other terms, vital experience is supported with the perceptible understanding of the potential for expansion, with the anticipation and memory of sequentially ordered places, and with the desire for the openness and flexibility of loosely programmed places. And is there any other way Downing's architecture—or any architecture—can be art? Unless we are able to see and feel ourselves connected in some way to architecture and landscape, there can be no appreciation for it.

Downing wrote about design principles and designed houses based on democratic values outlined forty years before his birth. As Thomas Jefferson said, "the new society should not have an 'artificial' aristocracy 'founded on wealth and birth' but a 'natural' aristocracy based on 'virtue and talents.'"[6] And, we should add, hard work. Downing was a republican who believed in popular education, popular arts, and popular manners. He concluded his essay on "Our Country Villages" by saying that "we confidently wait for the time when public parks, public gardens, public galleries, and tasteful villages, shall be among the peculiar features of our happy republic" (Fig. C.3).[7] In this confidence he expressed himself with true American spirit. He believed that everyone could and would live in houses and in communities that provided both real and apparent support for dwelling—and this belief is his legacy.

Downing's designs of relative and absolute beauty that express feelings of domesticity do so through their consistent use of elements that support the experiences satisfying our sense of dwelling, because they have a direct correspondence with inherent human tendencies. Ours is a continuous search for design based on eternal principles. We also have a desire for the whole-

Fig. C.3. Downing Park, Newburgh, New York.

ness possible in life-supporting, satisfying, and respectful dwelling in the landscape. As Downing continually argued, the universal, eternal essence of dwelling fundamental to the tendencies of the human spirit required the expression of these sensibilities in forms associated with experience. This approach is causal—one thing causes another—a familiar Aristotelian framework that is the basis for much Western thought. Downing's legacy includes the vital association he made when he observed that "man's dwelling, in its most complete form, may be regarded as the type of his whole private life."[8]

The theory of type as the originating reason of a thing is more than the imitation of a model. For Quatremère, it "is based on the nature of things, on historical notions, on the most ancient opinions, on the most constant facts and on the most evident testimony of every architecture."[9] Distinguishing type in design is an exercise that separates the basic and economic form from the accidental and arbitrary characteristics of specific models. Looking at the origins of how and why a thing is formed promotes fabrication that is grounded in inherent human nature. Downing asserted, "every material object that becomes the type of the spiritual, moral, or intellectual nature of man, becomes at once beautiful, because it is suggestive of the beautiful in human nature."[10]

The commonality of common sense is something Downing found appealing in Loudon's work based on eighteenth-century Scottish philosophy, and American Transcendental writers who argued for the authority of first principles that carry their truth as self-evident. Conventions allow a certain degree of socially acceptable conduct, communication with appropriate language defined through common use, and an objective appreciation of the building arts. After all, there is something of the brave hunter, reflective wanderer, and ingenious inventor in all of us. When Downing designed examples of the complete house and grounds that deeply touched common and inherent qualities of humanity, he showed us how dwelling is possible.

GLOSSARY OF TERMS

Any study of nineteenth-century landscape and architecture design finds terminology whose definitions are changed. This glossary is primarily limited to nouns whose evolving definitions may be of interest in considering how some of the richness of perceptible experience may have been lost due to the abstraction of descriptive terminology. Not all definitions from each dictionary and glossary are included here, or every definition an author offers; rather, selections were made to reveal shifts in meaning through time. For instance, today the terms "passage," "corridor," and "hall" are often used interchangeably, but had distinct characteristics in Downing designs.

One notable omission from this glossary is the term "living room." This term does not appear at all in *Cottage Residences*; Downing's sketches for *The Architecture of Country Houses* say "family room" (Design XVII), which Davis changed to "living room" (designs V, VII, XII, XIV, XV, and XIX). Nineteen designs identify a space as a living room and fifteen do not, but these are primarily villas designed by other architects. In 1881, Clarence Cook uses "living room" instead of "parlor" because, as he put it, "I am not intending to have anything to say about parlors . . . as none but rich people can afford to have a room in their houses set apart for the pleasures of idleness"(see note 1). Contemporary science and medical writer Gina Kolata notes that "as the second decade of the twentieth century wound to a close, the memory of a world stalked by infectious disease had dimmed. People had become complacent, almost smug, about disease and death. It was a time when death had nearly lost its sting, an era when the miracles of medicine were portrayed as almost a new religion. And it was a time when death became separate from everyday life. *The Ladies Home Journal* proudly declared that the parlor, where the dead had been laid out for viewing, was now to be called the 'living room,' a room for the living, not the dead"(see note 2).

And so with the passage of time—from the industrial advancements of Downing's Victorian-era America to innovations in transportation, food preparation and storage, medicine, and more in the twentieth and twenty-first centuries—our way of living continues to change, and so do the names we use to designate the particulars of our dwellings. Knowing their difference helps us to understand domestic operations then and now—and perhaps see our way into the future.

The descriptions for each term in this glossary are organized chronologically and span two hundred years, from their appearance in Samuel Johnson's 1806 dictionary to mid-nineteenth century encyclopedias by Joseph Gwilt, Richard Brown, Minard Lafever, and Noah Webster (see note 3) to James Stevens Curl's current resource. I have taken basic definitions and word origins from the *Oxford English Dictionary* and *The Oxford Dictionary of English Etymology* edited by C. T. Onions (Oxford: Clarendon Press, 1995). For each entry, the source follows the description in italics.

TERMS

ante-room, ante-chamber, n. [F. *antichambre*] The room through which the passage is to a principle apartment (*Johnson*). An apartment through which access is obtained to another chamber or room. One in which servants wait and strangers are detained till the person to be spoken with is at leisure (*Gwilt*). A waiting-room, within a house, situated near the entrance-hall (*Brown*). A room before or in front of another (*Webster*). A room before, or forming an entrance to, another (*OED*). Room leading to an apartment beyond, often used as a waiting-room (*Curl*, 1999 ed. only).

apartment, n. [l. *partimentum*, F. *appartement*] A part of a house allotted to the use of any particular person; a room (*Johnson*). A space enclosed by walls and a ceiling, which latter distinguishes it from a court or area (*Gwilt*). A room in a building; a division in a house, separated from others by partitions; a place separated by inclosure (*Webster*). A portion of a house or building, consisting of a suite or set of rooms, allotted to the use of a particular person or party (*OED*). Self-contained set of rooms for domestic use (also called a flat) on one floor, usually one of several in a large building (*Curl*).

arboretum, n. [l. *arborētum*] A place in a park for foreign plants (*Brown*). A place in a park, nursery, &c., in which a collection of trees, consisting of one of each kind, is cultivated (*Webster*). A place devoted to the cultivation and exhibition of rare trees; a botanical tree-garden (*OED*). Garden containing a collection of trees. Nursery for growing trees (*Curl*).

arcade, n. [F., *arcus*, sp. *arcada*] A continued arch; a walk arched over (*Johnson*). A series of apertures or recesses with arched ceilings or sofites (*Gwilt*). A piazza formed by a row of piers and arches attached to one or more buildings (*Brown*). A covered passage, or a vaulted avenue (*Lafever*). A long, continued arch, or series of arches, elevated on piers or columns; a walk arched above. A long, arched building or gallery, lined on each side with shops (*Webster*). A vaulted place, open at one or both sides; an arched opening or recess in a wall (*OED*). Series of arches on the same plane, supported by colonnettes, columns, piers, or pilasters (*Curl*).

aspect, n. [L. *aspectus*] Look; air; appearance; view (*Johnson*). The quarter of the heavens to which the front of a building faces (*Gwilt*). Look; view; appearance to the eye or the mind; as, to present an object or a subject in its true aspect, or under a double aspect. In astrology, the situation of one planet with respect to another, or the angle formed by the rays of light proceeding from two planets, and meeting the eye. The aspects are five: sextile, 60° (favorable); quartile, 90°; trine, 120° (favorable); opposition, 180°; and conjunction, when they are in the same degree (*Webster*). The action of looking at anything; beholding, contemplation; gaze, view (*OED*).

attic, n., a. [Gr. *ατtikos*, L. *atticus*] Belonging to Athens; and hence, pure; classical; elegant (*Johnson*). A low order of architecture, commonly used over a principal order, never with columns, but usually with antæ or small pilasters (*Gwilt* and *Lafever*). A low crowning story above the main cornice of the front of a house (*Brown*). Pertaining to Attica, in Greece, or to its principal city, Athens. A story in the upper part of either in or above the cornice. A small square pillar with its cornice on the uppermost part of a building. Attics properly form the crown of the building, or a finishing for the other orders, when they are used in the structure (*Webster*). A decorative structure, consisting of a small order (column and entablature) placed above another order of much greater height constituting the main façade (*OED*). (STOREY) In Classical architecture, a storey erected over the main entablature, often with an Attic Order relating to the Orders below, but sometimes treated very plainly (*Curl*).

balcony, n. [F. *blacon*; it. *balcone*] A frame of iron, wood, or stone, before the window of a room (*Johnson*). A projection from the external wall of a house, borne by columns or consoles, and usually placed before windows or openings, and protected on the extremity of the projection by a railing of balusters or ironwork (*Gwilt* and *Lafever*). A stone platform in front of a house projecting from the first-floor, and constructed with a balustrade breast-work (*Brown*). In architecture, a platform or projection from the external wall of a house, or other building, supported by columns, pillars, or consoles, and encompassed with a balustrade. Balconies are common before windows (*Webster*). A kind of platform or open gallery projecting from the wall of a house, supported by pillars, brackets, consoles, and enclosed by a balustrade (*OED*). Platform or open gallery built out from the naked of a wall, supported on brackets, consoles, corbels, or columns, or cantilevered. Normally constructed in front of windows or other apertures, it is unroofed, with a balustrade, parapet, or railing around the platform, is capable of bearing the weight of one or more persons, and is usually slightly below the floor-level within the building. Projecting gallery with seats in an auditorium at a higher level than the stalls (*Curl*).

basement, n. [base, L. *basis*, a pedestal, foot, base] A continued base, extended a considerable length; as around a house, a room, or other piece of building (*Johnson*). The lower story of a building, whether above or below the ground (*Gwilt*). The floor underground or below the ground-floor (*Brown*). In architecture, the ground floor, on which the order or columns which decorate the principal story are places. In modern architecture, a story below the level of the street (*Webster*). The lowest or fundamental portion of a structure (*OED*). Lower part of the walls of a building, especially if distinguished by an architectural treatment, such as rustication or battering, as in Palladian compositions. Storey behind the wall described above, above the ground or wholly or partly underneath it, supporting the principal storey (*Curl*).

bath (room), n. [Sax. *bað*] A bath is either hot or cold, either of art or nature (*Johnson*). An apartment or series of apartments for bathing (*Gwilt*). An apartment for bathing (*Webster*).

bay, n. [F. *baie*] In architecture, a term used to signify the magnitude of a building. In buildings also, used to signify any kind of opening in walls; as a door, window, or even chimney (*Johnson*). The division of a barn or other building (*Gwilt*). A division of a roof, or vaulting of a building, consisting of the space between the beams or arches. A part of a window between the mullions is often called a bay (*Lafever*). Any kind of opening in walls (*Webster*). An opening in a wall; esp. the space between two columns (*OED*). Regular structural subdivision of a building, such as a church: in the latter case the building is divided along its long axis by bays defined by the buttresses, piers, and vaults, with windows inserted into the curtain-wall of each bay. Part of a framed building between the main supporting timbers (*Curl*).

bay window, n. A window jutting outward, and therefore forming a kind of bay or hollow in the room (*Johnson*). A window placed in the bay or bow of a window: called also an oriel window (*Gwilt*). A polygonal window, generally hexagonal or octagonal; they are sometimes carried up to the parapet of the building (*Brown*). A window jutting outwards; called also a bow-window, and an oriel window (*Lafever*). A window jutting out from the wall, as in shops (*Webster*). A window forming a bay or recess in a room, and projecting outwards from the wall, either in a rectangular, polygonal, or semicircular form often called a boy-window (*OED*). Projection from a house-front, circular, rectangular, segmental, or canted on plan, largely filled with windows (*Curl*).

belvedere, n. [L. *bellus*, fine and It. *vidēre*, to see] A raised turret or lantern raised for the enjoyment of a prospect; also a small edifice in gardens, not uncommon in France and Italy (*Gwilt*). An Italian turret-chamber above the roof for viewing the surrounding landscape (*Brown*). A turret, lantern, or cupola, raised above the roof of a building (*Lafever*). In Italian architecture, a pavilion on the top of an edifice; an artificial eminence in a garden (*Webster*). A raised turret or lantern on the top of a house, or a summer-house erected on an eminence in a garden or pleasure-ground, for the purpose of viewing the surrounding scene (*OED*). Any raised structure or tower erected over the roof of a dwelling-house or on a vantage-point in a landscape from which pleasant scenery may be viewed. Such a building in a garden might be in the form of a Classical temple, and is also termed a gazebo, mirador, or summer-house (*Curl*).

boudoir, n. [F. *boudoir*, a place to sulk in] A lady's dressing-room (*Brown*). A small, private room for curiosities (*Webster*). A small elegantly-furnished room, where a lady may retire to be alone, or to receive her intimate friends. Formerly sometimes applied to a man's private apartment (*OED*).

bower, n. [sax. *būr*] A chamber; a private retirement; an arbour in a garden; a shady recess (*Johnson*). An arbour for a summer-seat, a recess arched overhead with a woodbine or other climbing plants (*Brown*). A shelter or covered place in a garden, made with boughs of trees bent and twined together. It differs from arbor in that it may be round or square, whereas an arbor is long and arched (*Webster*). A dwelling, habitation, abode. In early use *lit.* a cottage; in later use a poetical word for abode (*OED*). Room in medieval houses for the exclusive use of women, therefore the precursor of the boudoir. Small dwelling in the country, or a cottage, therefore a cottage orné or deliberately rustic building in a Romantic, Picturesque landscape. Gazebo or other similar garden-building. Shady recess, leafy covert, or place closed in or overarched with branches, deliberately created to look "natural" in a garden or landscape (*Curl*).

cabinet, n. [F. *cabinet*, and L. *cavea*, an excavated place, a cavity] A closet; a small room; a hut or small house; a cot or tent (*Johnson*). A retired room in an edifice set apart for writing, study, or the preservation of any thing curious or valuable. The term is also applied to an apartment at the end of a gallery in which pictures are hung, or small pieces of sculpture, medals, bronzes, and other curiosities are arranged (*Gwilt*). A closet; a small room, or retired apartment. A private room, in which consultations are held. A hut; a cottage; a small house [Obs.] (*Webster*). A little cabin, hut, repository. A room devoted to the arrangement or display of works of art and objects of *vertu* (object of virtue); a museum, picture-gallery (*OED*). Cabin. Relatively small room used for interviews or private conferences by e.g. a sovereign. Small room, often richly ornamented, designed for the display of valuable objects (*Curl*).

ceil or ceiling, n. [L. *caelestia,* the heavenly bodies and *cēlō*, to hide, cover] The inner roof, the upper part (*Johnson*). The upper horizontal or curved surface of an apartment opposite the floor, usually finished with plaster work (*Gwilt* and *Webster*). The action of lining (the roof or walls of) an apartment with boards, or (more rarely) with plaster, etc. A screen of tapestry, a curtain. The wooden lining of the roof or walls of a room; paneling; wainscoting (*OED*). To furnish with a canopy or screen. A ceiling is therefore the visible covering of the underside of a floor which provides the roofing of a room or other space below, and can take many forms (*Curl*).

cell, n. [L. *cella* or *celo*, to conceal] A small close room; hollow place; cave, cavity (*Johnson*). In ancient architecture the part of a temple within the walls (*Gwilt*). An enclosed space within the walls of an ancient temple (*Lafever*). A small or close apartment, as in a prison, or a bath. A cottage; a cave; a small or mean place of residence (*Webster*). A small apartment, room or dwelling (*OED*). Small apartment of any sort, such as a room in a dormitory or inn, but especially a confined study-bedroom allotted to a monk or nun in a monastery (*Curl*).

cellar, n. [L. *cellarium*, and F. *cellier*] A place under ground, where stores and liquors are reposited (*Johnson*). The lower story of a building, when wholly or partly under the level of the ground (*Gwilt*). A room under a house or other building, used as a repository of liquors, provisions, and other stores for a family (*Webster*). A store-house or store-room, whether above or below ground, for provisions; a granary, buttery, or pantry (*OED*). Subterranean or partly underground room or rooms within a building, normally without windows, for the storage of fuel, provisions, wines, etc. rather than as living-space (*Curl*).

chamber, n. [F. *chambre* and L. *camera*] An apartment in a house (*Johnson*). Properly a room vaulted or arched, but the word is now generally used in a more restricted sense to signify an apartment appropriated to lodging (*Gwilt*). An apartment in an upper story, or in a story above the lower floor of a dwelling-house, often used as a lodging-room (*Webster*). A room or apartment in a house; usually one appropriated to the use of one person; a private room, in later use esp. a sleeping apartment, a bedroom. A hall appropriated to the meetings of a deliberative, legislative, or judicial body. An enclosed space; a cavity (*OED*).

closet, n. [F. *clos*] A small room of privacy and retirement. A private repository of curiosities and valuable things (*Johnson*). A small apartment frequently made to communicate with a bed-chamber, and used as a dressing room. Sometimes a closet is made for the reception of stores, and is then called a store closet (*Gwilt*). A small room or apartment for retirement; any room for privacy. An apartment for curiosities or valuable things (*Webster*). A room for privacy or retirement. A private repository of valuables or curiosities. A small side-room or recess for storing utensils, provisions, etc.; a cupboard (*OED*). Private audience-chamber. Oratory. Dressing-room adjacent to a larger room. Cupboard. Secluded study. Private pew in a church. Store. Water closet (*Curl*).

colonnade, n. [L. *columnātus*, supported by pillars] A peristyle of a circular figure, or a series or range of pillars or columns (*Johnson*). A range of columns. When a colonnade is in front of a building, it is called a portico, when surrounding a building a peristyle (*Gwilt*). A row or columns, sometimes consisting of two, between which is a passage (*Brown*). A range of columns, whether attached or insulated, and supporting an entablature (*Lafever*). In architecture, a series or range of columns, placed at regular intervals (*Webster*). A series of columns placed at regular intervals and supporting an entablature (*OED*). Series of columns in a straight line supporting an entablature: when standing before a building, supports a roof, and serves as a porch, it is a portico; and if it is carried around three or four sides of a building exterior or round a court or garden it is a peristyle (*Curl*).

conservatory, n. [L. *cōnservātiō*, a keeping, preserving] A place where anything is kept in a manner proper to its peculiar nature; as, fish in a pond, corn in a granary (*Johnson*). A building for preserving curious and rare exotic plants (*Gwilt*). A house with much glass and attached to a dwelling-house for preserving exotic plants (*Brown*). A large green-house for exotics, in which the plants are planted in beds and borders, and not in tubs, or pots, as in the common green-house (*Webster*). A place where things are preserved or kept securely; a storehouse, a repository. A greenhouse for tender flowers or plants; now, usually an ornamental house into which plants in bloom are brought from the hot-house or greenhouse (*OED*). Grander and more ornamental version of a glasshouse or greenhouse used for conserving plants, either a detached structure or one joined to a dwelling, heated and kept humid. Public building devoted to the cultivation of, and instruction in, any branch of art or science, especially music (*Curl*).

corridor, n. [F. and L. *currō*, to hasten, hurry, and It. *corridore*] A gallery or long isle round a building, leading to several chambers at a distance from each other (*Johnson*). A gallery or passage round a quadrangle leading to the various apartments. Also, any gallery of communication to them (*Gwilt*). A passage open on the sides, but covered above (*Brown*). A gallery or open communication to the different apartments of a house (*Lafever*). In architecture, a gallery or open communication round a building, leading to several chambers at a distance from each other. In fortification, the covered way lying round the whole compass of the fortifications of a place (*Webster*). A passage, covered walk, or avenue between two places (*OED*).

cottage, n. [Sax., from *cot*] and L. *cottīdiānus*, everyday, ordinary] A hut, a mean habitation; a cot; a little house (*Johnson*). A small house or dwelling for a poor person (*Gwilt*). A cot; a hut; a small habitation for poor persons (*Webster*). A dwelling-house of small size and humble character, such as is occupied by farm-labourers, villagers, miners, etc (*OED*). Small, single-storey dwelling, sometimes with sleeping-quarters in the roof-space, inhabited by agricultural workers, built of cheap materials such as adobe, cob, pisé, rubble, etc., and roofed with thatch, turf, etc (*Curl*).

dining or dinner room, n. [dine, F. *dîner*] The principal apartment of the house; the room where entertainments are made (*Johnson*). Generally one of the largest rooms in a dwelling-house (*Gwilt*). Room for dining in (*Brown*). A room for a family or for company to dine in; a room for entertainments (*Webster*). The room in a private house or public establishment in which dinner and other principal meals are taken, and which is furnished for this purpose (*OED*).

drawing or withdrawing room, n. [OE. *dragan*, pull] The room in which company assemble at court (*Johnson*). The apartment to which the company *withdraw* after dinner (*Gwilt*). Withdrawing-room—commonly called drawing-room, a handsome and elegant room to which the family in the best houses retire after dinner (*Brown*). A room appropriated for the reception of company; a room in which distinguished personages hold levees, or private persons receive parties (*Webster*). A room to withdraw to, a private chamber attached to a more public room; now, a room reserved for the reception of company, and to which the ladies withdraw from the dining-room after dinner (*OED*).

dressing room, n. [F. *dresser*, to make straight] The room in which clothes are put on (*Johnson*). A room generally adjoining to and communicating with the sleeping room, used, as the name implies, for dressing in (*Gwilt*). A small room adjoining the bedroom (*Brown*). An apartment appropriated for dressing the person (*Webster*). A room for dressing and the toiler, usually opening from a bed-room (*OED*).

dressing(s), n. Attire; ornament; habiliment; outward appearance (*Johnson*). All kinds of mouldings beyond the naked walls or ceilings are called by the general name of dressings (*Gwilt*). The mouldings and sculptured decorations of all kinds, which are used on the walls and ceilings of a building for the purpose of ornament (*Lafever*). In architecture, dressings are mouldings round doors, windows, &c (*Webster*). Applied to various technical processes in arts and manufactures (*OED*). General term for all finishes, mouldings, ornaments, dressed stones, and the like (often projecting) around an aperture such as a door or window, and distinguished from the rest of the plain surface of the naked of a wall (*Curl*).

entrance, entry, n. [L. *intrā*, towards the inside and F. e*ntrée*, to put into a trance] A passage; the act of entering (*Johnson*). The door, gate, passage or avenue, by which a place may be entered. Commencement; initiation; beginning. The act of taking possession, as of land . . . or into office (*Webster*). The action of coming or going in (*OED*). Term used to describe the position of the main entrance to a medieval timber-framed house (*Curl*).

floor, n. [OE., Sax. *floꞃe*] The bottom of a room; the part on which one treads; a story; a flight of rooms (*Johnson*). The pavement or boarded lower horizontal surface of an apartment (*Gwilt*). That part of a building or room on which we walk; the bottom or lower part, consisting, in modern houses, of boards, planks, or pavement (*Webster*). The layer of boards, brick, stone, etc. in an apartment, on which people tread; the under surface of the interior of a room. In legislative assemblies, the part of the house where the members sit, and from which they speak. The right of speaking; as to get or obtain the floor. An artificial platform, or leveled space, for the carrying on of some industry, esp. threshing (*OED*). Division between one storey and another. Set of rooms and landings, on the same level, i.e. in one storey. Layer of boards, etc., on which people tread, and i.e. the surface of the floor in the room (*Curl*).

gable, n. [Brit. *gavel*] The fore-front or end of a house coming down right (*Johnson*). The vertical triangular piece of wall at the end of a roof, from the level of the eaves to the summit (*Gwilt*). The angle-pointed masonry above the end of a Tudor building, answering to the pediment of the Greek temple (*Brown*). The upright triangular end of a building, from the level of the cornice or eaves to the summit (*Lafever*). The triangular end of a house or other building, from the cornice or eaves to the top. In America, it is usually called the gable-end (*Webster*). The vertical triangular piece of wall at the end of a ridged roof, from the level of the eaves to the summit (*OED*). Wall of a building, closing the end of a pitched roof: its top may be bounded by the two slopes of the roof forming parged verges or overhangs with barge-boards, or it may be a parapet following (more or less) the slopes of the roof behind (*Curl*).

gallery, n. [F. *galerie* and L. *galea,* a helmet, metal covering] A kind of a walk along the floor of a house, into which the doors of the apartments open; in general, any building of which the length much exceeds the breadth (*Johnson*). An apartment of a house, for different purposes. A common passage to several rooms in any upper story is called a gallery (*Gwilt*). An oblong room for pictures or statues (*Brown*). An apartment generally of greater length in proportion to the width; a common passage to several rooms in any upper story; a long room for the reception of pictures; also, the platform on piers, or projecting from the wall of a church or other building, and open in front to the central space. The term is, moreover, used to denote porticoes formed with long ranges of columns on one side (*Lafever*). In architecture, a covered part of a building, commonly in the wings, used as an ambulatory or place for walking. An ornamental walk or apartment in gardens, formed by trees. In churches, a floor elevated on columns, and furnished with pews or seats. A similar structure in a play-house. In fortification, a covered walk across the ditch of a town, made of beams covered with planks and loaded with earth (*Webster*). A covered space for walking in, partly open at the side, or having the roof supported by pillars; a piazza, portico, colonnade (*OED*). Large internal passage, often a grand room on the upper floor of an Elizabethan or Jacobean house, called long gallery, extending the full length of a façade, and used to display pictures and tapestries, for recreation, and as a connecting corridor (*Curl*).

garret, n. [Scot. *garret*, a watch-tower, from the same root as guard] The uppermost room of a house (*Johnson*). The upper story of a house taken either partially or wholly from the space within the roof (*Gwilt*). A room in the roof (*Brown*). That part of a house which is on the upper floor, immediately under the roof (*Webster*). A turret projecting from the top of a tower or from the parapet of a fortification; a watchtower. A room on the uppermost floor of a house; an apartment formed either partially or wholly within the roof, an attic (*OED*). Space in a building beneath the roof-covering and above the uppermost storey of flat-ceilinged rooms, therefore with sloping sides. It may be unlit, or illuminated with roof-lights, dormers, etc. Not to be confused with an Attic (*Curl*).

greenhouse, n. [Teut. root *gro*, grow, and *hus*] A conservatory for plants, &c. A house in which tender plants are sheltered from the weather (*Johnson*). A building for sheltering in pots plants which are too tender to endure the open air the greater part of the year. It is constructed with a roof and one or more sides of glass, and being one constructed for luxury should not be far away from the dwelling-house, so that the greatest enjoyment may be had from it. At the same time it should, if possible, be near the flower-garden, as being of similar character in use (*Gwilt*). A house in which tender plants are sheltered from the weather, and preserved green during the winter or cold weather (*Webster*). A glass-house in which delicate and tender plants are reared and preserved (*OED*). See conservatory (*Curl*).

hall, n. [Sax. *heall*] A court of justice; the first large room of a house (*Johnson*). A name applied indifferently to the first large apartment on entering a house, to the public room of a corporate body, a court of justice, or to a manor house (*Gwilt*). An ancient mansion-house. The first open space or room on entering a mansion; a dining-room for servants (*Brown*). In architecture, a large room at the entrance of a house or palace. An edifice in which courts of justice are held. A room for a corporation or public assembly; as, a town-hall (*Webster*). A large place covered by a roof; in early times applied to any spacious roofed place, without or with subordinate chambers attached; a temple, palace, court, royal residence (*OED*). Main roof of a medieval house or the large, communal room of a college, etc., often an open-hall, open to the roof, and sometimes with an open hearth. Any large roofed volume (*Curl*).

hip, or hipped roof, n. [OE *hype*, projection] A roof whose ends slant back at the same angle with the adjacent sides, also called hip-roof (*Gwilt* and *Webster*). A projecting inclined edge on a roof, extending from the ridge or apex to the eaves, and having a slope on each side (*OED*). Sloping salient angle of a roof where two sides (*skirts*) join. Rafter at this angle (*Curl*).

kitchen, n. [Sax. *cyćene*; g. *küche,* F. *cuisine*, and L. *coquere*, to prepare by cooking] The room in a house where the provisions are cooked. A room used for cookery, &c (*Johnson*). The apartment or office of a house wherein the operations of cookery are carried on (*Gwilt*). A room for dressing victuals in; during the middle period, these rooms were spacious and noble (*Brown*). A cook-room; the room of a house appropriated to cookery (*Webster*). That room or part of a house in which food is cooked; a place fitted with the apparatus for cooking (*OED*).

laundry, n. [F. *lavanderie* and L. *lavātiō*, a washing] The room in which clothes are washed (*Johnson*). It should be spacious and well supplied with every convenience for mangling, drying, and ironing the linen of a family (*Gwilt*). A room for drying and ironing clothes (*Brown*). The place or room where clothes are washed (*Webster*). An apartment or establishment, where linen, etc. is washed and "got up" (*OED*).

library, n. [L. *librārium* and *liber*, any writing material, book, treatise] A large collection of books, publick or private (*Johnson*). An edifice or apartment for the reception of a collection of books (*Gwilt*). A room for books, situated at the east end of a house (*Brown*). A collection of books belonging to a private person, or to a public institution or a company (*Webster*). A place set apart to contain books for reading, study, or reference (*OED*).

loggia or loggie, n. [It. *loggia*] An inner open gallery or colonnade round a building, with a court in the middle (*Brown*). In its strict meaning, a lodge; but usually signifying an open gallery (*Lafever*). A gallery or arcade having one or more of its sides open to the air (*OED*). Roofed structure, open on at least one side, essentially a gallery, an arcade, or colonnade, affording a protected seating-place with a view, common in Italy, and often with architectural pretensions. Lodge, in the sense of a building in a park (*Curl*).

museum, (see note 4) [L. *mūsēum*, a seat of the muses, library, academy, study, and Gr. *μουσειον*] A repository of learned curiosities (*Johnson*). A repository of natural, scientific, and literary curiosities, or of works of art (*Gwilt* and *Webster*). A house or apartment dedicated to the pursuit of learning or the arts; a "home" of the Muses; a scholar's "study." A building or portion of a building used as a repository for the preservation and exhibition of objects illustrative of antiquities, natural history, fine and industrial art, or some particular branch of any of these subjects, either generally or with reference to a definite region or period. Also applied to the collection of objects itself (*OED*).

nursery, n. [L. *nūtrīcāre*, to nourish, to bring up] A place where children are nursed and brought up; a plot of ground for raising young trees for transplantation (*Johnson*). Ground, in which various shrubs and young plants are reared and propagated (*Brown*). The place or apartment in a house appropriated to the care of children. A place where young trees are propagated for the purpose of being transplanted. The place where any thing is fostered and the growth promoted. That which forms and educates (*Webster*). Fosterage, upbringing, breeding; nursing (*OED*).

office(s), n. [F. and L. *officium*, a kind of service, to make or do, duty] To perform; to discharge; to do public employment, agency (*Johnson*). The apartments wherein the domestics discharge the several duties attached to the service of a house; as kitchens, pantries, brewhouses, and the like (*Gwilt* and *Webster*). A house or apartment in which public officers and others transact business (*Webster*). A place for the transaction of private or public business of some kind; often including "staff" by which the business is conducted, or denominating the department of which they are officers (*OED*). Place for the transaction of private or public business, e.g. room or department in which the paperwork of an establishment is dealt with. In the plural, those parts of a house, or buildings attached to it, used for the kitchens, pantry, laundry, scullery, etc., sometimes including stables, barns, out-houses, etc (*Curl*).

oriel, or oriol, n. [Old F. *oriol* and L. *orīrī*, to rise, to get up] A little waste room next to the hall, where particular persons dine. A sort of recess (*Johnson*). A large bay or recessed window in a hall, chapel, or other apartment. It ordinarily projects from the outer face of the wall either in a semi-octagonal or diagonal plan, and is of varied kinds and sizes (*Gwilt*). A small semicircular window projecting from an upper story, and resting on clustered mouldings. Their origin is eastern, and in the monastic edifices, those recesses were appropriated to places of prayer for the abbot

(*Brown*). A large bay or recessed window in a hall, chapel, or other apartment. It projects from the outer face of the wall, mostly of a triagonal or pentagonal form (*Lafever*). A small apartment next a hall, where particular persons dine; a sort of recess (*Webster*). A large recess with a window, of polygonal plan, projecting from the outer face of the wall of a building, usually, in an upper story, and wither supported from the ground or on corbels. Formerly sometimes forming a small private apartment attached to a hall, or the like (*OED*). Large bay-window projecting from the naked of a wall on an upper storey, supported on brackets, corbels, a pier, or engaged column (*Curl*).

ornament, n. [F. *orné*, ornate and L. *ōrnāmentum*] Embellishment; decoration; connect to particular style (*Johnson*). The smaller and detailed part of the work, not essential to it, but serving to enrich it; it is generally founded upon some imitation of the works of nature (*Gwilt*). In architecture, ornaments are sculpture or carved work. Embellishment; decoration; additional beauty (*Webster*). Any adjunct or accessory (primarily for use but not excluding decoration or embellishment); equipment, furniture, attire, trappings (*OED*). Decorative devices, not essential to structure, but often necessary to emphasize or diminish the impact of structural elements, sometimes with iconographic roles (*Curl*).

pantry, n. [F. *paneterie* and L. *pānis*, bread] A place formerly used solely for the keeping of bread. A room in which provisions are reposited (*Johnson*). A room or apartment in a house, etc., in which bread and other provisions are kept; also, one in which the plate, linen, etc., for the table are kept (*Brown* and *OED*). An apartment or closet in which provisions are kept (*Webster*).

parlor or parlour, n. [F. *parler*, to speak and L. *pariter*, equally] A room in houses on the first floor, elegantly furnished for reception or entertainment (*Johnson*). A room for conversation, which in the old monasteries adjoined the buttery and pantry at the lower end of the hall. At the present day it is used to denote the room in a house where common visitors are received (*Gwilt*). A small room set apart to receive visitors, a room for conversation (*Brown*). Primarily, the apartment of a nunnery where the nuns are permitted to meet and converse with each other; hence, with us, the room in a house which the family usually occupy, and where when they have no company, as distinguished from a drawing room intended for the reception of company, or from a dining room, when a distinct apartment is allotted for that purpose. In most houses, *the parlor* is also the dining room (*Webster*). An apartment in a monastery for conversation with persons from outside, or among inmates. A smaller room set aside apart from the great hall, for private conversation or conference (*OED*). Apartment in, e.g., a monastery for conversation with outsiders or among inmates. Room set apart from the larger hall for private conversations, e.g. mayor's parlour in a town hall. Sitting-room in a dwelling-house. Dining- or supper-room (*Curl*).

partition, n. [L. *partīre*, to share, part] The act of dividing, division (*Johnson*). A wall of stone, brick, or timber, dividing one room from another. When a partition has no support from below, it should not be suffered to bear on the floor with any considerable weight, and in such cases it should have a truss formed within it, in which case it is called a trussed partition (*Gwilt*). That by which different parts are separated; as a partition of wood or stone in a building (*Webster*). The action of parting or dividing into parts; division (*OED*). Screen. Non-loadbearing wall dividing a space into parts (*Curl*).

passage(s), n. [F. and L. *pāssim*, by spreading] The act of passing; journey; incident; road; narrow street; part of a book (*Johnson*). The avenues leading to the various divisions and apartments of a building. When there is only one series of rooms in breadth, the passage must run along one side of the building, and may be lighted by apertures through the exterior walls. If there be more than one room in breadth, it must run in the middle, and be lighted from above or at one or both ends (*Gwilt*). The act of passing or moving by land or water, or through the air or other substances (*Webster*). The action of passing; a going or moving onward, across, or past; movement from one place or point to another, or over or through a space or medium; transition, transit (*OED*).

pavilion, n. [F. *pavillon* and L. *pāpiliō*, a butterfly, tent (like butterfly wings), and It. *padiglione*] A tent; a temporary or movable house (*Johnson*). The term is also applied to the projecting parts in the front of a building (*Gwilt* and *Webster*). An oriental palace or princely summer residence (*Brown*). A turret or small building, generally insulated and comprised under a single roof (*Lafever*). In architecture, a kind of turret or building, usually insulated and contained under a single roof; sometimes square and sometimes in the form of a dome. Sometimes a pavilion is a projecting part in the front of a building; sometimes it flanks a corner. A movable habitation (*Webster*). A tent: chiefly applied to one of a large or stately kind, riding to a peak above (*OED*). Central, flanking, or intermediate projecting subdivision of a monumental building or façade, accented architecturally by more elaborate decoration. Feature at the angle of a building, or terminating feature of a wing of a larger structure, as in a symmetrical Palladian composition. One of several distinct buildings or blocks, linked by e.g. corridors, as in a hospital or gaol, for reasons of hygiene or security. Detached ornamental building, such as a gazebo or a summer-house, often, but not always, dependent on a larger or principal building. Temporary building. Covering or canopy, so a tent-like structure, such as a canopied litter or the velarium over an amplitheatre (*Curl*).

piazza, n. [F. *place*, It. *plazza* and Sp. *plaza*] A walk under a roof supported by pillars (*Johnson*). A square open space surrounded by buildings. The term is very frequently and very ignorantly used to denote a walk under an arcade (*Gwilt* and *Webster*). Generally understood of an arcade or colonnade; though, properly speaking, it is the square which the colonnade surrounds (*Brown*). An open area or square; a covered walk or portico (*Lafever*). A portico or covered walk supported by arches or columns (*Webster*). A public square or market-place; originally, and still usually, one of an Italian town; but in 16th to 18th c. often applied more widely to any open space surrounded by buildings, as the parade ground in a fort or the like (*OED*). Open space, square, or market-place, surrounded by buildings and approached by various streets. Any covered way, colonnade walk, or pentice. Open porch or verandah (*Curl*).

plan, n. [L. *plānus,* level, flat, even] A scheme, form, draught, model (*Johnson*). The representation of the horizontal section of a building, showing its distribution, the form and extent of its various parts (*Gwilt*). A draught or form; properly, the representation of any thing drawn on a plane, as a map or chart, which is a representation of some portion of land or water. A scheme devised; a project; the form of something to be done existing in the mind, with the several parts adjusted in idea, expressed in words or committed to writing (*Webster*). A drawing, sketch, or diagram of any object, made by projection upon a flat surface, usually a horizontal plane (*OED*). Horizontal section through a building showing the arrangement of rooms, etc. It is a drawing that represents an object in horizontal projection, to scale, as distinct from those representing vertical sections or elevations, and might show an exterior of an object as seen from above, as in a roof-plan (*Curl*).

porch, n. [F. *porche,* It. *portico* and L. *porticus*] A roof supported by pillars before a door; an entrance (*Johnson*). An exterior appendage to a building, forming a covered approach to one of its principal doorways (*Gwilt* and *Lafever*). A projecting entrance inclosed at the two sides, and open with an arch in front (*Brown*). An exterior appendage to a building, forming a covered approach to one of its principal doorways; a kind of vestibule supported by pillars. Any small portico considerably lower than the main structure to which it is attached may be so termed, in contradistinction from one carried up the height of the building, or as high as the principal cornice (*Lafever*). In *architecture*, a kind of vestibule, at the entrance of temples, halls, churches or other buildings. A portico; a covered walk. By way of distinction, the porch was a public portico in Athens, where Zeno, the philosopher, taught his disciples (*Webster*). An exterior structure forming a covered approach to the entrance of a building; sometimes applied to an interior space serving as a vestibule (*OED*). Covered place of entrance and exit attached to a building and projecting in front of its main mass, such as the south porch of a medieval church, often with a room over it (*Curl*).

portico, n. [L. *porticus*] A covered walk, a piazza (*Johnson*). See colonnade (*Gwilt*). A projecting entrance formed with pillars supporting an entablature, and pediment roof above (*Brown*). In architecture, originally, a colonnade or covered ambulatory; but at present, a covered space, inclosed by columns at the entrance of a building (*Lafever* and *Webster*). A covered ambulatory consisting of a roof supported by columns placed at regular intervals, usually attached as a porch to a building, but sometimes forming a separate structure; a colonnade; a pergola in a garden (*OED*). Covered ambulatory consisting of a series of columns placed at regular intervals supporting a roof, normally attached as a colonnaded porch to a building, but sometimes forming a separate structure. The volume so created can be open or partly enclosed at the sides, stand before a building such as a temple, and often have a pediment over the front, in which case it is described as a temple-front (*Curl*).

prospect, n. [L. *prōspectāre,* to look forward, view] A view; an object of view; view of something distant (*Johnson*). A view of things within reach of the eye. View delineated or painted; picturesque representation of a landscape (*Webster*). The action or fact of looking forth or out, or of seeing to a distance; the condition (of a building, or station of any kind) of facing or being so situated as to have its front in a specified direction; outlook, aspect, exposure (*OED*). (TOWER) Tall building on high ground commanding a view, called a look-out or standing tower (*Curl*).

roof, n. [Sax. *rof,* to cover] The cover of a house; the inside of the arch that covers a building; the palate (*Johnson*). The exterior covering of a building (*Gwilt* and *Lafever*). The cover or upper part of a house or other building, consisting of rafters covered with boards, shingles, or tiles, with a side or sides sloping from the ridge, for the purpose of carrying off the water that falls in rain or snow (*Webster*). The outside upper covering of a house or other building: also, the ceiling of a room or other covered part of a house, building, etc (*OED*). Covering of any building by which its fabric and habitants are protected from the inclemencies of the weather (*Curl*).

room, n. [Sax., Dan., Sw. *rūm*, space, G. *raum*, and L. *rūs*, the country] Space, extent of place great or small; stead; chamber (*Johnson*). An interior space or division of a house, separated from the remainder of it by walls or partitions, and entered by a doorway (*Gwilt*). Space; compass; extent of place, great or small. Space or place unoccupied. Place for reception or admission of any thing. Place of another; stead; as in succession or substitution. Unoccupied opportunity (*Webster*). Space; dimensional extent. A seat. To make room, to open a space or place for any thing. To give room, to withdraw; to leave space unoccupied for others to pass or to be seated (*OED*).

rural, a. [L. *ruralis, rūs*, the country] Belonging to the country (*Johnson*). Pertaining or belonging to the country, as distinguished from a city or town; suiting the country, or resembling it (*Webster*). Of persons: living in the country; having the standing, qualities, or manners of peasants or country-folk; engaged in country occupation; agriculture or pastoral (*OED*). (ARCHITECTURE) Buildings associated with the countryside, but especially C18 and C19 cottages ornés and fremes ornées or other buildings designed to suggest the rural ideal, as in a Picturesque landscape, using free compositions, asymmetry, vernacular detail, and materials such as roughcast, thatch, rubble, etc (*Curl*).

rustic, n. [L. *rūsticātiō*, country-life] Rural, rude, simple, plain, rough, savage (*Johnson*). (ORDER) A species of building wherein the faces of the stones are hatched or picked with the point of a hammer (*Gwilt*). (WORK) A mode of building masonry wherein the faces of the stones are left rough, the sides only being wrought smooth where the union of the stones takes place (*Gwilt* and *Lafever*). (BUILDING) A building composed of rough stones of any kind (*Brown*). (COTTAGE) A cottage built with rough stones and flints, and unbarked pollard-trees for pillars, casement windows, picturesque roofs, and diagonal chimney-shafts (*Brown*). In architecture, a term denoting a species of masonry, the joints of which are worked with grooves or channels, to render them conspicuous. The surface of the work is sometimes left or purposely made rough, and sometimes even or smooth (*Webster*). Species of masonry characterized by surfaces artificially roughened or left rough-hewn, or by having the joints, notably the horizontal ones, emphasized by being deeply sunk or chamfered (*Curl*).

scullery, (see note 5) [Scot. *skul, skoll,* a bowl, shell, skull] A place to clean and keep dishes (*Johnson*). The apartment for washing up the dishes and utensils wherein the scullion works (*Gwilt*). A place where dishes, kettles and other culinary utensils are kept (*Webster*). The department of a household concerned with the care of the plates, dishes, and kitchen utensils. Also the room or rooms in which the work of this department is carried on (*OED*).

terrace, n. [F. *terrasse,* It. *terrazzo,* and L. *terra,* earth] A mound or earth covered with grass or gravel (*Johnson*). An area raised before a building above the level of the ground to serve as a walk. The word is sometimes but improperly used to denote a balcony or gallery (*Gwilt*). A raised walk in front of a house, laid with gravel, and inclosed with a dwarf balustrade wall (*Brown*). A raised level space or platform of earth, supported on one or more sides by a wall or bank of turf &c., used either for cultivation or for a promenade. A balcony or open gallery. The flat roof of a house (*Webster*). A raised level place for walking, with a vertical or sloping front or sides faced with masonry, turf, or the like, and sometimes having a balustrade; esp. a raised walk in a garden, or a level surface formed in front of a house on naturally sloping ground, or on the bank of a river (*OED*). Embankment or prepared and leveled mass of earth in e.g. a garden. Any artificial or built level platform for promenading, with a vertical or sloping front or sides faced with masonry, turf, etc., and sometimes having a balustrade, often adjacent to a country-house. Loggia or external usable space, e.g. roof-garden. Series of houses joined together in one row (*Curl*).

umbrage, n. [F. *ombrage* and L. *umbra*] Shade; shadow; offence, resentment (*Johnson*). A shade; a screen of trees. Shadow; slight appearance (*Webster*). Shade or shadow cast by trees or the like. A shadowy appearance or indication, a semblance, outline, or faint representation, a glimmering or trace, of something. A feeling or suspicion or doubt (*OED*).

veranda(h), n. [Hindi, *varandā*] An oriental word denoting a kind of open portico, formed by extending a sloping roof beyond the main building (*Webster*). An open portico or light roofed gallery extending along the front (and occas. other sides) of a dwelling or other building, freq. having a front of lattice-work, and erected chiefly as a protection or shelter from the sun or rain (*OED*). Light external open gallery, or covered way, with a sloping or lean-to roof carried by slender (usually metal) columns or posts, attached to a building, often in front of the windows of the principal rooms, affording shelter from the sun as well as a pleasant external seating area with access from French windows. Sometimes it can be very decorative, with trellis-work and plants, and may extend all round a house, forming a skirt-roof. It was a feature that became popular from the early C19 (*Curl*).

vestibule, n. [F. and L. *vestibulum* and *vesta*, goddess of the fire burning on the hearth, and of domestic life] The porch or first entrance of a house (*Johnson*). An apartment which serves as the medium of communication to another room or series of rooms (*Gwilt*). An ante-hall, lobby, or inner porch (*Brown*). The porch, or the first entrance of a house (*Lafever*). The porch or entrance into a house, or a large open space before the door, but covered. A little antechamber before the entrance of an ordinary apartment. An apartment in large buildings, which leads into a hall or suit of rooms or offices (*Webster*). The enclosed or partly enclosed space in front of the main entrance of a Roman or Greek house or building, an entrance-court or fore-court. A chamber or hall immediately between the entrance-door and the interior of a building or house (*OED*). Enclosed or partly enclosed space in front of the main entrance of a Greek or Roman house or building, i.e. an entrance-court or fore-court. Entrance-lobby or hall immediately between the entrance-door and the interior of a building. Ante-chamber acting as a baffle between e.g. a corridor and a room, really a communication-lobby (*Curl*).

villa, vill, n. [F. and L. *villa*] A small collection of houses; a country seat; a village (*Johnson*). A country-house for the residence of an opulent person. Among the Romans there were three descriptions of villa, each having its particular destination, namely, the *villa urbana*, which was the residence of the proprietor, and contained all the conveniences of a mansion in the city. The *villa rustica*, which contained not only all that was essential to rural economy, such as barns, stables, &c., but comprised lodging apartments for all those who ministered in the operations of the farming establishment. The *villa fructuaria* was appropriated to the preservation of the different productions of the estate, and contained the granaries, magazines for the oil, cellars for the wine, &c (*Gwilt*). A Roman country-seat, some of which were most splendid and extensive (*Brown*). A country seat; usually one for the residence of a wealthy person (*Webster*). A country mansion or residence, together with a farm, farm-buildings, or other houses attached, built or occupied by a person of some position and wealth; a country seat or estate; in later and more general use, a residence in the country, in the neighbourhood of a town, usually of some size and architectural elegance and standing its own grounds (*OED*). Antique Roman country-house or farmstead of three basic types: *villa rustica*, house in the country with spacious accommodation for the owner and his family, and quarters for staff and workers, stores, and animals (the latter called *villa fructuaria*). It was really a grand farmhouse with refinements; *villa suburban*: house near a town, lacking service buildings; *villa urbana*: essentially a retreat, with spacious rooms, access to agreeable gardens, fine views over the landscape and the sea (if possible), galleries, and parts suitable for summer and winter use. Renaissance country-house that was almost a cultural centre, where the like-minded could enjoy civilized life in beautiful surroundings, with fine gardens, works of art, and pleasant views. Detached C19 house set in its own grounds on the fringes of a town, often with outbuildings and winds. Small detached house in a modest garden in the suburbs in the late C19 and C20 (*Curl*).

wall, n. [L. *vallum,* stakes for palisading, a palisaded rampart, entrenchment] A partition of brick or stone, &c (*Johnson*). A body of materials for the enclosure of a building and the support of its various parts (*Gwilt*). A work or structure of stone, brick, of other materials, raised to some height, and intended for a defense or security (*Webster*). A rampart of earth, stone, or other material constructed for defensive purposes (*OED*). Structure of stone, brick, etc., serving to enclose a room, house, or other space, and, in most cases, load-bearing, i.e. supporting the floors, roof, etc. It may also be a screen-wall for privacy or enclosure (*Curl*).

water closet, n. [OE *wæter*] A closet for easing nature, having a contrivance for carrying off the discharges by a stream of water through a waste-pipe below (*Webster*). A closet or small room fitted up to serve as a privy, and furnished with water-supply to flush the pan and discharge its contents into a waste-pipe below (*OED*).

window, n. [Dan. *vindue*, Sp. *ventana* and OE. *ēağ duru*, an eye door] An opening in a house for light and air; the glass it contains (*Johnson*). An aperture in a wall for the transmission of light to an apartment (*Gwilt*). An opening in the wall of a building for the admission of light, and of air when necessary. An aperture or opening. The frame or other thing that covers the aperture. Lattice or casement; or the network of wire used before the invention of glass (*Webster*). An opening in a wall or side of a building, ship, or carriage, to admit light or air, or both, and to afford a view of what is outside or inside (*OED*). Aperture in a wall to allow light and air to enter a building (*Curl*).

NOTES

In the notes and figure captions, Downing's books are cited with the following abbreviations:

ACH	page and figure numbers from the 1968 reprint of *The Architecture of Country Houses* (1850).
CR	page and figure numbers from the 1981 reprint of the 4th edition of *Cottage Residences* (1852 edition).
RE	page and figure numbers from the 1974 reprint of *Rural Essays* (1853).
TPLG	page numbers from the 1991 reprint of the 4th edition of *A Treatise on the Theory and Practice of Landscape Gardening* (1849 edition).

INTRODUCTION

1. Downing, "A Few Words on Rural Architecture," *The Horticulturist* 4 (July, 1850), 11, and *RE*, 208.
2. Lynes, *The Tastemakers*, 22.
3. Editorial, *The Horticulturist* 9 (September, 1852).
4. "It's hard to imagine any book with the words 'theory' and 'practice' in the title being so popular today, but that doesn't mean it's not needed." Carmer, *The Hudson*, 177.
5. Sedgwick in Bremer, *The Homes of the New World*, 46.
6. Tucker, *The Cultivator* VI (June, 1849), 200. Tatum, *Andrew Jackson Downing*, 66.

CHAPTER 1

1. Letter from Downing to Robert Donaldson, January 21, 1842 (Courtesy of Richard H. Jenrette).
2. Tax records show a 16' x 20' single frame house with a 12' x 24' joiner's shop on a 4¼ acre property valued at $150 (Newburgh Free Library).

3. Charles lived a few miles north of Newburgh in Balmville and was one of the country's foremost pomologists.
4. Carmer, *The Hudson*, 172, and Handlin, *The American Home, Architecture and Society*, 41, 42. For further Downing biographical information, see Tatum, *Andrew Jackson Downing.*
5. The population in America rose between 1830 and 1850 from a little less than thirteen million to over twenty-three million of which many were English, Irish, German, Dutch, Belgian, Swiss and Scandinavian immigrants entering through Eastern ports. Fish, *The Rise of the Common Man*, 110.
6. Irving, *Letters*, 40–42.
7. Historians use DeWint, although De Windt is the spelling on Caroline's tombstone.
8. Bremer, *The Homes of the New World*, 19–22.
9. DeWint and Downing were in a financial lawsuit from 1846 to April of 1849 when it was settled in Downing's favor. See Schuyler, *Apostle of Taste*, 89. For an account of the Fishkill area in 1817 in general and DeWint in particular, see Haydon, *Upstate Travels*, 33–35.
10. A full description of the house and grounds was published in Hovey's *Magazine of Horticulture*, Vol. VII, No. XI (November, 1841), 401–14, and are reprinted in De Wolf, Jr., "Andrew Jackson Downing and Pomology," in Tatum and MacDougall, eds., *Prophet with Honor*, 153–63. Also see text by C. C. (Clarence Cook) and drawings by Withers in *The Horticulturist* 8 (January and February, 1853). For a complete history and description see Downs, "Downing's Newburgh Villa." For images see Tatum, *Andrew Jackson Downing*, fig. 62, and fig. 63 for a Davis designed barn. See Kowsky, *Country, Park & City*, fig. 2.1 for a photograph of the run-down south façade from the early 1920s. For Downing's first-floor plan sketch, see A. J. Davis Documents, Department of Prints and Photographs, Vol. III, Leaf 87 tipped onto Leaf 79 [24.66.1402] (Metropolitan Museum of Art).
11. Kowsky, "The Architectural Legacy of Andrew Jackson Downing," in Tatum and MacDougall, eds., *Prophet with Honor*, 277. Another contemporaneous author, Nathaniel Parker Willis, also wrote about Downing. Vaux designed Willis's house called Idlewild in Moodna, New York in 1853 and published it as Design No. 23, *Villas and Cottages* (2nd ed.).
12. See Kowsky, *Country, Park & City*, 43; and *The Architecture of Frederick Clarke Withers and the Progress of the Gothic Revival in America after 1850*; and Tatum, "Introduction: The Downing Decade (1841–1852)," in Tatum and MacDougall, eds., *Prophet with Honor*, 38, ft. 81.
13. Later, one unrealized purpose of the American Institute of Architects, formed in 1857, was to establish a college of architecture. William R. Ware, translator of Vignola's systematic study of the classical orders, founded the first curriculum of architecture at the Massachusetts Institute of Technology in 1865.
14. Gutman, *Architectural Practice*, 120.
15. Hunt (1827–1895) was one the American Institute of Architects' twenty-three founding members formed in Richard Upjohn, Esq.'s New York office. Downing included an Upjohn design in *ACH* as Design XXVII. Hunt passed his entrance exam to the École on his second try, and having won several mentions, gained admission to the first class. He received no other competition awards and ended his studies in 1852. He is best known

for parts of New York's Metropolitan Museum of Art, begun in 1894 and completed by his son in 1902, and the base for the Statue of Liberty. Richardson (1838–1886) has the distinction of having an architectural style—Richardsonian Romanesque—named after his work.

16. See Schuyler, *Apostle of Taste*, 156–60, for a full account. Davis worked for Ithiel Town (1784–1844), designing many Greek Revival and Gothic style public buildings and residences. Town was one of the founding members of the National Academy of Design in 1825, an organization of artists who agreed to meet three evenings a week for drawing by the light of a large oil lamp. For more on the Academy see Clark, *History of the National Academy of Design,* 10, 11, 187; and Reiff, *Houses from Books*, 80. For information about Town's library, see Newton, *Town and Davis, Architects and Pioneers in American Revivalist Architecture*, 66–75. For more on early American architects' libraries, see Hafertepe and O'Gorman, *American Architects and their Books to 1848.* Davis was elected an Associate of the Academy in 1828, the year he gives as the start of his architectural practice. For more on Davis see Peck, *Alexander Jackson Davis, American Architect.*
17. "Domestic Notice," *The Horticulturist* 2 (February, 1848), 383.
18. The *New York Mirror* was a weekly reflex of news, arts, science, literature, and politics from 1820. D. T. Valentine's *Manual of the Corporation for the City of New York* (1841) contained 72 prints. For advertisements for Davis's *Rural Residences*, see [24.66.1182] (Metropolitan Museum of Art).
19. Emerson's older brother William was vice president of the Horticultural Association of the Valley of the Hudson in 1838. For more on this Association, see Schuyler, *Apostle of Taste*, 32–34. The contents of Downing's library include "a complete set of Loudon's works, including the *Arboretum Britannicum*; copies of the *Annales de Fromont*, and of the horticultural societies of Paris and Berlin; a copy of a beautiful French work, *L'Herbier de l'Amateur*, in eight octavo volumes, with finely colored plates; and another of a work very rare in this country, *Hofland's White Knights*, folio, with exquisite etchings of objects in landscape gardening." "Residence of A. J. Downing, Botanical Garden and Nurseries, Newburgh, New York," *The Magazine of Horticulture* (November, 1841, 407).
20. Downing to Robert Donaldson letter, December 26, 1840 (Courtesy of Richard H. Jenrette).
21. Downs, "Downing's Newburgh Villa," 53. Petrarch, the Humanist, is considered to be the first person to have an aesthetic view of nature based on his ascent of Mont Ventoux.
22. Tatum notes that Vaux "recalled he had heard his friend say that he read Hazlitt 'for assistance in forming a style.'" In Tatum and MacDougall, eds., *Prophet with Honor*, 21 and ft. 22. Hazlitt was one of Loudon's favorite essayists, according to Simo, *Loudon and the Landscape*, 217.
23. Loudon was not an architect and is not included in Colvin, *A Biographical Dictionary of English Architects.* See Downs for specific references to Loudon's magazine in *Downing and the American House*, 14, 15.
24. Archer, *The Literature of British Domestic Architecture*, 218. Also see Hunt, *Gardens and the Picturesque*, 286.
25. Hunt, *Gardens and the Picturesque*, chapter 5.
26. Upton, "Pattern Books and Professionalism," 126.
27. Downing referred to Claude (Gelée Lorrain) in "The Beautiful in a Tree," *The Horticul-*

turist 6 (February, 1851), and *RE*, 291, and in "The Beautiful in Ground," *The Horticulturist* 7 (March, 1852), and *RE*, 108. Downing compares the painters in *TPLG*, 63–75.

28. See Schuyler, *Apostle of Taste*, Appendix for a full account of all published writings, and Hitchcock, *American Architectural Books*, for printing runs.
29. Crowley, "The Invention of the Cottage as a Comfortable House," 2. See Bode, *The Anatomy of American Popular Culture*, 110, 111, for the book business and developments in distribution methods. The bound edition of *TPLG* sold for $3.50.
30. Robert Donaldson, Esq. (1800–1872) graduated from the University of North Carolina, Chapel Hill, a campus where Davis worked from 1844 to 1858 designing and building numerous projects, some financed by Donaldson. Davis remodeled Donaldson's house in Manhattan. Schuyler, *Apostle of Taste*, 50. In 1835, Donaldson bought a 95-acre estate called Annandale at Red Hook in Dutchess County from John C. Cruger for $19,000, renaming it Blithewood. Anderson, *Carolinian on the Hudson*, 161–66. See engravings of the Ravine Walk opposite page 350, and of the Cataract fig. 41, page 364, in Downing, *TPLG*. In 1853, Donaldson sold Blithewood to John Bard for $63,000. (Dutchess Co. Deed: 99–127). See Downs, "A Previously Unattributed Structure from the Partnership of Downing & Vaux." Donaldson then purchased Sylvania, the home of Mrs. Margaretta Livingston (Lowndes) Brown near Barrytown for $22,000 and renamed the estate Edgewater. For a photograph, see Eberlein and Hubbard, *Historic Houses of the Hudson Valley*, 93 and pl. 82. Davis designed a library for Edgewater in 1853. Regarding Montgomery Place, General Montgomery's widow, Janet Livingston Montgomery built the house in 1802. Her youngest brother Edward inherited the estate. In 1842, his widow Louise hired Davis to design a wing addition, front portico and north porch shown in *The Horticulturist* 2 (October, 1847). Downing designed the grounds at that time. See Smith, *The Great Estates Region of the Hudson River Valley*. The restored house and grounds that partially survive are open for tours. Regarding Wodenethe, Downing provided services for Sargent's estate in Fishkill, New York whose gardens he greatly admired. Sargent and Downing's brother Charles updated and supplemented an 1873 edition of *Cottage Residences* with eleven more designs, updated construction cost estimates and a more extensive treatment of horticulture and gardening. Downing said Parmentier was the first and finest landscape gardener in America. Parmentier practiced in Brooklyn and was responsible for importing many plant species to America. Parmentier also worked on Wodenethe's 700 acres from 1824 to 1850. Regarding Hyde Park, Donaldson knew Hyde Park and Anderson credits it with his enthusiasm for landscape design (in *Carolinian on the Hudson*, 160). Downing considers, "For a long time, this was the finest seat in America." *TPLG*, 46.
31. Reiff, *Houses from Books*, 70. John Notman, Esq. (1810–65) immigrated to America in 1831 and settled in Philadelphia. The City Directory of Philadelphia lists him as a carpenter in 1837 and an architect in 1841. Known for the Laurel Hill Cemetery in Philadelphia (1836–39), he designed numerous brownstone churches, houses and civic buildings. See Greiff, *John Notman, Architect*, and Jackson, *Early Philadelphia Architects and Engineers*, 213–25. Downs says, "There is some evidence of an early, evidently informal, partnership of Downing and Notman" (in *Downing and the American House*, 13, ft. 15). Blanche Linden lists three Notman houses with Downing designed landscapes: Harry Ingersolls's Medary (1847); Joshua Francis Fisher's Alverthorpe (1850) in Jenkintown, Pennsylvania; and Henry Pratt McKean's Fern Hill (1851–52) in Germantown, Mary-

land in Birnbaum and Karson, eds., *Pioneers of American Landscape Design*, 270. Also see Brownell, "The Italianate Villa and the Search for an American Style, 1840–1860"; Jaffe, ed., *The Italian Presence in American Art,* 210.

32. Downing used the title in setting his salary for the design of the Washington Mall.
33. Reissues of the 4th edition were in 1853, 1855, 1856, 1860, 1863, 1865, 1866, and 1868.
34. Anderson (1775–1870) was an intimate friend of Washington Irving and taught him how to play the clarinet. See Barr, *The Life and Works of Alexander Anderson, MD*; Knubel, "Alexander Anderson and Early American Book Illustration"; and Dingman, *Alexander Anderson.* See Hamilton, *Early American Book Illustrators and Wood Engravers*, for the involvement of Anderson as well as other engravers used by Downing including J. W. Orr, R. H. Carson and Joseph A. Adams, a pupil of Anderson (Tatum, *Andrew Jackson Downing*). Adams drew the illustrations for Davis's book.
35. Woods, "The First American Architectural Journals: The Profession's Voice," 118. For further discussion of recent advances in printing techniques, see Ackerman, *The Villa: Form and Ideology of Country Houses*, 240. Gloag notes Loudon's *Encyclopedia of Gardening* (1822)—a model book for Downing—besides being an "immense mass of useful matter" had inserted "a great number of finished wood-engravings being printed with the text instead of being in separate pages," and enjoyed "an extraordinary sale, and fully established the literary fame of its author" (*Mr. Loudon's England*, 200, 201).
36. Tatum in Tatum and MacDougall, eds., *Prophet with Honor*, 25.
37. The house was published with a different roof configuration and chimney location in Downing's first editorial essay, "Introduction," *The Horticulturist* 1 (July, 1846), as the "improved" view of "A Common Country House." Schuyler credits Downing and Davis for the design (*Apostle of Taste*, 76, 77). Davies credits Davis only, "Davis and Downing: Collaborators in the Picturesque," in Tatum and MacDougall, eds., *Prophet with Honor*, 92, 93. The word "Davis" is written on Downing's original sketch in pencil under the title [24.66.363], and Davis lists the project in his Index of Work, 1830–1880, vol. I [24.66.1400]. Also see vol. VI [24.66.1405], Leaf 21 for the house and Leaf 250 for a front door drawing (Metropolitan Museum of Art). On the other hand, Reiff claims Downing influenced Davis's project, the Delameter House in Rhinebeck, New York, built in 1843–44 (*Houses from Books*), 60, 61. Also see Downs, *Downing and the American House. CR* contains a note about its construction on Staten Island, New York, as well as other places, 46. In declining health and facing bankruptcy, George Downing leased the new house to Robert L. Case of New York City who purchased it in May, 1844 according to Downs, *Downing and the American House*, 45 and Errata. "C. L. Case May 3, 1843" is etched onto an original glass window pane and may be seen today. Case appears as the property owner on the Dripps 1850 map of Newburgh. R. L. The original house had additions built in 1870 and 1903. In about 1857, Vaux designed a new house in the Carpenter Gothic style for Case on the east portion of the property. See Design No. 8, Vaux, *Villas and Cottages*, (2nd ed.).
38. For publications before 1895, see Hitchcock, *American Architectural Books*; Park, *A List of Architectural Books Available in America before the Revolution*; and Schimmelman, *Architectural Books in Early America*. For British publication, see Wittkower, "English Literature on Architecture"; Harris, *British Architectural Books and Writers*; and Archer, *The Literature of British Domestic Architecture*.
39. Downing to Robert Donaldson letter, January 21, 1842 (Courtesy of Richard H. Jenrette).

40. Using the nomenclature of the London Horticultural Society as his guide, Downing gave the standard name for each fruit, the authorities who had given previous accounts and descriptive comment including the history, uses, how to gather and keep the fruit, propagation techniques, and guidelines on soil, situation and culture, diseases, and varieties organized by season so that home orchards in temperate climates could have fresh fruit for ten months throughout the year.
41. Tatum in Tatum and MacDougall, eds., *Prophet with Honor*, 28, 29.
42. Downing to Robert Donaldson letter, March 3, 1845 (Courtesy of Richard H. Jenrette).
43. "The New-York Park," *The Horticulturist* 6 (August, 1851) and *RE*, 152.
44. Hovey, *Magazine of Horticulture* 8 (1842).
45. Downing calls Luther Tucker (1802–1873) "the shrewdest & most experienced manager of all our agricultural papers." Tucker also published *The Genesee Farmer* from 1831; *The Cultivator* from 1840, whose motto was "To improve the soil and the mind"; and *The Country Gentleman* from 1853. Downing was offered "from $1500 to $2000 per annum to edit what he hoped to make 'a valuable periodical to the country at large.'" Downing letter to Robert Donaldson, July 9, 1846 (Courtesy of Richard H. Jenrette). Monthly payment receipts may be found at the Princeton University Library, Rare Book Room. In 1850, Bode counts over six hundred nonpolitical magazines published for eleven million literate Americans (in *The Anatomy of American Popular Culture*, 116).
46. Wightwick was the secretary and companion of London architect Sir John Soane and was probably the first English architectural journalist. See Brownell, "The Italianate Villa and the Search for an American Style, 1840–1860," in Jaffe, ed., *The Italian Presence in American Art*, 214. Brownell thinks Downing's Design VII, *CR* and Brown's "Anglo-Italian Villa" in *Domestic Architecture* were based on a plate from Wightwick's *Palace of Architecture*, 214–15, figures 131, 132.
47. Schuyler, *Apostle of Taste*, 130–32.
48. From a speech Downing gave at the Massachusetts Horticultural Society's annual Festival at Faneuil Hall in Boston and published the proceedings in *The Horticulturist* 3 (November, 1848), 235. On associationism and the common sense philosophical tradition, see Hersey, "J. C. Loudon and Architectural Associationism."
49. See Scully, *The Shingle Style and the Stick Style*, xxviii, ft. 19; Hitchcock, *American Architectural Books*; Woods "The First American Architectural Journals," 119; and Schuyler, *Apostle of Taste*, 72.
50. *CR*, 80.
51. Vol. XII, Leaf 36 and letters December 3, 11 and 20, 1849, and January 4 and 13, 1850 (Metropolitan Museum of Art).
52. Vol. II, [24.66.1401] (Metropolitan Museum of Art).
53. Downing to Robert Donaldson letter dated June 5, 1849 included sketches of five-, six-, and eight-sided buildings (Courtesy of Richard H. Jenrette).
54. *Rural Residences* cost Davis the equivalent of a year's salary even with the financial support of subscribers and two clients: Donaldson to whom it is discretely dedicated and James A. Hillhouse, a poet and patron of Thomas Cole. See Jane Davies's introduction in the 1980 reprint. *Rural Residences* is considered by some historians to be the first American house pattern book. Wood, "The New "Pattern Books" and the Role of the Agricultural Press," in Tatum and MacDougall, eds., *Prophet with Honor*, 182. Tatum disagrees with Wood because the book was too large, had only eight designs and was

too expensive due to the hand-colored lithographs. See Tatum's introduction in Holly, *Holly's Picturesque Country Seats*, vii. The book, meant to be a six-part issue with four designs each, and was sold for $2.00 colored or $1.50 uncolored through Davis's architecture office. Moss says that this book is the first American example of this coloring process (*Paint in America*, 60).

55. Downing to Davis letter, December 22, 1848 (Metropolitan Museum of Art).
56. "Letters from England," July, 1850, *RE*, 477.
57. Scott (1828–1919) from Columbia, South Carolina spent several months living and studying with Downing between 1846 and 1850, and again from 1851 to 1852. Scott dedicated his book *The Art of Beautifying Suburban Home Grounds of Small Extent* to Downing. Scott opened an office in Toledo, Ohio in 1852, and later served as a Central Park Commissioner and encouraged Frederick Law Olmsted to apply for the superintendent's position. See Tatum in Tatum and MacDougall, eds., *Prophet with Honor*, 39, ft. 86, and Birnbaum and Karson, *Pioneers of American Landscape Design*, 336–38. Downs mentions a professional British gardener Downing engaged who was in transit at the time of Downing's death (*Downing and the American House*, 13, ft. 16).
58. Downing to John Jay Smith letter, March 29, 1852, *The Horticulturist* 6 (April, 1856).
59. Downing to John Jay Smith letter, Oct. 30, 1851, *The Horticulturist* 6 (April, 1956).
60. Headley was a Presbyterian minister and "author of many popular travel and historical books" including *Letters from Italy*, *Sacred Mountain* and biographies of Napoleon, Cromwell, and Washington (Kowsky, *Country, Park & City*, 34). Downing notes the client's "object being to erect a picturesque rural home in keeping with the scenery, but without the least unnecessary outlay for decoration" (*CR*, 174). Mancari describes an extant ha-ha in the rear garden in "Downing's Design XIV is more than a cottage," 17. While it has had numerous additions and modifications (fig. 98 of the carriage porch was added to *CR* editions after Downing's death), it remains a well-preserved private residence. This house was used as the frontispiece in *CR*, 4th ed. Reiff notes Jacob W. Holt copied the design for his house in Warrenton, North Carolina, c. 1855–56, and Luther Briggs for the James F. Bigelow House in Boston, Mass., 1857–58 (*Houses from Books*, 71).
61. Vassar had the largest collection of Hudson River School landscape painted sketches. See Harvey, *The Painted Sketch*. Only the cottage's brick foundation is visible today. The entrance porch and front façade were moved to the State Museum in Albany in 1976 after a 1969 fire and substantial vandalism. Downing's sketch is on 5¼" x 8" paper, dated 1848, with the note "wood." [24.66.111 (4)] (Metropolitan Museum of Art).
62. Kowsky, *Country, Park & City*, 28. For a description and photographs see Alex, *Calvert Vaux, Architect & Planner*, 5–6, 70–73.
63. See the Historic American Buildings Survey, No. DC-246, DC GEO 116, 1–16. Robert and Francis Dodge were brothers whose family business was located along the Georgetown waterfront. They built their houses on Georgetown's northern border. See Reiff, *Washington Architecture*, 122–25. While the original building cost estimate was $10,000, "We find the cost of our houses to be much beyond what Mr. Downing led us to expect—say about $15,000 each; yet we have fine houses, and very comfortable and satisfactory in every respect" (Vaux, *Villas and Cottages*, 2nd ed., 235).
64. Culbert was "A homeopathic physician who over his long career in Newburgh earned the love and respect of many of his fellow citizens for his good judgment and fatherly

counsel" (Kowsky, *Country, Park & City*, 36).

65. "A nephew of Downing's wealthy Newburgh neighbor Thomas Powell, Parish and his brother Henry were among the richest men in New York City" (Kowsky, *Country, Park & City*, 39). For another photograph, see Downing and Scully, *The Architectural Heritage of Newport*, Pl. 167.
66. Newton, *Town and Davis*, fig. 15. Davies, "Davis and Downing: Collaborators in the Picturesque," in Tatum and MacDougall, eds., *Prophet with Honor*, 93.
67. Regarding Algonac, Kowsky notes that "several outbuildings that were undoubtedly designed by Downing and Vaux. One of these was a brick stable" (*Country, Park & City*, ft. 26, 325). Alex includes a Vaux drawing and photograph, c. 1877 (*Calvert Vaux, Architect & Planner*, 52, 53). See Reiff, *Washington Architecture*, 129, ft. 151, 130, with a site plan (fig. 194) and photograph (fig. 193) dated 1890. The Barber villa was demolished for the Navel Observatory designed by Richard Morris Hunt.
68. The best account of the estate is in Dutchess County Department of Planning, *Springside*. It includes many photographs and letters supporting preservation efforts. Also see Flad, "Matthew Vassar's Springside" in Tatum and MacDougall, eds., *Prophet with Honor*, and Bowen, *Great River of the Mountain*, for good photographs.
69. Downing's original drawings for Vassar may be found in the Vassar College Libraries, Special Collections. Other drawings preserved in this collection include designs for the Gate Lodge built in 1851, and a Lodge and Principal Residence, dated 1851, unbuilt. These construction drawings are executed in scale, in ink and color wash and indicate details such as sliding casement windows and roof leaders. Specifications for the Principal Residence are also preserved. Other documents include construction drawings for a Cottage, a Carriage House and Barn Stables complex.
70. For a descriptive narrative, see Lossing, *Vassar College and its Founder*, 63. Also see Dutchess County Planning Board, *Springside*, 9.
71. Significant landscape elements absent or no longer discernable according to the Visitor's Map (unfortunately out of date as of this writing with further landscape decline evident) are marked * including: Maple Hill* (*2*); Deer-park* (*3*); Stonehenge* (*4*); Group Gap (*5*); Rock Roost (*6*); Little Belt (*7*); Knitting Knoll (*8*); Jet Vale* (*13*); Walnut Row (*14*); Willow Spring*—the estate is named for this active spring (*15*); Lawn Terrace (*17*); Locust Grove Drive (*18*); Ever-green Parks (*19* and *20*); Center Circle* (*21*); Flower and Kitchen Gardens* (*25*); avenues, knolls and hills (*29–34*); and Meadow Girt* (*35*).
72. Flad, "Matthew Vassar's Springside," in Tatum and MacDougall, eds., *Prophet with Honor*, 244.
73. See Reiff, *Washington Architecture* and Miller, *Washington in Maps*, for more detail.
74. Thomas U. Walter's 1851 expansion plans for the Capitol were under consideration. Also in Washington, Mills designed the Treasury Building (1836), the General Post Office (1830) later the Tariff Commission and an unexecuted design for the Smithsonian Institution (1841). Mills's three landscape designs for the Mall reflected a French formalism influence complete with parterres and followed L'Enfant's Baroque design more closely than what Downing proposed.
75. Downing was unhappy about the Smithsonian's architecture and said, "a foreigner liberally bequeaths his fortune to the foundation of an institution 'for the diffusion of knowledge among men'—and the regents erect a college in the style of a Norman monastery—with a relish of the dark ages in it, the better to contrast with its avowed

purpose of diffusing light" ("A Few Words on Our Progress in Building," *The Horticulturist* 6 (June, 1851) and *RE*, 217.) In 1835, James Smithson left his estate to America should his nephew die without an heir. As a result and after a court battle, Smithson's will directed payment to the "United States of America, to found at Washington . . . (such an) establishment."

76. U.S. Congress, House, Report of the Secretary of War, 1867, 522, quoted in Scott, *Capital Engineers*, 73.
77. Downing wrote about his visit to Dropmore whose Pinetum contained every evergreen species that could grow in England in "The Horticultural Shows," *The Horticulturist* 5 (September, 1850), and *RE*, 538–40. Downing offered further remarks on how pine trees, when contorted by weather, add "to their picturesque power in sublime and grand scenery" ("The Beautiful in a Tree," *The Horticulturist* 6, February, 1851, and *RE*, 289).
78. For more information on the Mall, see Reps, "Downing and the Washington Mall"; Schuyler, *Apostle of Taste*; Longstreth, *The Mall in Washington*; and Washburn, "Vision of Life for the Mall."
79. See Beveridge and Schuyler, eds., *The Papers of Frederick Law Olmsted.*
80. And see Tatum, "The Emergence of an American School of Landscape Design," 34–41.
81. See Design 9 for the boat-landing, perhaps created with Withers's assistance; rustic bridge (Design 27); and shaded seats (Design 28) (Vaux, *Villas and Cottages*, 2nd ed., 1864).
82. "The New-York Park," *The Horticulturist* 6 (August, 1851), and *RE*, 147.
83. See Monell, "Burning of the Henry Clay," and Schuyler, *Apostle of Taste*, 220–21, who refers to multiple eyewitness accounts.
84. The tall monument adjacent to the grave markers is for Mary Wait Downing, Eunice Bridge Downing, and Samuel Downing. About fifteen feet away is a rustic cross monument on a piled stone base marking Mary E. Monell and Judge John J. Monell's graves.
85. See Tatum, *Andrew Jackson Downing*, for a complete list.
86. In 1850, the U.S. census valued the property at $15,000. The original Carson engraving of the house is in Vol. II, Leaf 6, [22.66.1401] (Metropolitan Museum of Art). Davis designed a villa for Alger in Berkshire, Massachusetts in 1845. Newton, *Town and Davis*, fig. 16; and see Tatum for a photograph (*Andrew Jackson Downing*, fig. 62). The Miller-Hurley Realty Company demolished the house.
87. The unexecuted studies include Frederick J. Betts House, "Villa Residence with Curved Roof," No. 20, 1864 ed. (see fig. 3.6). Betts was "A prominent figure in the New York State legal profession and a friend who had once helped Downing out of a difficult financial situation" (Kowsky, *Country, Park & City*, 36.) Downing designed the grounds according to Tatum, *Andrew Jackson Downing*, 100. Other unexecuted projects include Vassar's Villa, No. 30; the S. D. Dakin House, No. 37; and a Villa on a Large Scale, No. 39. (All design numbers from the 1864 ed.)
88. "On the Moral Influence of Good Houses," *The Horticulturist* 2 (February, 1848), 383.
89. Downing in Wightwick, *Hints to Young Architects*, xxvii.
90. *ACH*, 38.
91. Downing to John Jay Smith letter, February 19, 1847 (Yale University Library, Rare Book Room). Smith edited *The Horticulturist* after Downing's death and reprinted Downing letters in the January, February and April issues, 1856. Also see Handlin, *The American Home, Architecture and Society*, 42.

CHAPTER 2

1. *ACH*, 262.
2. *CR*, 1–25, and refined in *ACH*, 5–26.
3. *CR*, 15, and chart on page 16, in original editions.
4. TPLG, 371, quoting Loudon, *Encyclopaedia of Cottage, Farm, and Villa Architecture*, 4.
5. *ACH*, 260.
6. *ACH*, 396.
7. *TPLG*, Preface, x. For the evolution of Downing's design principles, see Handlin, *The American Home, Architecture and Society*, 30–46. For more on Loudon, see Simo, *Loudon and the Landscape*.
8. Loudon published among other essays, "Enquires on the Causes of the Colour of the Water of the Rhone" (September, 1834); and "Facts and Considerations on the Strata of Mont Blanc . . . etc." (December, 1834) in his *Magazine of Natural History*. He also published "Whether Works of Art may, with Propriety, be combined with the Sublimity of Nature; and what would be the most appropriate Situation for the proposed Monument to the Memory of Sir Walter Scott, in Edinburgh?" by Kata Phusin, Ruskin's *nom de plume* (January, 1939), 625–36. See Hunt, *The Wider Sea*, 56–59. Hunt considers Loudon to be Ruskin's mentor in the 1830s (*Gardens and the Picturesque*, 204).
9. Loudon, *Architectural Magazine* (January, 1837), 44. Also published was Quatremère's, "On the Use of Allegory in Architecture" (January, 1837), 1–3. Major counts nine translated essays beginning in 1835 (*To Live in the New World*, 55).
10. Archer, *The Literature of British Domestic Architecture*, 523.
11. Gloag, *Mr. Loudon's England*, 99, 100. Also see Hersey, "J. C. Loudon and Architectural Associationism," Ill. 92, and *High Victorian Gothic*.
12. Crowley distinguishes between *archaic* architecture, more aptly thought of as temporary, exemplified by rough timber houses with clay-lined wood chimneys, and *vernacular* houses meant to be permanent and with no pretension of style (*The Invention of Comfort*, 96–102).
13. Downing also included speaking tubes, rotary pumps and closets (considered a separate room increasing the house tax) in his list of innovative devices (*CR*, 5–7).
14. Alison, *Essays on the Nature and Principles of Taste*, has two essays. "Of the Nature of the Emotions of Sublimity and Beauty" discusses parts, and "Of the Sublimity and Beauty of the Material World" discusses the manner these parts may be combined. A third essay on the standards of perfection was not undertaken. For Alison's influence on Loudon, see Simo, *Loudon and the Landscape*, 42.
15. *ACH*, 5–35.
16. See Upton, "Pattern Books and Professionalism," 125, 126.
17. *ACH*, 201.
18. *ACH*, 23.
19. *ACH*, 258, 259.
20. See Harris, *The Artist in American Society*, 212–16, and Tatum, "The Emergence of an American School of Landscape Design," 34.
21. Archer, "The Beginnings of Association in British Architectural Esthetics," 244.
22. Tatum, "Nature's Gardener," in Tatum and MacDougall, eds., *Prophet with Honor*, 57, 58.

23. "A Few Words on Our Progress in Building," *The Horticulturist* 6 (June, 1851).
24. *ACH*, 265.
25. *ACH*, ft. 265.
26. "American versus British Horticulture," *The Horticulturist* 7 (June, 1852), and *RE*, 219.
27. For a discussion, see Major, *To Live in the New World*, 56–61.
28. "Some New World curiosities such as the sunflower and the yucca had arrived in Europe before 1600, but in the 1620s the trickle of American plants became a flood, which flowed unabated for the next hundred years." Pavord, *The Naming of Names*, 363. Also see the essays "The Contribution from America to British Gardens in the Early Nineteenth Century" by Taylor in MacDougall, ed., *John Cludius Loudon and the Early Nineteenth Century in Great Britain*, and "Approaches to planting in the late eighteenth century" by Mark Laird, and books by Fry (*The Plant Hunters*) and D. Chambers (*The Planters of the English Landscape Garden*).
29. *ACH*, 345.
30. "A Few Words on Rural Architecture," *The Horticulturist* 5 (July, 1850), and *RE*, 208.
31. *ACH*, v, vi.
32. Sweeting, *Reading Houses and Building Books*, 96. On Dickens's trip and others like it, see Haydon, *Upstate Travels*.
33. "A Talk about Public Parks and Gardens," *The Horticulturist* 3 (October, 1848), and *RE*, 138.
34. Schuyler, *Apostle of Taste*, 91.
35. *The Horticulturist* 3 (June, 1849), and *RE*, 229. Also see Schuyler, *Apostle of Taste*, 117.
36. See "Influence of Horticulture," *The Horticulturist* 2 (July, 1847), and *RE*, 14.
37. Maine was granted statehood in 1842, Oregon in 1846, Florida, Wisconsin, Texas and Iowa in 1848, Minnesota in 1849, and Utah, New Mexico and California in 1850.
38. Fish, *The Rise of the Common Man*, 125–27. Under the 1840s political vision of Manifest Destiny, U.S. government confiscated lands were surveyed, subdivided into parcels and sold to settlers in land office auctions through the Homestead Act of 1862. The minimum price was $1.25 per acre and the minimum purchase requirement was 80 acres. Land grants set aside parcels for local schools at a rate of one section per 36, and each township or two in each state had to provide land for a future university.
39. See de Tocqueville's commentary from a visit in 1831 in *Democracy in America*.
40. Ariès, *Centuries of Childhood*, 328.
41. Stilgoe quoting Grunds *The Americans in Their Moral, Social and Political Relations*, 263–64, in *Common Landscape of America*, 337.
42. *ACH*, 97.
43. "Introduction," *The Horticulturist* 1 (July, 1846), 11.
44. *TPLG*, 417.
45. Downing used Loudon's floor plan for Design XV, *ACH*. Hussey considers this the culminating book on the picturesque, indicating that "Every class of country building and style was copiously represented, but Loudon's picturesque attitude to them all is illustrated by his asserting: 'If there is one test rather than another by which the taste or no taste of an Architect can be detected with certainty (always supposing that he is master of the mechanical rules of the art), it is the degree of perfection which he has attained in sketching general scenery'" (*The Picturesque*, 229).

46. Peter Frederick Robinson (1776–1858) was a pupil of Henry Holland, an architect who worked with "Capability" Brown. His designs have descriptions of a scenic dwelling's identifiable characteristics and were to be no more expensive than a "less attractive structure." Such design would promote good behavior. Early considers Robinson the leader along with Loudon of the "second wave of the picturesque in England" (*Romanticism and American Architecture*, 80, ft. 8). Hussey considers him one of the Tudor style's first designers (*The Picturesque*, 225). *Rural Architecture* is a parallel study to Hunt's *Picturesque Domestic Architecture*. Archer considers Robinson and Hunt the most prolific domestic design book authors of the 1820s (*The Literature of British Domestic Architecture*). Loudon uses illustrations from the 1829 edition in his *Encyclopeadia*. Addison considers it a source for the American Gothic Revival style of the 1840s ("Early American Gothic," in Boas, ed., *Romanticism in America*). On the effect of Robinson's second book see Gloag, *Mr. Loudon's England*, 105, 106.
47. Downing used Robert Lugar's "A Cottage at Tillisheun" as a model for a reduced design as a Gate Lodge, Design V, *ACH*. Regarding *Villa Architecture*, Archer notes that "the design of a house must accommodate the pictorial characteristics of the surrounding landscape as well as the needs of the resident" (*The Literature of British Domestic Architecture*, 543).
48. Francis Goodwin (1784–1835). "He has let his eye for picturesque composition "serve in lieu" of classic or any other rules" (Hussey, *The Picturesque*, 228). The first edition was published in 1833 as *Domestic Architecture*, of which the first of two volumes were dedicated to Sir John Soane. The second edition of 1835 was called *Rural Architecture*. The name was changed back for the third and later editions. It includes designs from the author's portfolio, mostly executed. This book is important for associational and pictorial criteria, and appropriateness of style to environment. Thomas Frederick Hunt (c. 1791–1831). "Hunt was one of the earliest architects to make practical recommendations for producing picturesque texture" (Hussey, *The Picturesque*, 225). *Picturesque Domestic Architecture* described the Old English style. *Exemplars of Tudor Architecture* is considered the first lengthy account of Tudor architecture. Augustus Charles Pugin (1769–1832), French-born, was an assistant to John Nash and an engraver for numerous architectural publishers. His book argues for Gothic over Classical architecture. Addison considers it another source for the American Gothic Revival style of the 1840s ("Early American Gothic," in Boas, ed., *Romanticism in America*). "He produced some of the first archaeologically accurate images of medieval architecture" (Curl, *Dictionary of Architecture and Landscape Architecture*, 609). Hussey considers its contribution to be the use of Gothic style for picturesque architecture (*The Picturesque*, 194).
49. Marcus, *Apartment Stories*, 93, quoting Loudon, "Cottage Economy."
50. *ACH*, 305.
51. See Downs, "'Up-front' and Prominent Chimneys," for Downing's thoughts on fireplace and chimney placement on interior walls. Also *ACH*, 32, 174–80.
52. Downing thought thatch was unlikely to be used in America and no elevations show thatch roof material. He said, "Our snowy and changeable climate will soon destroy so frail a material, and it is therefore unfit for covering the roofs of buildings for habitation" (*CR*, 132). Downing predicted nine of ten houses would use wood shingles and the other roofs would be lead or tin. For shingle patterns see *ACH*, 181, fig. 83.
53. These manuscripts were called red books because they were bound in red Moroccan leather. See Daniels, *Humphry Repton*.

54. *ACH*, 79.
55. "How to Choose a Site for a Country Seat," *The Horticulturist* 2 (December, 1847), and *RE*, 161.
56. Hunt, *Gardens and the Picturesque*, 210, 216. In this regard, Ruskin thought Turner's work was superior.
57. Crowley, "The Invention of the Cottage as a Comfortable House," 19. Sweeting's book on nineteenth-century genteel romanticism challenges Downing's message as sentimental and snobbish, saying the good life depicted in Downing's work perpetuated gender segregation and designated those who failed to comply as immoral, uncouth and unpatriotic in their wastefulness and lack of civic attention. However, Downing's moral platitudes can be read as preaching a vision of improved cultivation and domestic harmony that would be elitist, except that he thought it was possible for everyone to achieve. Sweeting, *Reading Houses and Building Books*, 120, 121.
58. Archer, *The Literature of British Domestic Architecture*, 505. Ruskin's book was serialized in 1855 in *The Crayon* in America and published as a book in New York in 1873. See Hitchcock, "Ruskin and American Architecture, or Regeneration Long Delayed," 170.
59. *Architectural Magazine* (December, 1838). Also see Ruskin, *The Poetry of Architecture*, vi.
60. Ruskin, *The Poetry of Architecture*, 1 (emphasis added).
61. Ruskin's nine-volume book was published from 1843 to 1860. Downing refers to this book in *ACH*, 14. Gage considers Ruskin's work on Turner "still the most rounded and sympathetic treatment of his art" (*Color in Turner*, 7).
62. Crary, *Techniques of the Observer*, 94, 95. Of course, this is exactly what color lithographs would do in a few decades permitting color reproductions in books. Turner owned Goethe's *Theory of Colours*, translated by Eastlake in 1840; see Gage, *Color in Turner*, 216. Regarding the science of immeasurable thought, "It was this order of thought too, which must have attracted Turner at first to the world system of George Field, which attempted to unite all branches of knowledge in a scheme of universal analogy, based on the unity of nature," Gage, *Color in Turner*, 120. George Field, the English color maker and philosopher, improved the purity and range of pigments in the nineteenth century.
63. Major, *To Live in the New World*, 87.
64. Minkowski, *Lived Time*, 129 (emphasis added).
65. Proprietor, n., from the Latin *proprietās,* a property, peculiarity; and *proprius*, one's own. "An owner; the person who has the legal right or exclusive title to any thing, whether in possession or not." Webster, *An American Dictionary*.
66. Beecher, *Norwood*, 213. His contributions to *The Horticulturist* include "Do Varieties of Fruit run out?," (October, 1846); "The Strawberry Controversy," (December, 1846); "On the Practical Use of Leaves," (February, 1848); "A Few Words to Beginners," (May, 1850); and "Parlor-Flowers in Winter," (November, 1851).
67. Wilde, *The Decay of Lying*.
68. The Hudson River School was known by this name after 1879. Daniels, *Fields of Vision*, 169.
69. Stein thinks that Downing read the American edition (*John Ruskin and Aesthetic Thought in America*, xi). Also see Horatio Greenough's "American Architecture" in Small, ed., *Form and Function*, ft. 51. Pierson thinks that Downing, influenced by Emerson, formed his own ideas in *TPLG* published eight years before Ruskin's book (*American Buildings and Their Architects*, 359).
70. Jackson, *Crabgrass Frontier*, 340, ft. 55.

71. Stein, *John Ruskin and Aesthetic Thought in America*, 1.
72. Lynes, *The Tastemakers*, 32.
73. In 1800, Arthur Young said, "Everyone but an idiot knows that the lowest classes must be kept poor or they will never be industrious." Rykwert quoting Brian Inglis's *Poverty and the Industrial Revolution* (1971), 86, in *The Seduction of Place*, 25.
74. Simo, *Loudon and the Landscape*, 140.
75. See Giedion, *Mechanization Takes Command*, 346, 347, for the progress of machine-made ornament.
76. Ruskin, *The Seven Lamps of Architecture*, II, V, 35.
77. Lynes, *The Tastemakers*, 5.
78. Downing quoting, in part, Dr. Timothy Dwight, *Travels in America* in "On Moral Influence of Good Houses," *The Horticulturist* 2 (February, 1848), and *RE*, 211, 212.
79. *ACH*, 30; Downing specifically links truth to understanding, see *ACH*, 38, 137.
80. *ACH*, 25–26.
81. *ACH*, 32.
82. Ruskin, *The Crown of Wild Olive*, 51.
83. See Miller, *The Empire of the Eye*, 197.
84. Loudon, "Cottage Economy," v. A few pages later Loudon added the Gardenesque style for Repton's designs, viii, xi. Downing called the Geometric style Ancient or Formal in contrast to the Modern, Natural, or Irregular Style (*TPLG*, 21). The terms "Geometric" and "Modern" are shown in Loudon's plates CCCXLIII–CCCXLVI illustrating house and ground designs and defined in his entry "Landscape Gardening," 525–73.
85. For more on aspect and prospect, see the glossary.
86. Richard Brown's Design "A Villa in the Elizabethan Style" was Downing's Design XII, *CR*. Downing included it for its blunder in chimney and fireplace locations as well as its faulty exterior ornamental details. Downing first published the design in *The Horticulturist* 5 (September, 1850). See Brown, *Domestic Architecture*, 330 and footnote.
87. One lingering consequence of this proposition explains curved walks to suburban houses where the short distance between street and front door seldom warrants such an artificial treatment.
88. *TPLG*, ft. 69.
89. *TPLG*, 416.
90. George William Curtis described Downing's house in this way; see his introduction to *RE*, xxxii.
91. Hunt, *The Wider Sea*, 204.
92. *CR*, 147, 148.
93. "The first point in order for the proprietor's selection is, undoubtedly, situation and aspect, in respect to which Mr. Repton's remarks, as founded upon much experience, are entitled to particular attention. He observes no beauty of prospect can compensate for a cold exposure to the north, the glaring blaze of a setting sun, or the frequent boisterous winds and rain from the west and south-west; while in a southern aspect, the sun is too high to be troublesome in summer, and during the winter it is seldom an unwelcome visitant" (Lugar, *Villa Architecture*, vii, quoting Repton, *Observations on the Theory and Practice of Landscape Gardening*, 180).
94. *CR*, 2. For houses designed in the newly popular Italian style, Downing suggests the top floor of a belvedere or campanile "may be a museum or a prospect gallery." This, then, is

a raised place for viewing collected curiosities or observing the surrounding landscape, both activities in the pursuit of learning. Downing calls it a square tower or campanile, see Designs VI and VIII, *CR* and in *ACH*, Designs VII and XXI; and for a belvidere [sic] (Romanesque style), see Design XXXII, *ACH*.

95. Loudon, *Encyclopedia of Cottage, Farm, and Villa Architecture*, 541. Knight's *The Landscape, a Didactic Poem*, Price's *Essay on the Picturesque*, and Gilpin's *Observations* and *Three Essays* were contributors to the English debate on the picturesque. See Hussey, *The Picturesque*, 108; Hunt, *The Picturesque Garden in Europe*; and Macarthur, *The Picturesque*, 2 and 20 on Price, 43 and 36 on Gilpin.
96. Crary, *Techniques of the Observer*, 9. Also see Abrams, *The Mirror and the Lamp*, 57–65.

CHAPTER 3

1. *CR*, x.
2. Downs, "Downing's Newburgh Villa," 19, ft. 14.
3. "On Simple Rural Cottages," *The Horticulturist* 1 (September, 1846), and *RE*, 245, 246.
4. See Hamlin on the issue, the development of Downing's thoughts, the legacy of the Greek Revival movement, and the Greek versus the Gothic Revival movement ("The Greek Revival in America and Some of Its Critics," 255, 256).
5. *TPLG*, 383.
6. *CR*, 22.
7. *TPLG*, 374.
8. Kimball, *Nineteenth and Twentieth Century Architecture*, 110.
9. Scully, *The Shingle Style and the Stick Style*, xxvii.
10. *ACH*, 28.
11. *ACH*, 262–63.
12. See "The houses and their plans," for a detailed discussion of floor plan forms in Franklin, *The Gentleman's Country House and its Plan*.
13. Downing's specifications for Vassar's villa joists are 3" x 11" spaced 16" apart, to be made of sound, seasoned hemlock.
14. According to Reiff, this design influenced Christian G. Schneider House in Washington, D.C., built in 1864, fig. 191 and page 71; Stafford Place in Port Hope, Michigan, built in 1866, page 71; George Green House near Mayville, New York, built in c. 1867, fig. 111; Jones-Butler House in Utica, New York, built in c. 1852, page 70; and John C. Hopewell Villa in Flemington, New Jersey, built in c. 1854, page 70. See Reiff, *Houses from Books*.
15. Davies, "Davis and Downing: Collaborators in the Picturesque," in Tatum and MacDougall, eds., *Prophet with Honor*, 88.
16. Designs published in Downing's two books on architecture that have specific floor plan shapes include for: T-shapes, Design V (*CR*) and Designs II, III, V, VI, VIII and XXX (*ACH*); L-shapes, Designs VI, VII and VIII (*CR*) and IV, X, XVI, XXI and XXVII (*ACH*); H-shapes, Designs XXIV, XXIX and XXXII (*ACH*); and cross shapes (+), Designs XI, XIII and XV (*CR*) and XX, XXII, XXIII and XXXI (*ACH*).
17. *ACH*, 101.
18. Downing specified the interior partitions for Vassar's villa with wood framing members cut to 3"x 4" and spaced at 16" apart, plaster finishes and a 1" x 12" high wood base with

moulding. The exterior wall was 16" thick, hollow wall masonry construction with the same interior finishes of plaster on lath with wood trim.

19. See Kaufmann, *Architecture in the Age of Reason*, 195–201, for ways to arrange subdivided elements.
20. *TPLG*, 383.
21. Price, *As Essay on the Picturesque*, 268.
22. *CR*, 120.
23. See Schuyler, *Apostle of Taste*, 153, and letter from Calvert Vaux to Marshall P. Wilder, Aug. 18, 1852 (John Jay Smith Papers, Historic Society of Pennsylvania, Philadelphia).
24. "The Philosophy of Rural Taste," *The Horticulturist* 4 (August, 1849), 59, and *RE*, 105. Slavery was abolished in New York State in 1817, although its full effect was not felt until the Year of Emancipation ten years later. This is decades before the Civil War. Downing was surely aware of the labor changes in the landscaping business where "freed slaves drifted to such cities as Newburgh, Poughkeepsie, and Albany, creating a labor pool for the new industrialism" (Adams, *The Hudson Through the Years*, 241).
25. Burke, *A Philosophical Enquiry. . .* , 13, 25.
26. Downing uses this term when offering an alternate appropriate setting for Design VIII, *CR*, 140. See also "The Beautiful in Ground," *The Horticulturist* 7 (March, 1852), and *RE*, 106–9; and Downing in Wightwick, *Hints to Young Architects*, xix.
27. *ACH*, 263.
28. *CR*, 140.
29. *ACH*, 123. This house was the estate of E. P. Prentice, Esq. in Mount Hope near Albany, New York. Also published in *The Horticulturist* 3 (December, 1848), 287.
30. *CR*, 128.

CHAPTER 4

1. *ACH*, 3.
2. Davis, *Rural Residences*, unnumbered page entitled "American House."
3. *CR*, 95. Gloag notes that Loudon used Wotten's terms in his *Elements of Architecture* in his version of the Vitruvian principles, saying "the Fitness of a Building for the End in View, ought not only to be real, but apparent" (*Victorian Taste*, 49).
4. See Rykwert, *On Adam's House in Paradise*, 192. Also Argan for an argument about analogy, "On the Typology of Architecture."
5. *ACH*, 32. I prefer the word "element" as the current use of the word "feature" has been corrupted suggesting an additive approach to design as if each feature was a checklist amenity item from a "quality of life" agenda rather than an integral part of a composition.
6. Downing read Quatremère's "On the Principles of Taste" in Loudon's *Architectural Magazine* 2 (1835) according to Simo, *Loudon and the Landscape*, 132. Downing calls Quatremère, "a clever, French artist" (*ACH*, 377). See Aldo Rossi, "Typological Questions," in *The Architecture of the City*; and Vidler, "The Third Typology," "Type in *Encyclopédie Méthodique*," and "The hut and the body."
7. See Pevsner, *A History of Building Types*.
8. See Dripps, *The First House*, for an account of the first house and its architectural paradigms.

9. Rykwert, *On Adam's House in Paradise*, 192. Rykwert notes the label "primitive" refers to technological advances, and not social or cultural development (conversation with author).
10. Moneo, "On Typology," 28. Moneo defines "Type . . . as the *frame within which change operates*" (27).
11. Younés, *The True, the Fictive and the Real*, 254–57.
12. *ACH*, 21.
13. See Crowley, "The Invention of the Cottage as a Comfortable House." Wright counts 450 model house designs published between 1846 and 1898 in *Building the Dream*, 82. Major notes that *Cottage Residences* was first entitled *Model Cottages and Gardens* (*To Live in the New World*, 67).
14. Younés, *The True, the Fictive and the Real*, 255.
15. Herrmann discusses the eighteenth-century French arguments of taste as apart from the rules of proportion, the national superiority of certain countries and of certain people (*Laugier and Eighteenth Century French Theory*, 40, 41).
16. "How to Arrange Country Places," *The Horticulturist* 4, March 1850, 393, and *RE*, 166 (emphasis added).
17. Rykwert begins with an "implied house" (*On Adam's House in Paradise*, 13); for a full discussion of origins see pages 61–73. For another interpretation, see Harries, *The Ethical Function of Architecture*, 136–41.
18. Vitruvius, Book II.1.2. Dripps interprets Vitruvius's primitive hut differently. The discovery of fire led to social gatherings, the development of language and the architectural elements of wall, terrace, hearth and roof; an observation taken from Gottfried Semper.
19. Alberti, *On the Art of Building in Ten Books*, 39.
20. Quatremère, *De l'architecture Égyptienne*, 15, 16, 239. See Lavin, *Quatremère de Quincy and the Invention of a Modern Language of Architecture*, 86–100; Younés, *The True, The Fictive, and The Real*, 37–42; Rykwert, *On Adam's House in Paradise*, 62, 63; and Vidler, "The hut and the body," 111. Rykwert emphasizes the difference between the *found* cave and the *fabricated* tent and hut.
21. Loudon, *Encyclopedia of Cottage, Farm, and Villa Architecture and Furniture*, 5. Laugier is included for his position against proportional systems believing decisions about scale are more intuitive. Laugier wanted the Orders to be used structurally. John Wood (1704–1754), "sharply criticized the Vitruvian thesis that mankind naturally and progressively evolved techniques, styles, and forms of architecture over the course of centuries. Instead he argued that, according to Scripture, architecture was suddenly and divinely revealed to mankind, and that all subsequent architecture, including that of ancient Greece and Rome, derived from this divine revelation" (Archer, *The Literature of British Domestic Architecture*, 840). While this seems counter to Loudon's point of view, I take David Watkin's interpretation of Soane's interest in this book as evidence of its general influence on architects interested in Enlightenment theory. Wood's son, also named John Wood (1728–1781), is worth noting. Harris claims that "the superior reputation that Wood gained in the 1770s from the Royal Crescent and other building at Bath enabled him in 1781 to publish with impunity what 'no architect had yet thought it worth his while to offer,' a Series of Plans for Cottages for the working-classes and impotent poor" (*British Architectural Books and Writers*, 470). Francesco Milizia (1725–1798) was "the most important architectural theorist of the Enlightenment in eighteenth-century

Italy" (Watkin, *Sir John Soane, Enlightenment Thought and the Royal Academy Lectures*, 135). See Rykwert for a discussion, *On Adams House in Paradise*, 66–69.

22. Loudon, *A Treatise on Forming, Improving and Managing Country Residences*, 101, 102. See Cooper for the discussion of Ruskin's "The Nature of Gothic" (*Knights of the Brush*, 68).
23. Simo, *Loudon and the Landscape*, 172.
24. Loudon, *Gardeners' Magazine* (Dec., 1837), 598, and see Major, *To Live in the New World*, 64.
25. Simo, *Loudon and the Landscape*, 132. Also see Major, *To Live in the New World*, 56, 59.
26. Major, *To Live in the New World*, 64.
27. Emerson, "Thoughts on Art," in McCoubrey, ed., *American Art, 1700–1960*, 78.
28. "On Simple Rural Cottages," *The Horticulturist* 1 (September, 1846), and *RE*, 244–51. The examples Downing uses are Designs I and V, in *CR*.
29. *ACH*, 44.
30. *ACH*, 47.
31. *ACH*, 91.
32. See Scully, *The Cottage Style*, for a full treatment. Also, Horatio Greenough, "American Architecture," in Small, ed., *Form and Function*. Downing quotes a contributor as saying that "there is something native and true in the remarks on the kind of building recommended for rural purposes, which would lead me to hope that we may, by and by, have a style of building of our own, founded on just and sound principles, which shall be to us what the original ideas involved in the classical and pointed styles were to the ancients" ("On Country Houses," *The Horticulturist* 1, October, 1846, 153).
33. "A Few Words on Our Progress in Building," *The Horticulturist* 6 (June, 1851), and *RE*, 216.
34. "On Simple Rural Cottages," *The Horticulturist* 1 (September, 1846), and *RE*, 245.
35. *ACH*, 38.
36. Vidler, *The Architectural Uncanny*, 202.
37. Expressions indicating special status due to infrequent occurrence include *annèe cave* for lunar year (253 days), or *mois cave* for lunar month (29 days). See "cellar" and "basement" in the glossary.
38. Norberg-Schulz, *Intentions in Architecture*, 125.
39. For examples: bookcase cabinet-like recesses, Design XXXI (*ACH*); niches found in wall thicknesses, Design V (*CR*); alcoves, Design VIII (*CR*) and XXXII (*ACH*); bay windows, Designs I, II, III, V, VI, VIII, IX and X (*CR*) and VI, XVI, XIX and XXVII (*ACH*); and oriel windows, Designs XXV, XXVIII and XXX (*ACH*). See Summerson, "An Interpretation of Gothic," in *Heavenly Mansions*, for a discussion of the *aediculae*.
40. These are often places that attract attention providing a visual hierarchy in the room. See Vidler about the feeling of the uncanniness and fundamental insecurity brought about by a lack of orientation (*The Architectural Uncanny*, 23).
41. Over time, the cabinet of curiosities had expanded to room-size spaces and now museums are a specialized building type, often losing its intimate scale with the shift from private collection to public display.
42. Downing quoting Lord Bacon, *CR*, 51 and 129.
43. For examples: boudoir, Designs V and VIII (*CR*) and XXVIII, XXIX, XXX and XXXII (*ACH*); book closet, Designs I and XI (*CR*); and pantry closet, Designs II, III, IV, V, VI, VIII and XIV (*CR*) and I, II, III, IV, V, VI, VII, X, XII, XIV, XIX, XXVI, XXVIII (*ACH*).

44. See Girouard, *Life in the French Country House*, especially chapter 6, "In and Around the Boudoir."
45. *ACH*, 324. Also see a similar retreat is noted for Design XXXI, where the top floor of the tower "may be the private *sanctum* of the master of the house, or a general belvidere or 'look-out' for visitors, as the taste of the proprietor may lead him to appropriate it" (351). See Figs. 5.3 and 5.4.
46. Bachelard, *The Poetics of Space*, xxxviii.
47. For urban sites, see Hall, *A Series of select and original modern designs for dwelling houses,* and Walter and Smith, *Two Hundred Designs for Cottages and Villas.*
48. Ariès, *Centuries of Childhood*, 398.
49. Evans, *Translations from Drawings to Building and Other Essays*, 86.
50. For examples, see Design V (*CR*) for a bower called a rustic summerhouse; and Design VII (*CR*) for a bower called a rustic arbor.
51. For examples: arcade, Designs VIII (*CR*) and XXXII (*ACH*); balcony, Designs I, II, III, V, VI, VIII, IX and X (*CR*) and VI, XVI, XIX and XXVII (*ACH*); gallery, Designs X and XIV (*ACH*); loggia, Design XXVII (*ACH*); pavilion, Design XXXII (*ACH*); piazza, Design IV (*ACH*); porch, Designs V, VI, VIII, IX, XI, XII and XIII (*CR*) and III, IV, V, VI, XI, XIII, XV, XIX, XX, XXI, XXIII, XXV, XXVIII, XXIX, XXX and XXXI (*ACH*); stoop, Designs II and XI (*CR*) and I and II (*ACH*); terrace, Designs VI and VIII (*CR*); umbrage, Designs II, III and X (*CR*) and IV (*ACH*); veranda, Designs I, IV, V, VI, VII, XI, XIII and XIV (*CR*) and V, VII, VIII, IX, XI, XII, XVI–XXXI (*ACH*).
52. Kaye notes, "to children they (sleeping porches) were casual, festive sleeping places, rather like camping out in a tent" (*There's a Bed in the Piano*, 104).
53. Published in *The Horticulturist* 4 (December, 1849). Brownell claims this house is the first Loggia-Villa with Corner Tower's variation of Italianate style in America. See "Italianate Villa and the Search for an American Style, 1840–1860," in Jaffe, ed., *The Italian Presence in American Art*, 212, 213. For a photograph see Downing and Scully, *The Architectural Heritage of Newport*, Plate 163.
54. "The British term, 'verandah' (with or without the *h*), did not enter the American scene until the nineteenth century, coming from India by way of England." Kaye, *There's a Bed in the Piano,* 88.
55. See Kaye, *There's a Bed in the Piano*, Chapter 4.
56. *CR*, 141.
57. *ACH*, 120.
58. *TPLG*, 375.
59. Referring to Design V, *ACH*, 96.
60. *CR*, 29.
61. Referring to Design II, *CR*, 43.
62. "On Country Houses," *The Horticulturist* 1 (October, 1846), 154.
63. Irving to George Harvey, November 23, 1835, *Letters*, 845. Harvey was a local architect who drew plans for improvements to Irving's Sunnyside. Original floor plan drawings are in the Davis Collection, box labeled "Buildings not by Davis" (Metropolitan Museum of Art).
64. See Van Rensselaer, *Art Out-of-Doors*, for a description of how these different apartments were used.
65. *CR*, 136.

66. Younés, *The True, The Fictive, and The Real*, 171.
67. Cline, *A Hut of One's Own*, 65.
68. *CR*, 12, 13. Also see *TPLG*, 374, 375.
69. Ruskin, *The Stones of Venice*, discussed in Middleton and Watkin, *Neoclassical and 19th Century Architecture*, 65.
70. See the glossary for the evolving definitions of bathroom and water closet. Also see Downs, "Andrew Jackson Downing & the American Bathroom," 31–34.
71. For examples in *ACH*: piped kitchen sink, Designs VI and XVI; water closet, Designs V, VII and XIX; wind powered water-raising device, Design VIII; Chilson furnace, Design XXV; bathroom, Designs XXI, XXV, XXVIII, XIX, XXIX, XXXI and XXXII; hot-air heated greenhouse, Design XXV; water stored in a garret cistern, Design XXVIII; and roof ventilator, Designs XXVI and XXIX.
72. For examples: lifts, Designs No. 14, 16 and 20; furnace and skylight, Design No. 14; and gas piping and speaking tubes, Design No. 18.
73. *ACH*, ft. 480 and 481.
74. See Downs, "Evolution of American Open Planning."
75. See Crowley, *The Invention of Comfort*.
76. *CR*, 5.
77. *CR*, 3.
78. Leatherbarrow, *Uncommon Ground*, 157.
79. Ierley, *The Comforts of Home*, 99.
80. Downs, "Downing's Newburgh Villa," 23.
81. Borgmann, *Technology and the Character of Contemporary Life*, 140.
82. Crowley, "The Invention of the Cottage as a Comfortable House," 19.
83. Borgmann, *Technology and the Character of Contemporary Life*, 124, 125. Also of interest is Ivan Illich, "Dwelling," *In the Mirror of the Past*.
84. Burke, *A Philosophical Enquiry*, "Proportion further considered," Section V, 93.

CHAPTER 5

1. *ACH*, 275.
2. Quatremère, *Encyclopédie méthodique*, 1:508, in Lavin, *Quatremère de Quincy and the Invention of a Modern Language of Architecture*, 185.
3. See Wood, "Asher Benjamin, Andrew Jackson Downing," in Hafertepe and O'Gorman, eds., *American Architects and their Books to 1848*, for a comparison of Benjamin's *Builder's Guides* and Downing's *TPLG*.
4. *ACH*, 32.
5. *CR*, 13.
6. Berlin, *The Roots of Romanticism*, 58.
7. *CR*, 12.
8. Emerson, "The Transcendentalist," in *The Complete Writings of Ralph Waldo Emerson*, 101–10.
9. *Oxford English Dictionary*. Webster attributes this quotation to Milton (*An American Dictionary*). *OED* gives it to Johnson, 1755.
10. Wittkower, "Imitation, Eclecticism, and Genius," in Wasserman, ed., *Aspects of the Eighteenth Century*, 144.

11. Loudon, *The Architectural Magazine*, January, 1837: 1–3.
12. Stair towers are part of Design XX, XXI and XXXI in *ACH*.
13. *CR*, 163.
14. Webster, *An American Dictionary* (1860 ed.) (emphasis added).
15. See Simo, *Loudon and the Landscape*, for an account of Derby Arboretum.
16. Cassell's *New Latin Dictionary*.
17. *ACH*, 356.
18. Foucault, *The Order of Things*, 92–96.
19. Hussey, *The Picturesque*, 186–90.
20. Leupen et al, *Design and Analysis*, 48.
21. Downing's initials are on the elevation drawing. This floor plan resembles Downing's house, and Downs considers it a proposal Downing had in mind for future renovations ("Downing's Newburgh Villa," 74). Other designs with halls include: Design II where it is used as a winter dining room, III, V, VII "An Irregular Cottage," and VIII, (*CR*); and Design XIX "A Villa Farm House," XXV, XXVI, and XXXI (*ACH*).
22. Loudon, *A Treatise on Forming, Improving and Managing Country Residences*, 363, 414, 422.
23. Lindley, *Theory of Horticulture*, 1–4. Lindley criticized Downing's *TPLG* and Loudon's *Encyclopedia of Gardening*; see Major, *To Live in the New World*, 72, 73. Later Lindley called on Downing along with Harvard Professor Asa Gray to edit and provide notes to the American edition of his book published in 1852. Also see Schuyler, *Apostle of Taste*, 30–34.

CONCLUSION

1. Downing, "On the Moral Influence of Good Houses," *The Horticulturist* 2 (February, 1848), and *RE*, 209–10.
2. *ACH*, 312.
3. *ACH*, 315.
4. *CR*, 90.
5. Rykwert, *The Seduction of Place*, 109.
6. Thomas Jefferson letter to John Adams, 1813, in Tavernor, *Palladio and Palladianism*, 204.
7. Downing, "Our Country Villages," *The Horticulturist* 4 (June, 1850), 541, and *RE*, 243.
8. *ACH*, 22.
9. Younés, *The True, The Fictive, and The Real*, 255.
10. *ACH*, 23, 24.

GLOSSARY

1. *The House Beautiful: Essays on Beds and Tables, Stools and Condlesticks*, 1877. Reprint, New York: Dover, 1995, 45.
2. *Flu: The Story of the Great Influenza Pandemic of 1918 and the Search for the Virus That Caused It*, New York: Farrar Straus & Giroux, 1999, 48.
3. Webster prepared an elementary work in 1783 and published in Hartford, Connecticut. It was soon followed by additional work, the total of which comprised a spelling book,

an English grammar book, and a reader. Webster's first full dictionary was published in 1828, and enlarged and revised in 1832. See Lossing, *Eminent Americans*, 277, 278.

4. Downing called the top floor of a *campanile* a museum or prospect gallery. See Design XXI, *ACH*, 286.
5. This room was likely to contain the sink, especially in English houses as a kitchen was used only for cooking, and not for food or dish storage or cleaning up. There were sometimes separate sinks and cisterns for rainwater and well water as well as ingenious devices for measuring the water levels.

BIBLIOGRAPHY

WORKS BY ANDREW JACKSON DOWNING

- *A Treatise on the Theory and Practice of Landscape Gardening, Adapted to North America; with a view to the Improvement of Country Residences. Comprising historical notices and general principles of the art, directions for laying out grounds and arranging plantations, the description and cultivation of hardy trees, decorative accompaniments to the house and grounds, the formation of pieces of artificial water, flower gardens, etc. With remarks on rural architectures . . .* New York and London: Wiley & Putnam, 1841. Reprint of 4th ed., 1849, intro. Therese O'Malley, Washington, D.C.: Dumbarton Oaks Research Library and Collection, 1991. Also published as *Landscape Gardening and Rural Architecture*, an unabridged and unaltered republication of the 7th ed., 1865, intro. George B. Tatum, New York: Dover, 1991.
- *Cottage Residences; or A series of designs for Rural Cottages and Cottage-Villas, and their Gardens and Grounds, Adapted to North America*, New York: Wiley and Putnam, 1842. The 4th ed. in 1852 adds five new designs. The 1873 ed. includes additional designs and revised costs by Charles Downing and Henry Winthrop Sargent. The 1873 ed. has been reprinted as *Victorian Cottage Residences* with new preface Adolf K. Placzek, New York: Dover, 1981.
- *The Fruits and Fruit Trees of America; or, The culture, propagation, and management, in the garden and orchard, of fruit trees generally; with descriptions of all the finest varieties of fruit, native and foreign, cultivated in this country*, New York and London: Wiley and Putnam, 1845.
- *The Architecture of Country Houses; including Designs for Cottages, Farm Houses, and Villas, with Remarks on Interiors, Furniture, and the Best Modes of Warming and Ventilating*, New York: D. Appleton & Co., and Philadelphia: Geo. S. Appleton, 1850. Reprint with new intro. George B. Tatum, New York: Da Capo, 1968, and New York: Dover, 1969.

Rural Essays, Memoir of the Author by George William Curtis and a Letter to his Friends by Frederika Bremer, New York: Putnam, 1853. Reprint, George William Curtis, ed. with Memoir of the Author by George William Curtis and a Letter to His Friends by Frederika Bremer, and new intro. George B. Tatum, New York: Da Capo, 1974.

OTHER SOURCES

Abrams, Meyer Howard, *The Mirror and the Lamp: Romantic Theory and the Critical Tradition*, Oxford: Oxford University Press, 1953.

Ackerman, James, *The Villa: Form and Ideology of Country Houses*, Princeton, N.J.: Princeton University Press, 1990.

Adams, Arthur G., *The Hudson Through the Years*, New York: Fordham University Press, 1998.

Alberti, *On the Art of Building in Ten Books*, c. 1450, trans. Joseph Rykwert, Neil Leach and Robert Tavernor, Cambridge, Mass.: The MIT Press, 1994.

Alex, William, *Calvert Vaux, Architect & Planner*, intro. George B. Tatum, New York: Ink, 1994.

Alison, Archibald, *Essays on the Nature and Principles of Taste*, Edinburgh: Bell & Bradfute, 1790. Reprint Hildesheim: Georg Olms Verlagsbuchhandlung, 1968.

Anderson, Jean Bradley, *Carolinian on the Hudson: The Life of Robert Donaldson*, Raleigh: Historic Preservation Foundation of North Carolina, 1996.

Archer, John, "The Beginnings of Association in British Architectural Esthetics," *Eighteenth-Century Studies*, Vol. 16, No. 3, Spring, 1983: 241–64.

———, *The Literature of British Domestic Architecture, 1715–1842*, Cambridge, Mass.: The MIT Press, 1985.

Argan, Giulio Carlo, "On the Typology of Architecture," trans. Joseph Rykwert, *Architectural Design*, 33, 1963: 564–65.

Ariès, Philippe, *Centuries of Childhood: A Social History of Family Life*, trans. Robert Baldick, New York: Vintage Books, 1962.

Bachelard, Gaston, *The Poetics of Space*, trans. Maria Jolas, foreword John R. Stilgoe, Boston: Beacon Press, 1994.

Barr, Frederic M., *The Life and Works of Alexander Anderson, MD, The First American Wood Engraver*, New York: Barr Brothers, 1893.

Beecher, Henry Ward, *Norwood; or, Village Life in New England*, New York: Scribner, 1868.

Berlin, Isaiah, *The Roots of Romanticism*, Princeton, N.J.: Princeton University Press, 1999.

Beveridge, Charles E. and David Schuyler, eds., "Creating Central Park, 1857–1861," *The Papers of Frederick Law Olmsted*, Vol. III, Baltimore: Johns Hopkins University Press, 1983.

Birnbaum, Charles A. and Robin Karson, eds., *Pioneers of American Landscape Design*, New York: McGraw-Hill, 2000.

Boas, George, ed., *Romanticism in America*, Baltimore: Johns Hopkins University Press, 1940.

Bode, Carl, *The Anatomy of American Popular Culture, 1840–1861*, Berkeley: University of California Press, 1959.

Borgmann, Albert, *Technology and the Character of Contemporary Life: A Philosophical Inquiry*, Chicago: University of Chicago Press, 1984.

Bowen, Croswell, *Great River of the Mountain: The Hudson*, intro. Carl Carmer, New York: Hastings House, 1941.

Bremer, Frederika, *The Homes of the New World: Impressions of America*, trans. Mary Howitt, 2 vols., New York: Harper & Bros., 1853.

Brown, Richard, *Domestic Architecture*, London: G. Virtue, 1842.

Burke, Edmund, *A Philosophical Enquiry into the Origin of Our Ideas of the Sublime and Beautiful*, 1757. Reprint, intro. Adam Phillips, Oxford: Oxford University Press, 1998.

Carmer, Carl, *The Hudson*, New York: Fordham University Press, 1998.

Cassell's New Latin Dictionary, New York: Funk & Wagnalls, 1959.

Chambers, Douglas, *The Planters of the English Landscape Garden: Botany, Trees, and the* Georgics, New Haven, Conn.: Yale University Press, 1993.

Cline, Ann, *A Hut of One's Own*, Cambridge, Mass.: The MIT Press, 1998.

Clark, Eliot, *History of the National Academy of Design, 1825–1953*, New York: Columbia University Press, 1954.

Colvin, Howard, *A Biographical Dictionary of English Architects, 1660–1840*, Cambridge, Mass.: Harvard University Press, 1954.

Conron, John, "The American Dream Houses of Andrew Jackson Downing," *Canadian Review of American Studies*, 18, 1987: 9–40.

Cook, Clarence, *A Description of the New York Central Park*, 1869. Reprint, New York: B. Blom, 1972.

———, *The House Beautiful, Essays on Beds and Tables, Stools and Candlesticks*, 1877. Reprint, New York: Dover, 1995.

Cooper, James F., *Knights of the Brush: The Hudson River School and the Moral Landscape*, New York: Hudson Hills, 2000.

Crary, Jonathan, *Techniques of the Observer: On Vision and Modernity in the Nineteenth Century*, Cambridge, Mass.: The MIT Press, 1998.

Crowley, John E., "The Invention of the Cottage as a Comfortable House: The Designs of Catherine Beecher and Andrew Jackson Downing," Delaware: Winterthur Museum and Gardens, 1996.

———, *The Invention of Comfort: Sensibility & Design in Early Modern Britain & Early America,* Baltimore: Johns Hopkins University Press, 2001.

Curl, James Stevens, *Dictionary of Architecture and Landscape Architecture*, Oxford: Oxford University Press, 2nd ex. ed., 2006.

Daniels, Stephen, *Fields of Vision: Landscape Imagery and National Identity in England and the United States*, Princeton, N.J.: Princeton University Press, 1993.

———, *Humphry Repton: Landscape Gardening and the Geography of Georgian England*, New Haven, Conn.: Yale University Press, 1999.

Davis, Alexander Jackson, *Rural Residences*. Reprint of 1838 ed. with intro. Jane B. Davies, New York: Da Capo, 1980.

Dickens, Charles, *American Notes*, London: Chapman and Hall, 1842.

———, *The Life and Adventures of Martin Chuzzlewit*, New York: G. W. Carleton, 1849.

Dingman, John F., *Alexander Anderson, 1775–1870, and the background of wood-engraving in America*, San Marcos, Calif.: J. F. Dingman, 1984.

Donnell, Edna, "A. J. Davis and the Gothic Revival," *Metropolitan Museum Studies*, V/VI, 1934/35: 183–233.

Downing, Antoinette F. and Vincent J. Scully, Jr., *The Architectural Heritage of Newport,*

Rhode Island, New York: Bramhall House, 196?.
Downing Family, *Papers, 1802–1981*, Newburgh, New York: Historical Society of Newburgh Bay and the Highlands.
Downs, Arthur Channing, "Andrew Jackson Downing & the American Bathroom," *Historic Preservation*, 23, Oct./Dec. 1971: 31–34.
———, "Downing's Newburgh Villa," *Association for Preservation Technology*, IV, 1972.
———, *Downing and the American House*, Newton Square, Pa.: Downing & Vaux Society, 1988.
———, "Evolution of American Open Planning," Preliminary Report V, Newton Square, Pa.: Downing & Vaux Society, Feb. 1990: 126–63.
———, "The Picturesque and Truthful Roof," Preliminary Report V, Newton Square, Pa." Downing & Vaux Society, Feb. 1990: 99–103.
———, "'Up-front' and Prominent Chimneys," Preliminary Report V, Newton Square, Pa.: Downing & Vaux Society, Feb. 1990: 91–98.
———, "A Previously Unattributed Structure from the Partnership of Downing & Vaux," Report VII, Newton Square, Pa: Downing & Vaux Society, July, 1995.
Dripps, Robin, *The First House: Myth, Paradigm, and the Task of Architecture,* Cambridge, Mass.: The MIT Press, 1997.
Dutchess County Planning Board, *Springside: A Partnership with the Environment*, Poughkeepsie, N.Y.: Department of Planning, 1968.
Early, James, *Romanticism and American Architecture*, New York: A. S. Barnes, 1965.
Eberlein, Harold Donaldson and Cortlandt Van Dyke Hubbard, *Historic Houses of the Hudson Valley*. Reprint, New York: Dover, 1990.
Emerson, Ralph Waldo, *The Complete Writings of Ralph Waldo Emerson*, New York: Wm. H. Wise, 1929.
Evans, Robin, *Translations from Drawings to Building and Other Essays*, Cambridge, Mass.: The MIT Press, 1997.
Fish, Carl Russell, *The Rise of the Common Man, 1830–1850*, New York: Macmillan, 1927.
Foucault, Michael, *The Order of Things: An Archaeology of the Human Sciences*, New York: Vintage Books, 1994.
Franklin, Jill, *The Gentleman's Country House and its Plan, 1835–1914*, London: Routledge & Kegan Paul, 1981.
Fry, Carolyn, *The Plant Hunters: The Adventures of the World's Greatest Botanical Explorers*, London: Deutsch, 2009.
Gage, John, *Color in Turner: Poetry and Truth,* New York: Frederick A. Praeger, 1969.
Giedion, Siegfried, *Mechanization Takes Command*, New York: Oxford University Press, 1955.
Gilpin, William, *Observations, relative chiefly to Picturesque Beauty*, London: R. Blamire, 1789.
———, *Three Essays: On picturesque beauty; On picturesque travel; and On sketching landscape*, London: R. Blamire, 1792.
Girouard, Mark, *Life in the French Country House*, New York: Alfred A. Knopf, 2000.
Gloag, John, *Mr. Loudon's England: The Life and Work of John Claudius Loudon, and His Influence on Architecture and Furniture Design*, Newcastle-upon-Tyne: Oriel, 1970.
———, *Victorian Taste, Some Social Aspects of Architecture and Industrial Design, from 1820–1900*, New York: David & Charles, 1972.
Goodwin, Francis, *Domestic Architecture, 1833–34.*, 3rd ed., 2 vols., London: H. G. Bohn, 1850.

Greenough, Horatio, *Travels, Observations and Experience of a Yankee Stonecutter*, New York: G. P. Putnam, 1852.

Greiff, Constance M., *John Notman, Architect, 1810–1865*, Philadelphia: The Athenaeum of Philadelphia, 1979.

Grund, Francis J., *The Americans in Their Moral, Social and Political Relations*, London: Longman Green, 1837.

Gutman, Robert, *Architectural Practice*, Princeton, N.J.: Princeton University Press, 1988.

Gwilt, Joseph, *An Encyclopaedia of Architecture, Historical, Theoretical, and Practical,* (1842), updated, London: Longman, Brown, Green, and Longmans, 1867.

Hafertepe, Kenneth and James F. O'Gorman, eds., *American Architects and their Books to 1848,* Amherst: University of Massachusetts Press, 2001.

Haley, Jacquetta M., ed., *Pleasure Grounds: Andrew Jackson Downing and Montgomery Place with illustrations by Alexander Jackson Davis*, Tarrytown, N.Y.: Sleepy Hollow Press, 1988.

Hall, John, *A Series of select and original modern designs for dwelling houses, . . . adapted to the style of building in the United States*, Baltimore: John Murphy, 1848.

Hamilton, Sinclair, *Early American Book Illustrators and Wood Engravers, 1670–1870*, Vol. I & II, Princeton, N.J.: Princeton University Press, 1958.

Hamlin, Talbot Faulkner, "The Greek Revival in America and Some of Its Critics," *Art Bulletin*, Vol. XXIV, No. 4, 1942: 244–58.

———, *Greek Revival Architecture in America*, New York: Oxford University Press, 1944.

Handlin, David P., *The American Home, Architecture and Society, 1815–1915*, Boston: Little, Brown, 1979.

Harries, Karsten, *The Ethical Function of Architecture*, Cambridge, Mass.: The MIT Press, 1997.

Harris, Eileen, *British Architectural Books and Writers, 1556–1785*, Cambridge: Cambridge University Press, 1990.

Harris, Neil, *The Artist in American Society: The Formative Years, 1790–1860*, Chicago: University of Chicago Press, 1982.

Harvey, Eleanor Jones, *The Painted Sketch: American Impressions from Nature, 1830–1880*, Dallas: Dallas Museum of Art, 1998.

Haydon, Roger, ed., *Upstate Travels: British Views of Nineteenth-Century New York*, Syracuse, N.Y.: Syracuse University Press, 1982.

Hazlitt, William, *The Plain Speaker: The Key Essays*, 1826. Reprint, Massachusetts: Blackwell, 1998.

Herrmann, Wolfgang, *Laugier and Eighteenth Century French Theory*, London: A. Zwemmer, 1985.

Hersey, George L., "J. C. Loudon and Architectural Associationism," *Architectural Review*, August, 1968: 89–92.

———, *High Victorian Gothic: A Study in Associationism*, Baltimore: Johns Hopkins University Press, 1972.

Hitchcock, Jr., Henry-Russell, *American Architectural Books: A list of books, portfolios, and pamphlets published in America before 1895 on architecture and related subjects*, Middletown, Conn.: By author, 1939. Reprint of 2nd ed., with new intro. Adolf K. Placzek, New York: Da Capo, 1976.

Hogarth, William, *The Analysis of Beauty: Written with a View of Fixing the Fluctuating Ideas of Taste*, 1753. Reprint. Pittsfield, Mass.: Silver Lotus Shop, 1909.

Holly, Henry Hudson, *Holly's Country Seats*. Reprinted as *Holly's Picturesque County Seats*, intro George B. Tatum, New York: Dover, 1993.

Hunt, John Dixon, *The Wider Sea, A Life of John Ruskin*, New York: Viking Press, 1982.

———, *Gardens and the Picturesque: Studies in the History of Landscape Architecture*, Cambridge, Mass.: The MIT Press, 1992.

———, *The Picturesque Garden in Europe*, London: Thames & Hudson, 2002.

Hunt, Thomas Frederick, *Half a Dozen Hints on Picturesque Domestic Architecture, in a series of designs for gate lodges, gamekeepers' cottages, and other rural residences*, 1825. London: Henry G. Bohn. 3rd ed. with additions, 1841.

———, *Exemplars of Tudor Architecture, Adapted to Modern Habitations*, London: Henry G. Bohn, 1830.

Hussey, Christopher, *The Picturesque: Studies in a Point of View*, New York: G. P. Putnam's Sons, 1927.

Ierley, Merritt, *The Comforts of Home: The American House and the Evolution of Modern Convenience*, New York: Clarkson Potter, 1999.

Illich, Ivan, *In the Mirror of the Past*, New York: Marion Boyars, 1992.

Irving, Washington, *Letters*, Ralph M. Aderman, Herbert L. Kleinfield and Jennifer S. Banks, eds., 4 vols., Boston: Twayne, 1979–82.

———, *The Complete Works of Washington Irving*, 1834. Ed. with intro. Charles Neider, New York: Da Capo, 1998.

Jackson, Joseph, *Early Philadelphia Architects and Engineers*, Philadelphia, [s.n.], 1923. Available at the Historical Society of Pennsylvania, Philadelphia, Pa.

Jackson, Kenneth T., *Crabgrass Frontier: The Suburbanization of the United States*, New York: Oxford University Press, 1985.

Jaffe, Irma B., ed., *The Italian Presence in American Art, 1760–1860*, New York: Fordham University Press, 1989.

Johnson, Samuel, *A Dictionary of the English Language*, 2nd American ed., Boston: W. Andrews, 1806.

Kaufmann, Emil, *Architecture in the Age of Reason: Baroque and Post-Baroque in England, Italy, France*, New York: Dover, 1968.

Kaye, Myrna, *There's a Bed in the Piano, The Inside Story of the American Home*, Boston: Little, Brown, 1998.

Kimball, Fiske, *Nineteenth and Twentieth Century Architecture*, New York: Garland, 1976.

Knight, Richard Payne, *The Landscape, A Didactic Poem. In three books. Addressed to Uvedale Price, Esq.*, London: W. Bulmer, 1794.

———, *An Analytical Inquiry into the Principles of Taste*. 4th ed., London: T. Payne, 1808.

Knubel, Helen M., "Alexander Anderson and Early American Book Illustration," *The Princeton University Library Chronicle*, Vol. I, No. 3, April, 1940: 8–18.

Kolata, Gina, *Flu: The Story of the Great Influenza Pandemic of 1918 and the Search for the Virus That Caused It*, New York: Farrar Straus & Giroux, 1999.

Kowsky, Francis R., *The Architecture of Fredrick Clarke Withers and the Progress of the Gothic Revival in America after 1850*, Middletown, Conn.: Wesleyan University Press, 1980.

———, *Country, Park & City: The Architecture and Life of Calvert Vaux*, New York: Oxford University Press, 1998.

Lafever, Minard, *The Architectural Instructor, containing a history of architecture from the earliest ages to the present times*, with Glossary, New York: G. P. Putnam, 1856.

Laird, Mark, "Approaches to planting in the late eighteenth century: some imperfect ideas on the origins of the American garden," *Journal of Garden History*, 11, No. 3, 1991.

Lamb, Martha, "Homes of America: Some New England Houses," *The Art Journal*, 6, 1878.

———, *The Homes of America, or, An Attempt to Explain the Principal Operations of Gardening upon Psychological Principles*, New York: D. Appleton, 1879.

Lavin, Sylvia, *Quatremère de Quincy and the Invention of a Modern Language of Architecture*, Cambridge, Mass.: The MIT Press, 1992.

Leatherbarrow, David, *Uncommon Ground: Architecture, Technology and Topography*, Cambridge, Mass.: The MIT Press, 2000.

Leupen, Bernard, Christoph Grafe, Nicola Körnig, Mark Lampe and Peter de Zeeuw, *Design and Analysis*, New York: Van Nostrand Reinhold, 1997.

Lindley, John, *The Theory of Horticulture; or, An Attempt to Explain Principal Operations of Gardening upon Physiological Principles*, American ed., Notes and Preface by A. J. Downing and Asa Gray, New York: Wiley & Putnam, 1841.

Longstreth, Richard, ed., *The Mall in Washington, 1791–1991*, intro. Therese O'Malley, Washington, D.C.: National Gallery of Art, 1991.

Lossing, Benson John, *Our Countrymen, or, Brief Memoirs of Eminent Americans*, Philadelphia: Lippincott, Grambo & Co., 1855. Reprint, the Michigan Historical Reprint Series.

———, *Vassar College and its Founder*, New York: C. A. Alvord, 1867. Reprint, the Michigan Historical Reprint Series.

Loudon, Jane, *Gardening for Ladies; and Companion to the Flower-Garden*, American edition, A. J. Downing, ed., New York: Wiley & Putnam, 1847.

Loudon, John Claudius, *A Treatise on Forming, Improving and Managing Country Residences; and on the Choice of Situations Appropriate to every Class of Purchasers . . .*, 2 vols., London: Longman, Hurst, Rees, and Orme, Paternoster-Row, 1806.

———, "Landscape Gardening," *The Edinburgh Encyclopaedia*, 1830: 525–73.

———, *An Encyclopaedia of Cottage, Farm, and Villa Architecture and Furniture*, 1833. 3rd ed. with numerous corrections, and with many of the plates re-engraved, London: Longman, Rees, Orme, Brown, Green & Longman, 1835.

———, "Cottage Economy," *Library of Useful Knowledge*, London: Baldwin and Graddock, 1840.

Lugar, Robert, *Plans and views of buildings, executed in England and Scotland in the castellated and other styles*, London: M. Taylor, 1823.

———, *Villa Architecture: A Collection of Views, with Plans, of Buildings executed in England, Scotland, &c.*, London: J. Taylor, 1828.

Lynes, Russell, *The Tastemakers*, New York: Harper, 1954.

Macarthur, John, *The Picturesque: Architecture, Disgust and other Irregularities*, London: Routledge & Kegan Paul, 2007.

MacDougal, Elisabeth B., ed., *John Claudis Loudon and the Early Nineteenth Century in Great Britain*, Washington, D.C.: Dumbarton Oaks Research Library and Collection, 1980.

Major, Judith K., *To Live in the New World: A. J. Downing and American Landscape Gardening*, Cambridge, Mass.: The MIT Press, 1997.

Mancari, Ann, "Downing's Design XIV is more than a cottage," *Mid-Hudson Times*, July 21, 1999: 17.

Marcus, Sharon, *Apartment Stories: City and Home in Nineteenth-Century Paris and London*, Berkeley: University of California Press, 1999.

McCoubrey, John W., *American Art, 1700–1960: Sources and Documents*, Englewood Cliffs, N.J.: Prentice-Hall, 1965.

Middleton, Robin and David Watkins, *Neoclassical and 19th Century Architecture*, New York: Harry N. Abrams, 1980.

Milizia, Francesca, *The Lives of Celebrated Architects, Ancient and Modern*, dedicated to Sir John Soane, trans. Elizabeth Cresy, London: J. Taylor, 1826

Miller, Angela, *The Empire of the Eye: Landscape Representations and American Cultural Politics, 1825–1875*, Ithaca, N.Y.: Cornell University Press, 1993.

Miller, Iris, *Washington in Maps, 1606–2000*, New York: Rizzoli, 2002.

Minkowski, Eugène, *Lived Time: Phenomenological and Psychopathological Studies*, trans. and intro. Nancy Metzel, Evanston, Ill.: Northwestern University Press, 1970.

Moneo, Rafael, "On Typology," *Oppositions* 13, 1978: 23–45.

Monell, Mrs. John J., "Burning of the Henry Clay," *The Knickerbocker, or New York Monthly Magazine*, V. XL, October, 1852: 342–44.

Moss, Roger W., ed., *Paint in America: The Colors of Historic Buildings*, Washington, D.C.: The Preservation Press, National Trust for Historic Preservation, 1994.

Newburgh Gazette, "Account of the Burning of the Henry Clay" and "Death of A. J. Downing," V. XV, No. 9, August 4, 1852.

Newton, Roger Hale, *Town and Davis, Architects, Pioneers in American Revivalist Architecture, 1812–1870, including a Glimpse of their Times and their Contemporaries*, New York: Columbia University Press, 1942.

Norberg-Schulz, Christian, *Intentions in Architecture*, Cambridge, Mass.: The MIT Press, 1973.

Oxford English Dictionary, Oxford: Oxford University Press, 1884–1928.

Park, Helen, *A List of Architectural Books Available in America before the Revolution*, new ed., revised and enlarged, foreword Adolf K. Placzek, Los Angeles: Hennessey & Ingalls, 1973.

Pavord, Anna, *The Naming of Names: The Search for Order in the World of Plants*, London: Bloomsbury, 2005.

Peck, Amelia, ed., *Alexander Jackson Davis, American Architect, 1803–1892*, intro. Jane B. Davies, New York: Rizzoli, 1992.

Pevsner, Nikolaus, *A History of Building Types*, Washington, D.C.: National Gallery of Art, 1976.

Pierson, William Harvey, *American Buildings and Their Architects: Technology and the Picturesque, the Corporate and the Early Gothic Styles*, New York: Oxford University Press, 1978.

Price, Uvedale, *An Essay on the Picturesque, as compared with the sublime and the beautiful; and, on the use of studying pictures for the purpose of improving real landscape*, London: J. Robson, 1842.

Pugin, Augustus Charles, *Examples of Gothic Architecture; selected from various Antient Edifices in England*, 3 vols., London: H. G. Bohn, 1828–1836.

Quatremère de Quincy, Antoine Chrysostôme, *Encyclopédie méthodique l'Architecture*, Paris: Panekoucke, 1788.

———, *De l'Architecture Égyptienne, considérée Dans son origine, ses principes et son goût, et comparée sous les mêmes rapports à l'Architecture Grecque,* 1823 trans. Sir John Soane, 1807, Paris: Chez Barrois l'aîné et Fils, 1803.

———, *An Essay on the Nature, the End, and the Means of Imitation in the Fine Arts* (1823), trans. J. C. Kent, 1837. Reprint, New York: Garland, 1979.

———, *Dictionnaire Historique d'Architecture; comprenant dans son plan les notions historiques, descriptives, archarologiques, biographiques, theoriques, didactiques et practiques de cet Art,* 1832, Paris. Reprinted in part in Younés, 1999.

Ranlett, William H., *The Architect, a Series of Original Designs, for Domestic and Ornamental Cottages and Villas; Connected with Landscape Gardening, Adapted to the United States,* 2 vols. New York: Dewitt & Davenport, 1848. Reprint, New York: Dover, 2006.

Reiff, Daniel Drake, *Houses from Books: The Influence of Treatises, Pattern Books and Catalogs in America, 1735–1950,* University Park: Pennsylvania State University Press, 2000.

———, *Washington Architecture 1791–1861 Problems in Development,* Washington, D.C.: U.S. Commission of Fine Arts, 1971.

Reps, John W., "Downing and the Washington Mall," *Landscape* 16, Spring, 1967: 6–11.

Repton, Humphry, *Observations on the Theory and Practice of Landscape Gardening. Including Some Remarks on Grecian and Gothic Architecture, collected from Various Manuscripts, in the possession of the Different Noblemen and Gentlemen, for whose use they were originally written; the whole tending to establish Fixed Principles in the Respective Arts,* London: J. Taylor, 1803.

Robinson, Peter Frederick, *Rural Architecture; or, A Series of Ornamental Villas,* 4th ed., greatly improved, London: Rodwell and Martin, 1836.

———, *Designs for Ornamental Villas,* 3rd ed., greatly improved, London: Henry G. Bohn, 1836.

Rossi, Aldo, *The Architecture of the City,* trans. Diane Ghirardo and Joan Ockman, New York: Rizzoli, 1982.

Ruskin, John, *The Poetry of Architecture: or, the Architecture of the Nations of Europe considered in its Association with Natural Scenery and National Character,* 1837–38. Reprint, London: George Allen, 1893.

———, *The Seven Lamps of Architecture,* 1849. Reprint, New York: Dover, 1989.

———, *The Stones of* Venice, 1853. Reprint, New York: Da Capo, 1960.

———, *The Crown of Wild Olive,* New York: H. M. Caldwell, 1868.

———, *Modern Painters: Their Superiority in the Art of Landscape Painting to all the Ancient Masters, Proved by Examples of the True, the Beautiful, and the Intellectual, from the Works of Modern Artists, especially from those of J. M. W. Turner, Esq., R. A.* in *The Works of John Ruskin,* E. T. Cook and Alexander Wedderburn, eds., London: George Allen, 1903.

Rykwert, Joseph, *On Adam's House in Paradise: The Idea of the Primitive Hut in Architectural History,* New York: The Museum of Modern Art, 1972.

———, *The Seduction of Place: The City in the Twenty-first Century,* New York: Pantheon Books, 2000.

Schimmelman, Janice Gayle, *Architectural Books in Early America: Architectural Treatises and Building Handbooks Available in American Libraries and Bookstores through 1800,* New Castle, Del.: Oak Knoll Press, 1999.

Schuyler, David, *Apostle of Taste: Andrew Jackson Downing, 1815–1852,* Baltimore: Johns Hopkins University Press, 1996.

Scott, Frank Jessup, *The Art of Beautifying Suburban Home Grounds of Small Extent*, New York: D. Appleton, 1870.

Scott, Pamela, *Capital Engineers: The U.S. Army Corps of Engineers in the development of Washington, D.C., 1790–2004*, Alexandria, Va.: U.S. Corps of Engineers, Office of History, 2005.

Scully, Vincent J., *The Cottage Style: An Organic Development in Later Nineteenth-Century Wooden Domestic Architecture in the Eastern United States,* Ph. D. Dissertation, Yale University, 1949.

———, *The Shingle Style and the Stick Style: Architectural Theory and Design from Downing to the Origins of Wright*, New Haven, Conn.: Yale University Press, 1974.

Simo, Melanie Louise, *Loudon and the Landscape: From Country Seat to Metropolis, 1783–1843,* New Haven, Conn.: Yale University Press, 1988.

Small, Harold A., ed, *Form and Function, Remarks on Art.* intro. Erle Loran, Berkeley: University of California Press, 1947.

Smith, McKelden, *The Great Estates Region of the Hudson River Valley*, New York: Historic Hudson Valley Press, 1998.

Stein, Roger B., *John Ruskin and Aesthetic Thought in America, 1840–1900*, Cambridge, Mass.: Harvard University Press, 1967.

Stilgoe, John R., *Common Landscape of America, 1580 to 1845*, New Haven, Conn.: Yale University Press, 1982.

Summerson, John, *Heavenly Mansions*, New York: W. W. Norton, 1963.

———, ed., *Concerning Architecture*, London: Allen Lane, 1968.

Sweeting, Adam, *Reading Houses and Building Books: Andrew Jackson Downing and the Architecture of Popular Antebellum Literature, 1835–1855*, Hanover, N.H.: University Press of New England, 1966.

Tatum, George, B., *Andrew Jackson Downing: Arbiter of American Taste, 1815–1852*, Ph.D. Dissertation, Princeton University, 1949.

———, "The Beautiful and the Picturesque," *American Quarterly*, III, Spring, 1951: 36–51.

———, "The Emergence of an American School of Landscape Design," *Historic Preservation*, Vol. 25, April/June, 1973: 34–41.

———, "Andrew Jackson Downing: Nineteenth Century Tastemaker," Preservation League of New York State, *Newsletter*, Vol. 10, No. 4, July/August, 1984: 4–5.

———, and Elisabeth Blair MacDougall, eds., *Prophet with Honor: The Career of Andrew Jackson Downing, 1815–1852*, Washington, D.C.: Dumbarton Oaks Research Library and Collection, 1989.

Tavernor, Robert, *Palladio and Palladianism*, London: Thames and Hudson, 1991.

Tocqueville, Alexis Charles de, *Democracy in America*, trans. Henry Reeve, ed. John Canfield Spencer, 4 vols., London: Saunders and Otley, 1835–1840.

Tuthill, Louisa C., *The History of Architecture, from the earliest times; its present condition in Europe and the United States; with a biography of eminent architects, and a glossary of architectural terms*, Philadelphia: Lindsay and Blakiston, 1848.

Upton, Dell, "Pattern Books and Professionalism: Aspects of the Transformation of Domestic Architecture in America, 1800–1860," *Winterthur Portfolio*, 19, Summer/Autumn, 1984: 107–50.

Van Rensselaer, Marina Griswold, *Art Out-of-Doors: Hints on Good Taste in Gardening*, 1893. Enlarged 2nd ed., New York: C. Scribner's Sons, 1925.

Vaux, Calvert, *Villas and Cottages; A Series of Designs Prepared for Execution in the United States*, New York: Harper & Brothers, 1857. Reprint of 2nd ed. with new preface, 1864, New York: Da Capo, 1968.

Vidler, Anthony, "The Third Typology," *Oppositions* 7, 1976: 1–4.

———, "Type in *Encyclopédie Méthodique*," *Oppositions* 8, 1977: 146–50.

———, "The hut and the body: The 'nature' of architecture from Laugier to Quatremère de Quincy," *Lotus International* 33, 1981: 102–11.

———, *The Architectural Uncanny: Essays in the Modern Unhomely*, Cambridge, Mass.: The MIT Press, 1992.

Vitruvius, Marcus Pollio, *The Ten Books on Architecture*, trans. Morris Hicky Morgan, New York: Dover, 1960.

Walter, Thomas Ustick, and John Jay Smith, *Two Hundred Designs for Cottages and Villas*, Philadelphia: Carey and Hart, 1846.

Washburn, Wilcombe, "Vision of Life for the Mall," *AIA Journal*, Vol. XLVII, No. 3, March, 1967.

Wasserman, Earl E., ed., *Aspects of the Eighteenth Century*, Baltimore: Johns Hopkins University Press, 1965.

Watkin, David, *Sir John Soane, Enlightenment Thought and the Royal Academy Lectures*, Cambridge: Cambridge University Press, 1997.

Webster, Noah, *An American Dictionary of the English Language . . . to which are now added Pictorial Illustrations*, 1828. 2nd ed., Springfield, Mass.: George and Charles Merriam, 1860.

Wightwick, George, *The Palace of Architecture: A Romance of Art and History*, London: James Fraser, 1840.

———, *Hints to Young Architects, calculated to facilitate their practical operations, With additional notes and hints to persons about building in the country by A. J. Downing*, London and New York: Wiley and Putnam, 1847.

Wilde, Oscar, *The Decay of Lying*, 1889. Reprint, London & New York: Syrens, 1995.

Wittkower, Rudolf, *Palladio and English Palladianism*, London: Thames and Hudson, 1974.

Woods, Mary, "The First American Architectural Journals: The Profession's Voice," *Journal of the Society of Architectural Historians*, V. XLVIII, No. 2, June, 1989: 117–38.

Wright, Gwendolyn, *Building the Dream: A Social History of Housing in America*, New York: Pantheon Books, 1983.

Younés, Samir, *The True, The Fictive, and The Real: The Historical Dictionary of Architecture of Quatremère de Quincy*, London: Andreas Papadakis, 1999.

Zukowsky, John and Robbe Pierce Stimson, *Hudson River Villas*, New York: Rizzoli, 1985.

INDEX

Images are on pages shown in italics.